Annapolis Vignettes

Ginger M. Doyel

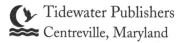
Tidewater Publishers
Centreville, Maryland

Cover art: Downtown Annapolis c. 1904. Painting by Ginger Doyel.

Library of Congress Cataloging-in-Publication Data

Doyel, Ginger.
  Annapolis vignettes / Ginger M. Doyel.— 1st ed.
      p. cm.
  A compilation of articles written by Ginger Doyel for her column,
"Annapolis from past to present" published weekly by The capital newspaper
since November 2002.
  Includes bibliographical references.
  ISBN-13: 978-0-87033-571-6
  1. Annapolis (Md.)—History—Anecdotes. 2. Annapolis Md.)—
Biography—Anecdotes. 3. St. John's College (Annapolis, Md.)—Anecdotes.
4. United States Naval Academy—Anecdotes. 5. Historic preservation—
Maryland—Annapolis—Anecdotes. I. Title.
  F189.A657D69 2005
  975.2'56—dc22
                                      2005020956

Manufactured in the United States of America
First edition, 2005; second printing, 2006

For my sister, Cathleen

Contents

Acknowledgments ix
Introduction xi

Part 1: People

F. Marion Lazenby and the Annapolis Dairy Products Company . . . 3
Peggy Kimbo Remembers Growing Up in a
    Segregated Urban Annapolis. 8
Orlando Ridout IV Recalls His Family's Woodlyn Farm Dairy . . . 13
J. Wilson Macey and The Annapolis Banking and Trust Company . . 18
Charles and Edward Weiss: Immigrants, Brothers,
    and Businessmen 24
The Troublesome Kate Kealy. 28
Pearl Gray's Runaway Wedding 33
Winston Churchill—The American 37
Robert Campbell Recalls Prohibition and Politics in Annapolis . . . 43
Henry Campbell, the Old Fish Market,
    and How "Old Bay" Came to Town 47
William Henry Hebron, the "Jewish" Fish Merchant. 52
Edward and Ella Burtis: Market Master, Market Mistress 55
Lou Hyatt, "the King of Shoeboxes" 65
James Strange Spoils Halloween for Local Youths 68
Peter and Helen Palaigos Recall Pete's Place 72
Francis R. Geraci, Jr., and the City's Former "Tonsorial Saloons" . . 76
Carolyn Martin's Sandwiches. 80
Dr. Faye Allen Reflects on Practicing Medicine
    and Marrying Dr. Aris T. Allen 84
Harry Klasmeier Recalls a "Quiet and Reserved" Annapolis 86

Part 2: Places

Market House on the Move (1698–1775) 93
Eight Generous Gentlemen 104
Save the Library!. 113
Save the Post Office!. 120
Gil Crandall Recalls the Opening of the
    "New" Severn River Drawbridge 123
Oscar and Jean Grimes Lament the Loss of Local Farmland 127

Annapolis High School Becomes
Maryland Hall for the Creative Arts 131
The Carroll Family—Buried Beneath a Shopping Center? 134
The J. F. Johnson Lumber Company Leaves Town 138

Part 3: St. John's College and the U.S. Naval Academy

Admiral Dewey Lays the Chapel Cornerstone 145
Alfred Schanze Records His Naval Academy Adventures 148
Why Midshipmen Toss Their Hats at Graduation 167
French Soldiers—Buried at St. John's? 169
Annapolis's Other Military School 172
How Spanish Influenza Attacked St. John's and the Academy . . . 180
"A Pretty Piece of Land:" How ROTC
Saved St. John's from the Academy 184
St. John's Artist Designs a Special Stamp 189
Ogle Hall's Many Owners 194
How Maryland Considered Taxing Bachelors to Fund Education . 197
Bygone Naval Academy Dating Traditions 200
The Naval Academy's Other Golf Course 204
Halligan Hall: Home to Marines and Midshipmen 211

Part 4: Preservation

Henry Sturdy's Colonial Guide Service 219
Rats: Unlikely Preservationists 223
Woodworkers Help to Preserve Local History 227
Anne St. Clair Wright: Annapolis's "First Lady of Preservation" . . 230
Saving the Historic Market House 234
Saving the Historic Market House—Again 240
Saving the Market—One More Time 243
"Hysteric, Historic Annapolis" 251
Making Sense of Annapolis's Historic Building Markers 255
Fireplace Mantel Preserves Century-old Letters 259
Preserving the Memory of British Convicts 263
Annapolis in December 1904 266

Appendix 1: Market Space Deed 269
Appendix 2: "Resolution Regarding City Market" 271
Notes 273
Bibliography 291
About the Author 297

Acknowledgments

Many people made this book possible. However two, above all others, were crucial to its completion: my parents, Roger and Michele Doyel. My father co-envisioned the newspaper column on which it is based, and my mother helped to prepare the final manuscript.

Special thanks must also be given to Linnell Bowen, my friend and role model. She encouraged me to write the column and presented the concept to Tom Marquardt, *The Capital*'s Executive Editor, on my behalf.

Those who offered valuable assistance, information about, and/or images of Annapolis's past were: Dr. Faye Allen, Michael Arndt, Nancy Avallone, Linnell Bowen, George T. Brown, Mr. and Mrs. Robert (Jane) Campbell, Carol Carman, Ronnie Carr, Lisa Mason-Chaney, Gilbert Crandall, Dr. and Mrs. Roger (Michele) Doyel, Robert Duckworth, the Governor Robert L. Ehrlich, Jr. Press Office, family and friends of Anne St. Clair Wright, David Fogle, Heather Foster, Claire Fowler, John Gadd, Francis R. Geraci, Jr., Mr. and Mrs. Walter (Mignon) Gerich, Joseph Getty, Mr. and Mrs. Oscar (Jean) Grimes, Jan Hardesty, David Hartcorn, Janice Hayes-Williams, Robert Henel, Jr., Esther Hokuf, Donna Hole, Captain Daniel Hunt, USN (Ret.), Louis Hyatt, Richard Israel, Ann Jensen, Matthew Kaler, Linda Keefer, Peggy Kimbo, Harry Klasmeier, Captain Richard D. Lazenby, USN (Ret.), Dr. Mark Leone, Anthony Lindauer, Carter Lively, Dr. Al Luckenbach, J. Wilson Macey, Mr. and Mrs. Joseph (Jo Ann) Francis Martin, Jr., Captain William Matton, USN (Ret.), Jane McWilliams, members of the Annapolis History Consortium, Melissa Moss, Ellen Moyer, Roger Moyer, Carole Markoff, Willard Mumford, Patrick Owen, Mr. and Mrs. Peter (Helen) Palaigos, Michael Parker, Terry Peterson, Lee Ann Plumer, L. Harvey Poe, Jr., Robert Reynolds, Mr. and Mrs. Orlando (Betty) Ridout IV, Orlando Ridout V, Ella Rowe, Dr. Jean Russo, Philip Sellars, Harold E. Slanker, Jr., Susan Smink, George Smyth, Charles Steele, Pringle Symonds, Mary Lee Thorsby, Donna Ware, Marion E. Warren, Edwin Weber, Mr. and Mrs. Robert (Norma) Worden, and many readers who contacted me with additional material.

The staff of the Anne Arundel County Public Library, especially Gloria Davis and Marion Francis; the Anne Arundel County Circuit Court; *The Capital*, especially John R. Bieberich, Lauren Brown, Bob Gilbert, J. Henson, Rick Hutzell, Tom Marquardt, and Erin O'Neill; Greenfield Library at St. John's College, especially Andrea Lamb, and Cara Sabolcik; the Hammond-Harwood

House, especially Heather Foster, Carter Lively, and Lisa Mason-Chaney; Historic Annapolis Foundation, especially Patricia Blick, Julie Fife, Jennifer Orrigo, Susan Steckman, and Dr. Gregory Stiverson; the Maryland Historical Society; the Maryland State Archives, especially Robert Barnes, Mimi Calver, Christopher Kintzel, Dr. Edward Papenfuse, and Robert Schoeberlein; the Maryland State Law Library; the St. John's College Communications Office, especially Rosemary Harty, and Beth Schulman; the U.S. Naval Academy Museum, especially James Cheevers; the U.S. Naval Academy Special Collections & Archives, especially Dot Abbott, Dr. Jennifer Bryan, Mary Catalfamo, Gary LaValley, and Beverly Lyall; and the U.S. Naval Academy Nimitz Library also offered valuable assistance and/or information.

All of you have my sincere thanks and appreciation.

Introduction

For many women—especially young, single, avid golfers—working with the PGA Tour would be an ideal job. Not for this fourth generation Annapolitan.

I returned to Annapolis, my hometown, from Charlottesville, Virginia, in June 2002. At the time, I only planned to stay briefly before moving to Florida to work with the Tour. Yet upon returning, I noticed that Annapolis had changed—and not just for the best. Development had transformed much of its landscape since I left for college in 1997, and it showed no sign of stopping. New developments—both residential and commercial—were emerging left and right: Park Place, Acton's Landing, the Annapolis Towne Centre at Parole, and so forth—the list seemed endless.

This trend disturbed me. And, although I was just twenty-two years old, I remembered a smaller, simpler Annapolis. I remembered going downtown, as a child, and seeing a harbor bustling with watermen and workboats—as well as tourists and pleasurecraft. I also remember my great-grandfather, David Jenkins, discussing the city's history, the importance of that history, and the sense of purpose with which he spoke.

That same sense of purpose prompted me to take a risk: I chose to stay in Annapolis rather than move, in order to help to preserve my hometown's heritage. Just how I was going to do that was a good question. After all, I was a golf artist with a B.A. in Leadership Studies.

I made my choice in late summer. Several weeks passed. Then, one evening, I had an idea. Actually, my father and I had the idea. We were playing Scrabble and discussing *The Capital*'s headlines when we reached this conclusion: *The Capital* was a fine newspaper; however, it didn't have a weekly history column: one that would inform readers about local heritage and encourage them to become stewards of that heritage.

We decided it should. We named it "Annapolis: From Past to Present." And, for the first time in the history of our father/daughter Scrabble rivalry, we stopped playing in order to pursue the concept. We started by brainstorming a list of topics for the column; we listed over 200 within an hour or so, and I wrote sample columns based on three of them within a month.

Meanwhile, my father mentioned the idea to Linnell Bowen: our friend, my role model, and Executive Director of Maryland Hall for the Creative Arts. Linnell had a strong background in history, historic preservation, and education. She also knew *The Capital*'s Executive Editor, Tom

Marquardt. And in early fall, she presented my sample columns to him, for his review, on my behalf.

To my surprise and delight, *The Capital* embraced the concept. I wasn't sure that it would—especially since I hadn't studied history, historic preservation, journalism, or any similar subject in college. Even so, the paper published my first column in November 2002.

Readers responded immediately. Some shared their complements in person; others called or wrote letters or emails to me or to the paper. All was going well—until the day I received "the call" from one of my editors. She said that several historians had contacted the paper and were concerned about the accuracy of my writing. She might have also listed their specific grievances—however, I don't remember. I was too flustered and heartbroken.

Later that night, once I had calmed down, I contacted the historians to apologize. They were most gracious. Not only did they advise me about what historical sources I could—and couldn't—trust. They also told me about, and invited me to participate in, the Annapolis History Consortium: an informal group of people with a professional or avocational interest in Annapolis history.

That was in 2002. Since then, many of the Consortium's members have become my friends and invaluable professional resources. Since then, I've also been asked to speak about writing as a career to many audiences, including a group of Girl Scouts the fall of 2004. After my speech they asked me "what I liked most" about writing my column. This was an easy question to answer, and this is what I told them:

> Writing *Annapolis: From Past to Present* has enabled me to make a small, but hopefully meaningful, contribution to my hometown. It's enabled me to meet and learn from people of all ages and backgrounds. It's also enabled me to learn about Annapolis's past, and in doing so, to understand its current issues more fully.

This book, *Annapolis Vignettes,* contains a collection of my columns that were written between November 2002 and February 2005. It has four parts, each of which contains stories, or "vignettes," relating to a specific theme. Part 1, "People," features two types of stories. Some are based on interviews with living Annapolitans who recall a "smaller, simpler" Annapolis, while others describe unique Annapolitans who are deceased. Each story relates to the next, so that they form a compelling, continuous narrative. Part 2, "Places," features sites that are essential to local history but are in danger of being forgotten. Many of them have been, or have the potential to be, razed and replaced by new developments. Part 3, "St. John's College and the U.S. Naval Academy," includes surprising stories in the history of these institutions. Finally, Part 4, "Preservation," celebrates historic preservation in Annapolis. It features key people, events, and organizations, as well as unexpected stories—such as how rats have helped to preserve the Hammond-Harwood House's history for over 200 years.

The stories have been edited slightly since *The Capital* published them. First and foremost, I tried to correct any historical errors that the original columns contained. I have tried to be as accurate as possible and apologize for any remaining mistakes. I also combined columns that had appeared as a series. The book also contains several chapters that the newspaper did not publish, but that I thought should be included. Among these is the final chapter that describes the illustration I created for the city of Annapolis's annual holiday open house invitation in 2004. It depicts Annapolis in December 1904, based on scenes reported by the *Evening Capital* that month.

I hope you'll enjoy the vignettes as much as I've enjoyed creating them.

Part 1: People

F. Marion Lazenby and the Annapolis Dairy Products Company

Captain Richard Lazenby has a clear view of Annapolis from his home on the Severn River. It's a sentimental view for the retired naval officer, as it reminds him of his father, Francis Marion Lazenby. Recently, Capt. Lazenby reflected on him, his local legacy, and on growing up in Maryland's capital.

F. Marion Lazenby had a goal in 1919: to bring pasteurized milk to Annapolis. To achieve his goal, he bought a failing dairy on West Street where Loews Annapolis Hotel is today. He called his venture the Annapolis Creamery Company, and it became the Annapolis Dairy Products Company in 1922. Locals simply called it the Annapolis Dairy.

Mr. Lazenby lived close to his business at 12 Taney (pronounced Tawney) Avenue. He "often walked from there to work, among other places in town," according to his son. The Dairy received its milk from farmers throughout Anne Arundel County. Its fleet of roughly sixteen dairy trucks traveled from West Street to farms along Forest Drive, and in St. Margaret's, Davidsonville, and southern Maryland. Farmers milked their cows, put the milk in large containers, then left them on the roadside to be picked up, and returned to the Dairy. There, workers in white uniforms converted the milk into cheese, heavy cream, plain milk, buttermilk, and chocolate milk.

The Dairy's milk was unique for two reasons. It was the first to be pasteurized in Annapolis. It also came in the company's signature curvy "cream-top" bottles, invented by Mr. Lazenby. The bottle's receptacle neck allowed cream to rise from the freshly pasteurized milk and to be removed easily with a curved, spoon-like tool.

"Customers kept the cream for cooking, or shook the bottle and drank the milk that way . . . But the Dairy stopped making its cream-top bottles once milk was homogenized and no longer separated," Capt. Lazenby said.

Later Annapolis Dairy bottles bore the company's hallmark, the "Annapolis Maid," which Mr. Lazenby also created. By the mid-1920s, bottles with this profile of a young woman wearing a bonnet were delivered countywide and on the Eastern Shore.

But the Dairy delivered more than milk. It also made and supplied the greater Annapolis area with ice. Mr. Lazenby acquired an ice plant and coal line in 1928. Horse-drawn trucks carrying 200- or 300-pound ice blocks delivered ice door to door. Each customer received a portion of the block (usually 25 pounds), which kept his or her icebox cool for about three days. The Dairy kept its ice and milk truck horses in stables across West Street, near Shaw Street.

Not only did the Dairy make ice; it also made delicious ice creams. Mr. Lazenby recalled how it sold its famous Eskimo Pies: "Each time a person bought a pie, he received a small, illustrated card located at the center of the pie. Customers collected the cards and stuck them on a master sheet. Once their sheets were full, they won a prize: A carton of Eskimo Pies . . . But filling the card was difficult. The Dairy printed very few of the final card needed to complete the sheet," he said.

In addition to Eskimo Pies, the Dairy sold pies, rolls, cakes, and cookies made by King's Bakery: an independent bakery at 56 West Street. Its frozen treats were most popular in the summer in downtown Annapolis and at a nearby community called Sherwood Forest. The Dairy supplied Sherwood's old "dug-out," which operated from beneath its general store. The "dug-out" sold countless Annapolis Dairy ice cream cones, floats, sodas, milkshakes, and more to residents and vacationers during hot months.

During the winter, however, the Dairy's ice cream and milk sales declined. So did its need for labor. This was a chief concern for Annapolis because the company employed more workers than any other local institution, aside from the military.

But Mr. Lazenby was a clever, compassionate man. In 1934, he founded Annapolis Utilities to keep his workers employed in the winter. This subsidiary of the Dairy stood across the street from it and sold fuel oil, oil burners, coal, wood, Frigidaires, and, at one point, LaSalle and Cadillac automobiles.

For many years, the Dairy's chief competitor was the U.S. Naval Academy Dairy in Gambrills, Maryland. Yet Mr. Lazenby's business often supplied the Academy with milk for two reasons. First, the school's dairy couldn't always produce enough milk for the entire Brigade of Midshipmen (who consumed 300 gallons of ice cream per week in 1938).[1] And second, the Naval

Courtesy of the Maryland State Archives SPECIAL COLLECTIONS (Robert G. Merrick Archives of Maryland Historical Photographs) The Annapolis Dairy Products Company, c. 1935 MSA SC 1477-1-6711.

The U.S. Naval Academy Dairy, 1920s. Courtesy of the Special Collections & Archives Division, Nimitz Library, U.S. Naval Academy.

Hospital used only pasteurized milk—a service offered exclusively by the Annapolis Dairy for some time.

Other dairies became viable competitors in the 1930s. "The competition became fierce as powerful dairy co-ops formed around the state and country," Capt. Lazenby said. His father's net profits were also slipping. A quart of milk cost his customers 11 cents and yielded only ¼ cent profit in the '30s. At the same time, the Dairy was paying $125,000 in annual salaries to its workforce of over 100 employees. When it could no longer make ends meet, Mr. Lazenby merged with Kress Farm Dairy in Baltimore, and eventually sold out to Greenspring Dairy.

The Dairy closed its doors permanently in the mid-40s. Even so, the property remained in the Lazenby family for many years, later serving as the Baltimore & Annapolis Bus Terminal.

Capt. Lazenby has fond memories of growing up in Annapolis while his father's business was still thriving. Like his father, he walked to many places in town. He walked to Annapolis Grammar School on Green Street, and later to Annapolis High School long before it became Maryland Hall for the Creative Arts.

In the winter, Capt. Lazenby and his peers often took alternate routes to school; they sledded on snow-covered streets, sidewalks, and yards or walked atop Spa Creek when it froze. Mr. Lazenby always tested the creek before they performed this daring feat. He fell through the ice while doing so in 1936, and, like father like son, the same fate befell Capt. Lazenby when he tried to save him. Fortunately two teenage boys rescued them by extending a long, sturdy tree branch.

Capt. Lazenby graduated from Annapolis High in 1937. He then attended Severn School in Severna Park for a year to prepare for the U.S. Naval Academy. Sometimes he commuted to Severn on a train, which he boarded at the bygone Bladen Street station. He recalled one amusing incident involving the train, which was operated by the Baltimore & Annapolis Railroad Company: "There had been a good heavy snow storm and some of the [Severn] students rolled a big snowball and put it on the tracks . . . This forced the train to stop. It caused a severe impasse near the school, which needless to say, displeased its Headmaster Roland Teel," he said.

Most days, however, Capt. Lazenby drove to Severn in a blue 1931 "Model A" Ford convertible with fellow students George "Bee" Weems, Walter "Boo" Smith, and John Clark. Each young man paid him $1 per week for gas, which he usually bought at the Severn Service Station at 260 King George Street (now Sandi's Flower Shop) for 32 cents per gallon.

Capt. Lazenby finished at Severn in 1938, attended the University of Virginia for one year, and entered the Naval Academy in 1939. This pleased Mr. Lazenby, even though he had attended its rival: the U.S. Military Academy at West Point.

Born in Baltimore in 1897, Mr. Lazenby was the last of three boys, and a younger sister born to Francis Allen and Sarah Deming Lazenby. The eldest son earned his medical degree at Johns Hopkins University—a pursuit that "took all of the family's money" Capt. Lazenby said. The second worked at the F. A. Lazenby Company, which made and sold cotton gins from Maine to Florida. Yet Marion, the youngest, "got little."

Family finances forced him to work as an insurance salesman through high school, while at Baltimore Polytechnic Institute, and later, while taking night classes at the University of Maryland law school. When World War I erupted, Mr. Lazenby enlisted immediately and was stationed at several camps around Baltimore. He was ordered to West Point, as a Class of 1919 cadet, just before his scheduled bar exam date.

Mr. Lazenby never took the bar. After the war, he moved from Baltimore to Annapolis, where he became a successful entrepreneur. In addition to founding the Dairy and Annapolis Utilities, he was an exemplary community servant. What follows are just a few of his contributions.

Annapolis Dairy advertisements from the Evening Capital *(May 4 and May 6, 1939).*

As president of the Annapolis Rotary Club, he founded Navy Night in 1931. Tensions were high between the city and Naval Academy that year. Naval officers were angry for this reason: There was a housing shortage on the Yard (the Academy's grounds) that forced those who were stationed there, and at the Naval Postgraduate School, to pay extremely high rents in town.

City merchants were equally angry. They were losing business to the midshipmen's store on the Yard. Only military officers were supposed to shop there. However, some civilians were taking advantage of its low prices by asking officers to shop there for them. Mr. Lazenby founded Navy Night to ease these tensions; it worked, and the event remains a strong, annual Annapolis Rotary Club tradition.

Capt. Richard D. Lazenby with his father, F. Marion Lazenby, at home at 12 Taney Avenue in spring or summer of 1942. Courtesy of Capt. Richard D. Lazenby, USN (Ret.).

Mr. Lazenby also contributed to St. John's College in the 1940s. The college was suffering from low enrollment at the time, which prompted him to meet with its president, Stringfellow Barr. Mr. Lazenby suggested that this trend could be reversed if St. John's became a co-ed institution, according to his son. And, although the first women were admitted in 1951 during president Richard Weigle's term, partial credit is due to Mr. Lazenby's consultations with both men.

Mr. Lazenby enticed his older brother Joe to move to Annapolis during the Depression. Joe formed the Joseph D. Lazenby Real Estate and Insurance Company and, like his brother, invested in St. John's—in a more controversial way.

The Naval Academy began its most aggressive attempt to annex St. John's campus in 1945. That year, the local Chamber of Commerce appointed Joe to chair "The Citizens' Committee for the Retention of the United States Naval Academy in Annapolis," which favored the proposed annex. Under his leadership, the Committee produced a petition supporting the move with over 4,000 signatures and presented it to Congress.

Meanwhile, Marion Lazenby was busy chairing Anne Arundel County's rationing board, a position he held from January 1942 until the end of World War II. After the war, he invested in the community in other meaningful ways. He chaired the committee that secured $350,000 to renovate the city's old hospital; he helped to restore historic sites such as the Hammond-Harwood House; and continued as Senior Warden of St. Anne's Church, later becoming a Senior Warden Emeritus there. A plaque that honors him and recognizes the unknown graves of Annapolitans in the churchyard, exists on the north side of the church.

Capt. Lazenby can see St. Anne's steeple from his home on the Severn. This view is a sentimental one—not just because it reminds him of his father's local legacy, but because it was also his father's view. In 1948, Mr. Lazenby moved his family from Taney Avenue, across the river, to where Capt. Lazenby lives now, and plans to stay.[2]

Peggy Kimbo Remembers Growing Up in a Segregated Urban Annapolis

Peggy Kimbo remembers the Lazenbys—and the Annapolis Dairy Products Company—very well. They often ate at the Little Campus Inn (now Galway Bay Irish Restaurant and Pub) on Maryland Avenue, where Peggy has worked since 1957. This is her story.

Annapolis was a different town when Miss Pink, a respected local midwife, delivered Peggy Kimbo in 1930. It was a smaller town with just 12,500 residents—about one-third of its current population. It was an "independent mom and pop shop" town with forty grocery stores. And it was a segregated town, which is why Peggy was born through a midwife, instead of at a hospital.

"That's the way most black women had their babies back then," Peggy said. "Miss Pink wore a knee length black dress and carried a black bag. We children thought that the babies came from inside her bag!"

Peggy and her older brother and sister, nicknamed Mickey and Mynie, were born and raised in downtown Annapolis, near the Naval Academy, at 18 College Avenue. Their grandmother Ethel, who lived next door at No. 20, was a "hat fanatic." She especially liked those at Mrs. Lillian Musterman's millinery at 197 Main Street.

"You'd think they wouldn't have let her try on hats because of her color, but they did," Peggy said. "People liked you because of you—the color of your skin didn't matter."

Peggy's "Uncle Notis," who lived across the street at 15 College Avenue, owned the family's only car. "We didn't have a car, that was a luxury, but our uncle did because of his upholstery business. He would take us driving out in the country, and call us city kids pointing out 'Now that's a cow,' and so on. Of course we knew what a cow was," she recalled.

"We used to have a lot of fun—good fun—even though we didn't have all the good stuff kids have now," Peggy said. "We made our own basketball

Peggy Kimbo, at far left, attending a tea at the YMCA on Northwest Street, 1947. Courtesy of Peggy Kimbo.

nets by taking the bottoms out of old veggie baskets and sticking them on polls . . . And where the fudge shop is today on Main Street—that was McCready's furniture store. We'd go there and collect large boxes that the store threw away, and used them as play benches—who could afford fancy things back then?"

Peggy and her siblings did have bikes, however, that they learned to ride on St. John's College campus. "St. John's and the Naval Academy were the two best playgrounds anyone could ask for," Peggy said. They also had tennis rackets and even though their father worked at the Naval Academy, its tennis courts were off-limits to them because they were black.

But this didn't stop the eager young athletes; they improvised by hitting balls against the Hanover Street wall next to the Academy's Gate No. 3. They often played while listening to music that came from a nearby home on Hanover. One time, as Peggy recalled, "the little white girl who played the music leaned out of her balcony and invited us in. We ate sandwiches, danced the jitterbug and sang 'Pennies From Heaven.' It was heaven."

When Peggy and her siblings weren't playing outdoors, they could be found at the movies. "We'd go to the movies—segregated movies," she said. "At the Star Theatre [at the corner of Northwest and Calvert Streets] we had Bank Night, and 3-2-1 Night when the first ticket cost $3, the second $2, and the last ticket just a dollar . . ." Sometimes after a matinee they would splurge and grab 5-cent ice cream cones at the Little Campus Inn.

Peggy, at left, with her sister Carolyn (Mynie) and Aunt Edith at 15 College Avenue, the home of Aunt Edith and Uncle Edward Notis, c. 1935. Courtesy of Peggy Kimbo.

Peggy attended St. Mary's Parochial Elementary School (the one for black children), while her friend, Jeanie Stewart, whom Peggy described as "a pretty girl with long red braids," attended the one for whites. The two would wait for each other after school, then stroll up Duke of Gloucester Street to the old Bladen Street station "for some girl talk," Peggy said. Several times she told Jeanie that she wanted to be a nun when she grew up, which made her friend "crack up laughing." Ironically, when their paths crossed years later Jeanie, not Peggy, had actually become a nun.

Peggy's family also worshiped at St. Mary's Roman Catholic Church, where they sat at the back left. "That's where most blacks sat during Mass," she said. Then, after church, they walked home to College Avenue via Green Street where "you could smell hot rolls cooking from all over town on Sundays."

Sunday was a special day for Peggy's family: a day of rest, worship, and celebration. "On Sundays Uncle Ernest, my father's brother, would read us the funnies or play horseshoes with us . . . He was the B.B. King of Annapolis and would sing his head off while sitting in the yard in a chair with his guitar," she recalled.

Advertisements for the Star Theatre from the Evening Capital *(December 12, 1923).*

Sunday brunch was a weekly tradition at 20 College Avenue, where Peggy's grandmother set a fine spread, using dishes from her china closet, and her lace tablecloth. Grapefruit halves topped with cherries started the meal, followed by platters of eggs, bacon, pork chops, fried potatoes, radishes, and sweet smelling hot rolls.

Most of the places Peggy's grandmother bought her food including the A&P at Market Space, a country store on Fleet Street, and two grocery stores on College Avenue have since disappeared. So has College Avenue Baptist Church, at the corner of College Avenue and St. John's Street, where Peggy and her friends would "race and sit on its steps out of breath on the way to catch a matinee." The Severn Service Station at 260 King George

The Little Campus Inn, as shown in the brochure, "Rambling thru Annapolis Maryland Spring-Summer 1968." From the author's collection.

11

Street, where Peggy's family purchased oil for wintertime heat, also belongs to the past.

Clearly, much has changed about Annapolis since Miss Pink delivered Peggy in 1930. Yet Peggy was right when she said, "It's still a pretty town. It's a town of memories . . . It's all built up, but the sentiment's still there."[1]

Galway Bay gave Peggy Kimbo a surprise party on March 15, 2005, eight days after her 75th birthday. Among the guests was Maryland Governor Robert L. Ehrlich, Jr., who issued a proclamation recognizing Peggy as an exceptional citizen. Courtesy of the Governor Ehrlich Press Office.

Orlando Ridout IV Recalls His Family's Woodlyn Farm Dairy

While Peggy was raised in downtown Annapolis, Orlando Ridout IV grew up in the city's rural surroundings. This is his story, and that of his family's farm, Woodlyn Farm Dairy.

Linda Keefer found an unexpected treasure in her backyard when Tropical Storm Isabel flooded Eastport in 2003. There on Back Creek, atop a pile of debris, she discovered a small glass bottle. Its unique shape and size, 2½ inches wide by 5½ inches tall, suggested that it was no ordinary bottle. And indeed, wiping the mud from its surface revealed these words: "Half Pint Liquid, Woodlyn Farm Dairy, Federal Tested Herd, O. Ridout, Jr. Annapolis, MD."

While the bottle's location just before Isabel is unknown, its first home was Woodlyn Farm Dairy. Owned and operated by the Ridout family, Woodlyn stood on the south side of Route 50 near the Chesapeake Bay Bridge. It thrived during a bygone era in Annapolis: an era when locals relied on small, independent dairies; an era when agriculture defined much of the landscape; and an era when "cows—not just cars—could be seen on Route 50," according to Orlando Ridout IV.

Born in 1922, Mr. Ridout IV was the Ridout family's oldest grandson. His father, Orlando Ridout III, was the last Ridout to be born at the family's estate called Whitehall. This grand property sits seven miles from Annapolis on a peninsula bounded by Whitehall and Meredith Creeks. Governor Horatio Sharpe, who governed Maryland from 1753–69, built Whitehall in 1764–65. Its ownership changed hands when he willed it to John Ridout, who came to Maryland in 1753 as his secretary. Whitehall remained in the Ridout family until about 1896, when it was sold to Mrs. Caroline Story, the wife of U.S. Army General J. P. Story, who was stationed in Washington, D.C.

Orlando Ridout III attended Maryland Agricultural College (now the University of Maryland) before serving in the Maryland National Guard during World War I.

Orlando Ridout IV, 1999. Courtesy of M. E. Warren. Copyright ©1999 by M. E. Warren.

5½" tall x 2½" wide

Woodlyn Farm Dairy bottle discovered by Linda Keefer in 2003. Illustration by the author.

He started operating Woodlyn Farm Dairy after the war and bought a milk route from his cousin, Orlando Duvall, in 1921. One year later he had his first son, Orlando IV, commonly called Lanny.

A daughter Katherine (Kit), and another son Folger (Mack) completed the family. Their mother, Mary McKinsey Ridout, was a homemaker and R.N. who graduated from Johns Hopkins with a nursing degree. After marrying, she used her skills to treat illnesses and accidents on their farm and in the St. Margaret's community.

As the family's eldest grandson, Mr. Ridout lived with his grandfather, Orlando Ridout, Jr., and his grandmother at Edenlawn Farms: a large, general-purpose farm that neighbored Woodlyn. Edenlawn had a spring garden on one of its sunny hillsides replete with peas, lettuce, radishes, and carrots, and a quince orchard. It also had five acres of market gardens containing strawberries, raspberries, gooseberries, currants, peach trees, and sweet potatoes. And nearby, in a pasture north of the farmhouse, there were a half dozen turkey houses.

In addition to turkeys, Orlando Ridout, Jr., raised sheep and beef cattle, which he sold to Annapolis merchants including the Childs family. William Childs and his son Roland owned Childs & Co. groceries at 169–71 Conduit Street. As Mr. Ridout recalled, "The son, Mr. Roland Childs, often drove out to my grandfather's farm to personally select stock: lambs, veal calves, ducks, geese, butter, and eggs. As a kid he always brought me a whole pack of Wrigley's gum."

While living at Edenlawn, Mr. Ridout attended Annapolis Grammar School on Green Street with Kit and Mack. Before and after school, and during the summer, he worked at Woodlyn with Mack, his father, and other laborers.

"Woodlyn was a working dairy farm—one of about eighteen or twenty very small local dairy farms that existed back then," he said. "We worked from 4 A.M. 'til sundown, seven days [per week], and everyone helped . . . two families lived on the farm, and other families who lived nearby also helped . . . Woodlyn produced five acres of kale and turnips in the winter, as well as sugar corn, and tomatoes—a lot of tomatoes—in the summer. Dad made three tomato plantings per year, planting 3,000 tomato plants each time. That was a lot of tomatoes to pick!"

After picking the tomatoes Mr. Ridout III brought them to local grocers including Rookie's Market at Market Space. In addition to tomatoes, "he always had something else to bring to customers or storekeepers such as eggs and chickens," according to his son.

Mr. Ridout's father also raised cows for milk. Woodlyn boasted eighty-four Guernsey cows, distinguished by their soft golden yellow color. Their milk was pasteurized at the farm, where it was also homogenized once cholesterol became a concern. When customers became even more cholesterol-conscious, the Ridouts replaced the Guernseys with black and white Holsteins, because they produced milk with lower butterfat content.

The cows' "first milking," a job done by hand until Mr. Ridout left for college, occurred at 4 A.M. Workers performed other chores while the milk cooled, and was bottled in glass quart bottles. Then, at about 6:30 A.M., the farm's trucks left to deliver milk throughout the greater Annapolis area.

Mr. Ridout received his own delivery route when he was old enough to drive. It stopped at roughly seventy homes and spanned from Sandy Point to West Severna Park. If Mr. Ridout was lucky, a "jumper" accompanied him on the drive. Jumpers were schoolboys, about fourteen or fifteen years old, who lived in the neighborhood. They carried full milk bottles to customers' doorsteps, where they retrieved and returned the empty ones to the vehicle.

Sometimes customers left more than empty milk bottles for Woodlyn's deliverymen on their doorsteps; they also left mousetraps holding their latest victims. As Mr. Ridout recalled, "Housewives who were afraid to remove the

Kit Ridout with her brothers, Lanny (mounted on the horse Pat) and Mack, at Woodlyn Farm Dairy, 1937. Courtesy of Mr. and Mrs. Orlando (Betty) Ridout IV.

Courtesy of the Maryland State Archives SPECIAL COLLECTIONS (Marion E. Warren Collection) Marion E. Warren, Woodlyn Farm Dairy Truck *MSA SC 1890-2-30,831.*

mice from the traps left them for us. We reset the traps as a 'customer service' and brought the mice back to the barn cats."

Mr. Ridout's route took about five hours to complete. If he had a jumper, he would "drop him off for school by quarter 'til nine," finish the route alone, and return to the farm. This happened at about noon, and then it was back to work. Lunch, like breakfast, was "grab and go," as there was little time for leisure.

After lunch, the second milking occurred from 2 to 4 P.M. The milk was then processed, bottled, and cooled in refrigerators; others baled hay and stored it in the barn. This was hard work, as each bale weighed about 80 pounds.

"Things continued 'til about 6," Mr. Ridout said, "or 'til dark if there was hay to get in when a thunderstorm might blow up and ruin it." At that point, the Ridouts gathered at their dining room table after a hard day's work. There they enjoyed goods from Woodlyn and Edenlawn including fresh fruits, vegetables, beef, pork, poultry, and of course—milk.

Like his father, Mr. Ridout left Annapolis for college. He attended the University of Maryland for three years and graduated before serving in World War II. Upon returning home in 1946, he married Elisabeth "Betty" Lawton of Washington, D.C. That year the newlyweds rented an 18th-century farmhouse located about one mile from Woodlyn, where Mr. Ridout continued to work.

The farm's operations had changed since he left for college; its cows, for instance, were no longer hand-milked. Yet much remained the same, including that work still started long before sunup. "Dad would jingle the party phone line at 4 A.M., signaling that it was time to rise and shine," he said.

Working weekends also remained a crucial part of life at Woodlyn: a fact that would soon change. As Mr. Ridout recalled, "When my brother and I finished college and married, we realized all three of us were working every weekend; we wised up and demanded of my father 'somebody is going to be off each weekend, by turns!' " Their persuasion worked, and soon, family members began to pursue other interests on weekends. For instance, his father and sister competed well in horse shows, and Mack enjoyed success in jousting tournaments. "As a family, these events were our fun occasions when dairy farming was a seven day, 4 A.M. to sundown workday reality," Mr. Ridout said.

On Monday, however, it was back to work. Mr. Ridout's weekday duties included delivering milk to the dairy's customers, as he had done as a teenager. Sometimes, civic duties prevented him from making his morning route. In 1950, at age twenty-eight, he was elected to the Maryland House of Delegates. He was one of six delegates, all Democrats, who represented Anne Arundel County at the time.

As a delegate, Mr. Ridout had to attend frequent morning committee meetings in Annapolis, in which case Betty finished his milk route. On days without committee meetings, he made his deliveries before attending the 2 P.M. session at the State House.

Mr. Ridout remained a delegate for twelve years until his father's cousin defeated him by eighteen votes (a loss he attributes to his stance against slot machines). This happened in 1962, the same year that Woodlyn ceased its door-to-door milk delivery operations. At that point, the dairy became a "milking parlor whose milk was collected by larger, co-op tank trucks," Mr. Ridout said.

This shift in Woodlyn's operations was part of a larger trend in Annapolis, as development redefined its landscape and the roles of local farmers and watermen. Mr. Ridout described this trend's impact on the city's market area.

"Gone are 1930s and '40s, when rows of trucks vending fresh fruits, vegetables, and flowers gathered there to sell their goods . . ." he said. He also noted the reduced abundance of local seafood, citing one of the market's bygone favorite faces, Florence Colbert, as an example. Ms. Colbert, an African-American woman who lived on Fleet Street, was renowned for her crab cakes, which she made from scratch with

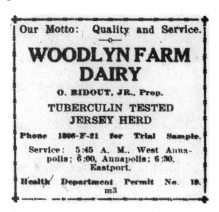

Woodlyn Farm Dairy advertisement from the Evening Capital (May 4, 1923).

17

crabmeat purchased at Rookie's. After making her specialty, she took them from bar to bar around Market Space, selling them on "saltine crackers with a dab of mustard" for just twenty cents each.

Beyond changes at the market area, Mr. Ridout has noticed "local shifts in attitude" and "how residents interact." "Now you have to go to Maryland Avenue to meet people you know . . . because Main Street is mostly chains . . . Storeowners used to live over their stores, and knew other storeowners and their families," he said.

Yet rather than passively lament the loss of an Annapolis "that was," Mr. Ridout has worked, and continues to work, to preserve its heritage. His preservationist activities began in 1938 when he joined the Society for the Preservation of Colonial Annapolis. He was a founding board member of Historic Annapolis, Inc. (now Historic Annapolis Foundation), and is one of only two surviving members from that original founding board. Later, his efforts expanded to include Anne Arundel County and the state of Maryland. In 1964, he became the first director of the Maryland Historical Trust, and concurrently, the first State Historic Preservation Officer.

Many in the Ridout family share their relative's commitment to preservation. Mr. Ridout's daughter, Mollie, is horticultural manager at the restored William Paca Gardens. His daughter-in-law, Barbara Cooper, is active at the Museum Store kept by Historic Annapolis Foundation on Market Space. Finally, his son and Barbara's husband, Orlando Ridout V, is Chief of the Office of Research, Survey & Registration at the Maryland Historical Trust. A leading expert on vernacular architecture, he is co-editor of the book *Architecture in Annapolis: A Field Guide.*

Although Mr. Ridout is now retired from the Maryland Historical Trust, he enjoys volunteer committee work on numerous historical projects. His brother Mack still owns and operates Woodlyn, where he boards show horses and nearby, champions the annual jousting tournament at St. Margaret's Church.[1]

J. Wilson Macey and The Annapolis Banking and Trust Company

Like Mr. Ridout, J. Wilson Macey was raised on one of the many farms that thrived in early 20th-century Annapolis. This is his story, and that of his longtime employer, The Annapolis Banking and Trust Company (AB&T).

Locals were recovering from a violent storm on May 15, 1905: the day AB&T opened for business. In the country, Sunday's downpour had destroyed acres of corn, peas, and fruit trees. Matters were worse in the city. Hailstones had cracked windowpanes, winds had torn signs from storefronts, and tree limbs lay scattered about the flooded streets.

Luther Gadd surveyed the aftermath as he walked through town. As the new bank's president he worried that it had also been damaged. Luckily it hadn't, and the bank opened at 9 A.M. as planned.

Well, almost. The bank's permanent home on Church Circle was still unfinished. Its interior was incomplete, which had forced the bank to assume temporary quarters in the Hotel Maryland Annex. Yet this probably did not bother Col. Gadd; over five years had passed since AB&T received its charter, and he was probably happy to have it open anywhere.

AB&T formed in April 1900, when Maryland's General Assembly passed "An Act to Incorporate the Annapolis Banking and Trust Company." However despite early enthusiasm surrounding the bank, progress was slow to follow. In response, Col. Gadd, a Maryland State Senator and AB&T stockholder, introduced a new bill regarding the company. It passed in March 1904 and amended the 1900 bill in several ways.[1]

First, it listed a new set of company incorporators including Col. Gadd, and then-Mayor of Annapolis, John De Peyster Douw. A native of New York, John Douw came to town in 1888 to attend a Bobby Werntz's Naval Academy preparatory school. He traveled in Europe with Mr. Werntz in 1890–91 and, in

Courtesy of the Maryland State Archives SPECIAL COLLECTIONS (Howard E. Hayman, Jr. Collection) E. H. Pickering, Annapolis Banking and Trust Company Building, *c. 1905 MSA SC 1804-2-265.*

1892, went aboard the school ship *St. Mary's* in New York. He graduated from there, first in his class, in 1894.

Upon graduating, John served as a mate aboard ocean steamers: a job that took him across the Atlantic thirty-four times by 1896. He married Harriet Tate that year, and they settled in Annapolis, where John quickly immersed himself in local affairs. He began volunteering for the Annapolis Fire Department at the Waterwitch Hook and Ladder Company No. 1 on East Street. He also became the Severn Cycle Club's president.

The bank's other incorporators included George Melvin, proprietor of the Hotel Maryland, and Richard Chaney, who owned a livery on West Street. Together, the incorporators elected AB&T's directors who in turn, chose the bank's secretary and treasurer: Mr. Asa Joyce. The *Evening Capital* praised Mr. Joyce as a "thoroughly capable man, of courageous and affable manner." He had earned this reputation while serving in Anne Arundel County's treasurer and tax collector's office. And, while Mr. Joyce was probably delighted by his new job, he faced the same problem as AB&T: he lacked a permanent home in Annapolis.

Just two weeks before the bank's scheduled opening, Mr. Joyce still lived near Odenton with his family, and the bank still lacked a site from which to operate. As the *Evening Capital* reported on May 1, 1905, "The directors are making every effort to secure temporary quarters in which to open up for business immediately. In the meantime work on their permanent quarters will be pushed ahead as fast as possible."

Several days later, the directors secured a space within the Hotel Maryland Annex on Main Street, where the bank opened on May 15.

Let's return now to Col. Gadd at AB&T that day in the afternoon. The bank closed its doors at 4 P.M. after a successful first day in business. Neither the storm, nor the bank's temporary home, had stopped customers from coming, as its ledger revealed.

He probably opened the heavy, canvas-covered book, *Individual Ledger No. 1* to read the day's entries. And, if he did, he was surely pleased. Several people had opened accounts ranging from $600 to $1—the minimum deposit required to open a savings account at AB&T in 1905. S. L. Paro, an Annapolis-area sign maker, deposited $1; Mr. Joyce deposited $90; and Phillip Cooper, an architect and contractor, deposited $600.

That was just the beginning. During its first few weeks in business, AB&T attracted sizeable accounts from Mayor Douw, author and attorney Elihu Riley, and other prominent locals. Companies also came to the bank including the C. W. Martin & Co. This business, which sold oystermen's and builders' supplies, opened an account with over $1,200—one of the largest deposits made in AB&T's early history. Days later, the Henry B. Myers Company, which sold wagons, buggies, and farm supplies on West Street, opened a $200 account. Other businesses followed suit including the Annapolis Ice Manufacturing Company, the Eastport Hiring and Livery Stable, the Colonial Theatre, and the Chesapeake and Potomac Telephone Company.

In addition to businesses, many businessmen opened personal accounts at AB&T in 1905. To cite just two examples, Charles Weiss, who owned one of the city's finest liquor emporiums, made a large first deposit on May 22; the next day, Fred Smith, a Maryland Avenue confectioner, opened his account.

Military personnel also chose AB&T such as Charles Zimmermann, the Naval Academy's longtime Bandmaster. Zimmermann lived at 138 Conduit Street and is best known for composing the Navy song "Anchors Aweigh" for the Naval Academy Class of 1907. Jonas Ingram, a member of that class and a famed athlete, also began banking with AB&T while attending the school.

Ingram, like others who chose AB&T, was wise to do so. The bank offered "absolute safety," to quote its motto, thanks to its Herring-Hall-Marvin Co. vault installed by Andrew Lohr. Mr. Lohr, a German immigrant, had twenty-three years of experience in the safe business when Herring-Hall sent him to Annapolis in 1905. He came to install two safes for AB&T. The first, a smaller safe, was placed in the bank's temporary quarters. This safe's first home had been the First National Bank of Baltimore, where it withstood the city's devastating fire of 1904.

The Annapolis

Banking and Trust Co.

NOW OPEN AND READY FOR BUSINESS

Temporary Location
Main Street Near Church Circle

Capital Stock, – $50,000
Authorized Capital, - $250,000

Secure and Reliable

Under Supervision of State Treasurer – as provided by law.

Your banking business large or small, is solicited; equal consideration given to both. We offer every accommodation consistent with good banking. Money loaned on approved real or personal estate security. Favorable terms extended. Correspondence invited.

Savings Department.

Special attention given to this department. Three per cent interest allowed on deposits, computed semi-annually. Accounts may be opened with deposits of $1 or more.

Trust Department.

This Company is authorized to execute TRUSTS of all kinds, and to act as Executor, Administrator, Guardian, Trustee, Receiver, Committee, etc. Careful and methodical management and settlement of estates.

Wills naming this Company as Executor or Trustee will be drawn, receipted for and deposited in the fire and burglar proof safe of the Company without charge.

Banking Hours.

Daily from.........9 a. m. to 4 p. m.
Saturdays..........9 a. m. to 6 p. m.

Officers—President, LUTHER H. GADD; First Vice-President, G. THOMAS BRASLEY; Second Vice-President JOSEPH F. BRENAN; Secretary and Treasurer, ASA A. JOYCE, Assistant to Secretary and Treasurer, J. FRANK LONG, formerly Cashier of the Reistertown Savings Bank; Counsel, RIDGELY P. MELVIN.

The Company's permanent quarters, Corner Main Street and Church Circle, will be completed on or about July 1st.

AB&T advertisements from the Evening Capital *(May 15, 1905).*

A SPECIAL
AUTO "ACCESSORY"
FOR OUR
SERVICE-LOVING
DEPOSITORS!

Our car-owning depositors enjoy the
special advantages of a particularly convenient "accessory": Our quick, free
Drive-In-Banking Window! They simply
roll up to the window, deposit or with-
draw money, and off they go. Join them!

Annapolis Banking & Trust

Member Federal Deposit Insurance Corporation
Member Federal Reserve System

Advertisement for AB&T's new branch at West Street and Chinquapin Round Road. Courtesy of the Annapolis Banking and Trust Company and Crosby Marketing Communications.

The second safe, which was placed in the bank's permanent home, was large, fireproof, and burglarproof. It boasted an impregnable combination of steel, concrete, railroad iron, glazed brick, and Sargent combination locks. Its locks protected a "vault proper" that was 6 feet long, 9 feet wide, and 7 feet high. Mr. Lohr finished installing this vault on August 21, yet it remained unused until the bank moved to its permanent home on November 2.

One of the first to open an account there was George Macey, who came to America from England in 1878. His grandson, J. Wilson Macey, joined the bank's staff on February 15, 1937.

J. Wilson Macey was born in 1911 on his maternal grandfather's farm, Hollywood Farm, in St. Margaret's, near downtown Annapolis. The Pettibone family owned this partial dairy farm, which stood on land now occupied by the Amberly community. As a child, Mr. Macey lived in West Annapolis, in a home hand-built by his father. Later he lived in the city, where he walked from his grandparents' home on Dean Street to Annapolis High School on Green Street.

Mr. Macey graduated from Annapolis High in 1930. This was a pivotal year for the school. Seniors usually received their diplomas at the Circle Theatre on Church Circle. However, it was too small to house that year's 130 graduates (the school's largest class ever at that point) and their guests. Instead, graduation took place inside Dahlgren Hall at the Naval Academy. About 3,500 gathered there for the ceremony on June 19, including seventy-five female and fifty-five male graduates. The girls wore white semi-evening gowns, and the boys donned white trousers, black jackets, and black ties.

Two of Mr. Macey's classmates, Dashilles LeTourneau and Emmerson Wiley, joined AB&T immediately after graduation. There, they joined George Velenovsky, a 1929 Annapolis High School graduate, who later became the bank's president.

Unlike his friends, Mr. Macey did not work for AB&T immediately after graduation; instead, he joined T. Kent Green's pharmacy at 170 Main Street.

Shortly thereafter, the Depression began to impact Annapolis. Fortunately, he remained employed and the city fared relatively well. As he recalled, "Annapolis survived the Depression because it was a stable town. It was the state capital, the County Seat, and it had the payrolls of the Naval Academy and other organizations."

Mr. Macey left Green's for AB&T after the Depression. "Annapolis was still a small town then [in 1937] . . . with no branch banks," he said. Mr. Macey's first job with the bank was as a "runner," which meant he "did a little bit of everything, including working long hours and weekends." His main task was to exchange checks between local banks at the end of the day. "Instead of going through regular clearinghouses, banks such as AB&T settled the difference in cash at the close of business," he said.

Mr. Macey was quickly promoted to teller and worked behind "Jesse James style bars that stretched to the ceiling." He remembers looking out into the bank's formerly narrow lobby and seeing "long lines of customers," many of whom he knew. He also remembers the bank's old-fashioned bookkeeping techniques, its original main entrance, which was located on Church Circle, and that it rented its upstairs to tenants including a radio station.

After several years at AB&T, Mr. Macey was drafted into the Army during World War II. At first, he was stationed at stateside locations such as Forts

Courtesy of the Maryland State Archives SPECIAL COLLECTIONS (Marion E. Warren Collection) Marion E. Warren, Annapolis Banking & Trust Co., Drive-in Bank Opening, *1954 MSA SC 1890-2-30,013D.*

Meade and Benjamin Harrison, where he attended finance school. Next, he served abroad; he was stationed in England, followed by France, where he remained for fifteen months. Mr. Macey returned to Annapolis in April 1947 and rejoined AB&T.

Thanks to his schooling at Fort Benjamin, Mr. Macey received what he called his first "desk job" at the bank in the mid-1950s. At that point, he helped to launch the bank's new branches: a task that required "wearing a lot of hats." In 1954, he helped to open its innovative branch at West Street and Chinquapin Round Road, which was one of the first to offer drive up banking in Maryland. "Customers were slow to come at first . . . probably because they did not know quite what to make of the new site," he said.

Mr. Macey recalled when AB&T joined Mercantile Bankshares Corporation, a Baltimore-based multi-bank holding company, in 1971. "This was not a merger," he said. Rather, AB&T retained its name, management, Board of Directors, and community identity. Five years later, Mr. Macey retired as the bank's treasurer. And although he is retired, he remains close to AB&T; he lives within a short walk of one of its banking offices, which he helped to establish.[2]

Charles and Edward Weiss: Immigrants, Brothers, and Businessmen

Like Mr. Macey, Edward and Charles Weiss had strong ties to AB&T. They helped to found the bank in response to the difficulty they—like other local Jewish immigrants—had in obtaining loans. This is their story.

Despite a dismal weather forecast, Annapolitans still planned to celebrate on Saturday, December 26, 1903. Many were going to the Christmas Hop at the Naval Academy's new Armory. There, surrounded by streamers, fresh greens, and white lights, they would dance 'til midnight. Others had dinner reservations at Carvel Hall. Located at 186 Prince George Street, this new, luxurious hotel offered the city's finest dining.

Next door to Carvel Hall, at 182 Prince George Street, Charles Weiss probably felt like celebrating too. It had been a year to remember for the local entrepreneur, and yesterday's unexpected good luck had made it even better.

Born in Austria in 1861, Mr. Weiss was among the many Jewish immigrants who came to America in the late 19th century. He arrived in 1883 and was naturalized in 1888. He lived briefly in New York, where he and his wife Fannie had their first two daughters: one in 1889 and the other in 1890.

That year, the Weiss family moved to Annapolis where a third daughter was born in 1900.

Mr. Weiss quickly established himself in Maryland's capital city. One year after arriving, he opened a liquor business at 8 Market Space that became a local favorite. In fact, the *Evening Capital's Historical and Industrial Edition* praised it as the "best liquor house in town" in 1908. The *Edition* compared the store to the "rock of Gibraltar" for its "firmly established trade," and lauded its appearance.[1]

The two-story brick building was attractive and inviting. Its plate glass windows were among the first in Annapolis, and four ornate signs decorated its facade. Its interior was equally impressive, with large mirrors, intricate woodwork, and a vast stock of goods that featured whiskeys from America, Canada, Scotland, and Ireland, and wines from France, Germany, Spain, Virginia, and California—all at unbeatable costs. For instance, customers could buy a bottle of champagne for just $3 on New Year's Eve, 1903.

Mr. Weiss displayed his stock on cherry wood shelves next to an oak bar and buffet. He also displayed his two business mottos near the buffet: "If you don't see what you want, ask for it; we have it;" and "We lead in prices others try to follow." The *Edition* claimed that these mottos were not "idle boasts" or "catch phrases." It stated, "For if Mr. Weiss does not have it, it is not made, and his prices are not equaled anywhere."

The *Edition* also praised Charles's brother, Edward Weiss. Born in Austria, Edward was about seven years younger than Charles. He immigrated to America in the late 19th century and stayed briefly in New York. He then moved to Baltimore and settled in Annapolis at about the same time as Charles.

Like his brother, Edward became a successful entrepreneur. And, like his brother, he was also in the liquor business. He was "one of the first to show Annapolitans what an up-to-date modern saloon [was]," said the newspaper. He lived above his saloon, the Leading West End Liquor House, at the corner of West and Calvert Streets. Some locals came to the "West End" to "while away a most pleasant and happy hour after the arduous duties of the day;" others took advantage of its

Charles Weiss, early 20th century. Courtesy of Carole Markoff.

Charles Weiss's Wine and Liquor Emporium at 8 Market Space, early 1900s. From the author's collection.

special home and business delivery service. The saloon also attracted visitors who could keep their horses at its hitching yard or stable.[2]

Although his brother was in the same business, Charles advertised that his store was "the best liquor house" in town in December 1903. Clearly locals were fond of it, as he was one of the city's wealthiest merchants at the time. His success enabled him to buy a lot on Prince George Street in 1900 for $1,225 and increase its size with a $140 purchase in 1901. Two years later, he built an impressive house onsite. The Weiss family moved in 1903 into what is now Sara-Beth's bed and breakfast.

Charles Weiss's granddaughter Carole Markoff, who was raised at 182 Prince George Street, recalled one of its defining features: A large stone block carved with the letters "C.WEISS" that once stood in front of the home. The block was raised above ground level to allow a person to tie a horse to it, or to help a rider mount or dismount with greater ease. Unfortunately, it has since been removed and its location is unknown.

In addition to owning a house and business in Annapolis, Charles maintained several properties across Spa Creek in Eastport. He owned a glass factory, a summer home called "Glen Echo," and stables on about 12 acres of land near Back Creek, where he pursued his favorite hobby: raising horses. He raised horses, including several trotters, and raced them on Camp Parole's track, where he won many trophies.

Yet poor weather and a hectic pace left little time for hobbies in

The Weiss family at home at 182 Prince George Street, early 1900s. Courtesy of Carole Markoff.

December 1903. It had been a busy month for Mr. Weiss and his fellow Market Space merchants. Louis Baer, who at age twenty-four became the city's first Jewish alderman, owned a shoe store at 36 Market Space. Thanks to an eye-catching ad, he had sold countless "famous Dorothy Dodd" women's shoes for $3.00 per pair. Nearby, men had flocked to Isaac Benesch & Sons that offered ladies' diamond rings for just $12.50. And, at 24 Market Space The Hub, "Annapolis' head to foot outfitters," had been equally swamped.

The Hub launched a plan to attract customers several weeks before Christmas. Starting in early December, the first 150 customers who spent $10 or more there were entered into a raffle. The raffle's grand prize was a pony, saddle, and bridle, or $50 if the winner didn't like horses. The contest would take place at The Hub, on December 25, at 10 A.M.

Although hoping for snow, Annapolitans received a wet, not white, Christmas that day. As the *Evening Capital* reported "As to weather, yesterday's was the most unpopular that the weather man could have meted out for Christmas . . . People carrying gifts to friends were wet and draggled with rain and mud or dropped the packages in pools of water . . . " However this downpour didn't stop people from heading to The Hub for the raffle.

Ticket holders and other spectators gathered there for the contest. Two young boys, Burgess and Brown, drew slips from a hat while a

Plain and Fancy

mixed drinks cocktails, etc., etc., perfectly blended, bottled and ready for instant use at home - appeal to the householder when unexpected visitors "drop in" of an evening. If you have an ounce of ice in the house, we can put in position to entertain your most exacting guest.

s29y

EDWD. WEISS,

..Liquor Dealer..

Cor. West and Calvert Sts., Annapolis.

GO TO

CHAS. WEISS'

Wine & Liquor Emporium.

A House worthy of your thought and attention. Do not take chances as to getting the value of your money by experiment with others, but go the house that has built up a reputation.

Purity and Strength is obtainable in our high grade WHISKIES, BRANDIES, FINE WINES, RUMS and GINS.

IF YOU ARE A GOOD JUDGE OF . . . .

LIQUORS,

CALL AT

CHARLES WEISS,

18 MARKET SPACE, Annapolis, Md.

Advertisements for Charles and Edward Weiss's businesses from the Evening Capital *(October 6, 1903 and October 30, 1900).*

Mr. Wahab and a Mr. Jacobson acted as judges. The winning ticket was number 40, which belonged to Mr. Weiss—a fitting victory given his love for horses. He was overjoyed and his friends congratulated him on his good fortune, according to the newspaper.

Clearly, much about Annapolis has changed since then. Yet much about it remains the same including the exterior of Mr. Weiss's former home at 182 Prince George Street. It appears almost exactly as it did a century ago—aside from missing the block where he probably tied his pony, before taking it to his stables on Christmas morning.

The Troublesome Kate Kealy

Charles Weiss probably knew Kate Kealy since they were practically neighbors. However, even if he didn't know her personally, he certainly knew about her. This tragic widow was the talk of the town in 1903, and this is her story.

The Naval Academy: The evening of September 16, 1903

All was quiet as the watchman made his usual rounds on the Yard. Then suddenly at midnight, a sound from Kate Kealy's house broke the silence. He turned, looked up, and saw Mrs. Kealy at her window aiming a revolver at him. He leapt behind a nearby tree just before she fired, and later eluded her in the darkness.[1]

Meanwhile, a stone's throw away, members of the Class of 1907 slept soundly after another arduous day of Plebe Summer. They arrived at a tumultuous time for the Academy, at the climax of its ongoing battle with Mrs. Kealy. For over a year, she had fought to save her home at 57 Hanover Street from the federal government, which planned to raze and replace it with new officers' quarters called Porter Row. The Academy had recently annexed the land on which her house stood and had enclosed the area with a wall.

Mrs. Kealy didn't want her house to be destroyed. However, if she had no choice, she demanded financial compensation for her loss. This would have been a logical request if the house were hers. The only problem was, it wasn't. Although she lived there, the property belonged to John Mulhall of New York, who purchased it after her husband John died in 1892.

John Kealy died without a will or children. His heirs-at-law inherited his estate, it was divided, and a house on the lot where Mrs. Kealy lived was given to her as part of her dower. Soon, however, the heirs learned that Mr. Kealy had died with an enormous amount of debt. This forced them to sell some of the property, including Mrs. Kealy's house, to Mr. Mulhall.

Some time between then and 1903, the old house in which she lived burned down, and was replaced by a new one. Mrs. Kealy also fell behind on her taxes, her house was sold at a tax sale, and Mr. Mulhall later repurchased it. Yet to quote the newspaper, he "could never get Mrs. Kealy out. Even the sheriff of the county, whose powers were invoked in Mr. Mulhall's behalf, failed to evict [the] sturdy party in possession."[2]

Mrs. Kealy was nearly twenty years younger than her husband; she was his second wife; her maiden name was also Kealy; and the two had been married for less than a year when he died. She claimed that he had planned to leave her his estate, but died before completing the necessary papers. Perhaps this prompted Mr. Mulhall to allow her to remain in the house as a boarder.

The government paid Mr. Mulhall when it confiscated his house for the Academy's use. However, Mrs. Kealy considered it hers and refused to move—until she too was paid. She threatened to shoot anyone who laid hands on the building, including the Academy's guards who she promised to "pump . . . full of lead."[3] She refused to speak with reporters and had allegedly attacked one with a frying pan.[4] Even those who came too close to "her home" risked being hit by pieces of china, or at least vile epithets.

Mrs. Kealy dominated local newspaper headlines in summer and fall of 1903. Consider this article that hit the *Evening Capital*'s front page on August 25:

Mrs. John Kealy—Refuses to Entertain Visitors At Her Home And Draws The Line on Strangers: Nothing will induce Mrs. Kate C. Kealy, who holds the fort within the government enclosure, and now occupies the one remaining house within the new walls, to entertain visitors.

Mrs. Kealy draws the line at seeing strangers. She will not answer repeated knocks at her doors, back and front, or on her shutters. Recently a lady who had a friendly feeling for the woman who lives alone, isolated from the rest of humanity, sought to gain an interview and took her flowers as a method of introduction, but she failed to accomplish her purpose in this manner.

Mrs. Kealy is still annoyed by the boys in the neighborhood, who throw brick[s], bats, and sticks at her doors and windows until her house is a mere shell. The front door is barricaded and she enters and exits at the back door. The shutters are broken, and there is not a single window, the panes of which are hot shattered. The boys take advantage of the situation, knowing that the city police have no right or authority to arrest them on government property.

When Mrs. Kealy comes out to church on Sunday morning, she is watched by the curious all along the route. . . .[5]

Officers' quarters on Porter Row, 1907. Courtesy of Special Collections & Archives Division, Nimitz Library, U.S. Naval Academy.

By September, the government had lost its patience. Mrs. Kealy had to move so that progress could be made on the new officers' quarters. And, since officials were ordered not to use physical force against her, they used more creative tactics: they cut off her water supply, placed two guards at the only nearby water spigot, and devised a clever plan. They posted two guards at the sole gate through which she could pass and ordered them not to let her return if she left the Yard.

Until then, Mrs. Kealy had left the Yard on Sundays to attend St. Mary's Church on Duke of Gloucester Street. Officials assumed she would do so on Sunday, September 13, and planned to start demolishing her house when she did.

Unfortunately, their plan became public knowledge. Therefore, when Sunday came, a large crowd gathered near her home to see what would happen when she emerged. They were brave, since she had recently "hurled a heavy piece of china" at "some curious person" for merely looking at her house.[6] The crowd must have made Mrs. Kealy suspicious, for she did not go to church that day; nor did she leave for food or water in the days to come.

Instead, she continued to ration $90 in groceries that had sustained her for six weeks and collected rain in pails for drinking water. As the paper noted in late September, "Whether it was an answer to her prayers or not, the heavy downpour of rain yesterday came in the nick of time for Mrs. Kate C. Kealy, who placed pails and other receptacles outside her door to catch the rain water and defied the guard, at the point of a pistol."[7] Later, on October 4, the paper reported, "Serves Mrs. Kealy's Purpose: During the rain storm yesterday afternoon Mrs. Kealy again made her appearance and filled several pails and other receptacles."[8]

By October, however, Mrs. Kealy's will began to break. On October 6 her friend (and the city's Police Chief) Travers Brown, passed her home while on his usual stroll. He heard someone call his name, followed by the sound of window shutters being thrown open. He looked up and saw Mrs. Kealy. She requested to see him, they met, and she asked him to contact Reverend Joseph Kautz, the Rector of St. Mary's Church, on her behalf.

Mr. Brown agreed, and left for the church. When several reporters intercepted him on his way, he said that Mrs. Kealy looked "no more haggard" than when he last saw her six weeks ago.[9]

Mr. Brown returned to Mrs. Kealy later that day bearing bad news. Rev. Kautz was away on vacation; however, he had left a message for her in case she called: to obey the government and move. (He would have told her this himself had she not refused to see him before he left for vacation.) The Reverend's message convinced Mrs. Kealy to admit defeat, and she consented to leave.

At that point, Mr. Brown sought housing for his soon-to-be displaced friend. Yet as the *Evening Capital* reported, "nobody wanted Mrs. Kealy. Some were afraid of her, others did not care to bring themselves into public notice by harboring a woman whose doings had made her public property."[10] Finally, after a lengthy search, the School Sisters of Notre Dame offered her refuge at a building adjacent to their convent in Annapolis—not as a permanent boarder but only until other arrangements could be made.

Mr. Brown arranged to move Mrs. Kealy to the convent via carriage on October 12. Secrecy was crucial to avoid the "curious crowd that would naturally follow"; even the carriage driver did not know he was part of the plan. So that he wouldn't know his true mission, he was ordered to a naval officer's home at 7:30 P.M. This time was chosen to coincide with the Short Line train's arrival from Baltimore, so that the late arrival to the convent would appear to be from the train.

According to the original plan, the driver would learn his final destination at the officer's home. He would proceed from there to Mrs. Kealy's, where she

Marriage entry for John and Kate Kealy, April 7, 1891. Marriage Records, St. Mary's Church, Annapolis, Maryland.

and Mr. Brown would board. However, upon hearing the plan's details, Mrs. Kealy said that she wanted only Mr. Brown to accompany her.

He accommodated her request. The driver left his first stop without the officer, picked up Mrs. Kealy and Mr. Brown, and proceeded to the convent at the base of Shipwright Street. The convent's Superioress greeted them, Mr. Brown departed, and the Sisters treated Mrs. Kealy to dinner and a bath before showing her to her room. The *Evening Capital* reported her move the next day; it's hard to believe its claim that she "and the Naval Academy authorities . . . parted the best of friends."[11]

Soon, Mrs. Kealy became restless at her new quarters. As the paper noted on October 24, "Mrs. Kealy is on the war path again. Tired of the quiet life behind convent walls, she has put on her war paint and feathers and gone on the rampage. Yesterday she visited a resident in the neighborhood of lower Main street and demanded to see the rent book, directing that the rent be turned over to her, or that the tenants vacate. The agent of the property . . . gave the tenants notice that they were not to recognize Mrs. Kealy . . . The agent says if Mrs. Kealy is obstreperous she will have to go to jail."

RAIN PLEASES MRS. KEALEY

SHE GETS WATER SUPPLY AND DEFIES THE MARINE GUARD.

The Government Having Turned Off Her Water Supply, She Has Her Thirst Quenched By The Use of Rain Water.

MRS. KEALEY'S SIEGE

STILL HOLDS THE FORT AND RESISTS GOVERNMENT AUTHORITY.

A Large Crowd Expected Her Removal From The Building Yesterday, But Were Greatly Disappointed.

MRS. KEALY'S REFUGE.

THE SISTERS OF NOTRE DAME WILL TAKE HER IN.

Their Protection Offered And Hospitality Extended To The Woman Who Resisted Government.

THE GOVERNMENT WINS

MRS. KATE KEALY CONSENTS TO LEAVE HER HOME AT LAST.

Chief of Police Travers T. Brown The Go Between—He Intercedes For Her—Provisions Running Low.

Evening Capital headlines regarding Mrs. Kealy, September 18, September 18, October 7, and October 12, 1903.

Mrs. Kealy remained at the convent for two weeks as planned. Then, on October 30, she traveled to Baltimore. The *Evening Capital* featured her trip in this article:

> Mrs. Kate C. Kealy, of hold-the-fort Naval Academy fame, made her first trip since the siege, to Baltimore today. Mrs. Kealy looks well and seems happy. She was the cynosure of all eyes on the way to the train. It is really a pity Baltimore reporters and snapshots do not know such a distinguished individual will alight from the train at Camden Station at 10 A.M. today. They might do her just ice for she is really not a bad looking woman although they pictured her as a hag.[12]

Upon returning to town, Mrs. Kealy requested an extension at the convent. It was granted; however, she began to cause trouble for her hosts. She became morose and angry, and in early November, she complained to the convent's leadership that several Sisters had spoken to her with "abusive language." Those she accused dismissed it as a misunderstanding, which made Mrs. Kealy even more irascible.[13]

At that point, the Sisters began to fear Mrs. Kealy. They gave her a week's notice to leave, which she did on November 16. She bought a roundtrip ticket and left Annapolis for Gotham, New York, on the 7:15 A.M. train. Those who suspected that she was going to live there permanently were mistaken. She said she was simply taking a "little vacation."[14]

What happened next is unclear. Officials have been contacted at St. Mary's Church in Annapolis, and at the School Sisters of Notre Dame in Baltimore. Yet no one seems to know what happened to her after she left town. She is not listed in future Baltimore or Annapolis City directories; she's missing from future Baltimore and Annapolis-area U.S. Census data; and the *Evening Capital* doesn't mention her in the months following her departure.

Dozens of individuals with the last name Kealy live in New York and Maryland. Perhaps one of them can shed light on what happened to the woman who defied the federal government and Naval Academy for over a year.

Pearl Gray's Runaway Wedding

Mrs. Kealy wasn't the only woman who made local headlines in 1903. So did Miss Pearl Gray. This is her story, and that of her runaway wedding in Annapolis.

Havre de Grace, Maryland: August 12, 1903

Conditions were ideal for a trip to Annapolis, as passengers boarded the steamer *Susquehanna*. The water was calm, the sky was clear, and yesterday's humidity had vanished.

Some of the boat's passengers were going to Annapolis to shop. One of the city's stores, Aaron L. Goodman's, was advertising prices up to 40 percent lower than its regional competitors. Others were going to tour the town, the Naval Academy, and its impressive new buildings. However two passengers, Miss Pearl Gray and her beau, Charles Puschell, had something more exciting in mind.

Pearl and Charles had a secret on August 12, 1903—a big one. It was their wedding day: a fact that they couldn't tell Pearl's mother, who was also aboard. A secret wedding was necessary because Mrs. Gray disapproved of Charles. She thought he was unlikely match for her daughter for many reasons. She was just eighteen and he was twenty-nine. He was born and raised in Cecil County; she hailed from Aberdeen in Harford County. He was 5-foot 10-inches tall, and weighed 160 pounds; in contrast, she stood at only 5-foot 2 and weighed 102 pounds. Yet despite these differences (and Mrs. Gray's objections) the two were in love and had been for a while.

They met thanks to a key form of transportation in 1903: the bicycle. Charles was an insurance salesman, who rode his bicycle to collect premiums. He encountered Pearl while riding one day, and they became immediately smitten with each other. Pearl's girlfriends used to tease her and Charles, who often deviated far from his regular collection route to see her. They even created and sang this rhyme about him: "Here comes Mr. Puschell. He wears a tall hat, and he's a great swell!"

Mrs. Gray knew that Pearl wanted to marry Charles. Yet she opposed the idea and had prevented their wedlock for some time. She became suspicious when Pearl suggested taking a last minute trip to Annapolis on August 12—a Wednesday. She became even more suspicious when she learned that Charles also happened to be aboard their boat.

Upon learning this fact, Mrs. Gray became "determined not to be caught napping." She kept a close eye on Pearl and Charles while on the water, and later, in town, which nearly ruined their plan. "She maintained such a relentless vigil all day," Mr. Puschell said at the time, which almost forced them to give up "in despair." Nevertheless, they made a bold, last minute move.[2] After several hours ashore, the excursionists

STEAMBOAT LINES.

TOLCHESTER COMPANY— STEAMERS FOR ANNAPOLIS AND WEST RIVER LINE, Mondays, Wednesdays, Fridays and Saturdays at 8.00 A.M.; Sundays at 8.30 A.M.; leave Annapolis for Baltimore at 4.30 P.M.; Sundays, 3.00 P.M. LITTLE CHOPTANK RIVER LINE, Tuesdays and Thursdays at 7.00 A.M. SASSAFRAS RIVER LINE, week-days, except Friday and Saturday, at 2.45 P.M., Saturdays at 10.30 A.M., for Betterton, Buck Neck and Sassafras river landings. Does not stop at Gales and Buck Neck on Monday and Wednesday. PORT DEPOSIT LINE, for Betterton, Havre de Grace and Port Deposit; Mondays at 2.00 P.M., Tuesdays, Thursdays and Saturdays at 1.00 P.M., Fridays at 3.30 P.M., Sundays at 9.00 A.M. Stops at Tolchester on Fridays only. Freight received at Pier 15, Light street.

Tolchester Steamboat Company schedule from the Baltimore Sun *(August 10, 1903).*

gathered for their return trip to Havre de Grace. They reconvened at the Prince George Street wharf, where the *Susquehanna* and similar vessels docked. Once everyone was aboard, and Mrs. Gray was sure that the danger had passed, she let Pearl and Charles stroll about the deck together without a chaperone. This wasn't a good idea.

Just as the boat was casting off, the young lovebirds sprang over its lower deck rail onto the wharf, rushed into town, and bolted for the State House. By the time Mrs. Gray realized what had happened, it was too late; the *Susquehanna* was already well out into the harbor.

What happened next isn't fully clear. The *Evening Capital* reported the wedding. So did the *Baltimore Sun* in a front page article titled "Wed in Senate Chamber: Runaway Couple Who Get Ahead of Watchful Mamma." It is this account that Pearl's descendents are familiar with, and it reads as follows:

"Frightened, but thoroughly happy, the prospective bride and groom encountered [at the State House] the gallant Secretary of State, Wilfred Bateman; John Z. Bayless, Chief Clerk in the State Treasurer's office, and several other well-known bachelors and told them of their adventure and asked for assistance in finding a minister. The alacrity with which these gentlemen responded and the air of great excitement they gave to all of Statehouse Hill because of the anticipated wedding was remarkable."

Courtesy of the Maryland State Archives SPECIAL COLLECTIONS (Robert G. Merrick Archives of Maryland Historical Photographs) Robert Sadler, The Steamer Susquehanna, *c. 1903 MSA SC 1477-1-6371. The Tolchester Steamboat Company built the iron-hulled, propeller-driven* Susquehanna *in 1898 for its subsidiary, the Port Deposit and Havre de Grace Steamboat Company. Author David Holly praised her as "by far the handsomest craft the Tolchester line ever owned," and a "lovely creature."* [1] *In 1923, the company sold her to New Orleans, due to a decreased demand for steam travel along the Susquehanna River route.*

The Maryland State House. Illustration by the author.

Next, Secretary Bateman and the others showered the young couple "with well-meant attentions" until Reverend Henry Lowndes Drew arrived from St. Anne's Protestant Episcopal Church. The group then went to the Senate chamber, where Rev. Drew performed the wedding. Finally, "a handsome contribution was presented to Mr. and Mrs. Puschell and they were warmly congratulated."

After the ceremony, Mr. Bateman asked Pearl if there were "any more damsels in Aberdeen" like her who were "available for marriage." She replied, "No, but we have several elderly maids up there, who would just suit you bachelors." The couple left Annapolis for Baltimore that evening, in order to "go home and ask for forgiveness."[3]

Pearl and Charles went onto enjoy a long, happy, fruitful marriage. They had ten children, including three boys and seven girls. One of them, Mrs. Esther P. Hokuf of North East, Maryland, contacted me after *The Capital* published this column, to share more about her family's history.

Mrs. Hokuf was born in Cecil County, in the home that her parents occupied when they were first married. She has been to Annapolis several times and has seen the State House where her parents were married. Unlike them, however, she didn't come by water. Over sixty years have passed since the last steamboat docked at the Prince George Street wharf, bringing shoppers, tourists, and occasionally, bold young lovers to town.

Winston Churchill—The American

Shortly after Pearl's wedding, the impressive Carvel Hall hotel opened on Prince George Street—four blocks from where the *Susquehanna* had docked. The hotel was named after the book *Richard Carvel*, which became a national bestseller in 1899. Here's the surprising story of this book's author, Winston Churchill—the American.

The Naval Academy: Winter of 1894

Another demerit? Naval Cadet Winston Churchill was dumbfounded. Granted he deserved last month's citation for having a dirty heater (and last week's for being late for breakfast) but today's was ridiculous. His bookshelves were not "dusty" as Lieutenant Charles Colahan, the overzealous inspector, had claimed.[1]

Churchill, nicknamed Spoony, received many demerits for minor violations while attending the Naval Academy. Yet he never spent a day aboard the *Santee:* the ship used to discipline the school's more unruly cadets. Churchill was a fine student; he graduated from the Academy thirteenth out of a class of forty-seven in 1894. He excelled in athletics and was one of the Cadet Battalion's four Cadet Lieutenants. He was also president of the school's Eating Club and had a healthy appetite, which earned him a second nickname: House.

Churchill was born November 10, 1871, in St. Louis, Missouri. Upon graduating from high school in 1888, he became a paper store clerk because college was financially impossible. His luck changed two years later. A St. Louis boy became ill in spring of 1890 and had to forfeit his appointment to the Naval Academy. Churchill seized this opportunity, contacted his U.S. Congressman, secured his own appointment to the school, and left home for Annapolis.

Churchill had it all upon becoming a plebe at eighteen: a sturdy 170-pound frame, intellect, and athleticism. He became a fencing expert and played on a champion intercollegiate football team at the Academy; however, his greatest athletic feat there was re-establishing crew as a sport. A violent storm had destroyed the school's shells and boathouse in 1870, and no effort was made to rebuild the program—until Churchill arrived.

His first published literary work was a letter to the editor in the August 6, 1892, *Army and Navy Register.* Titled "A Plea for the Revival of Boating interests at the Naval Academy," it contained what he called "a glorious appeal to all those interested in the Navy" to support crew at the school. As he wrote,

Naval Cadet Winston Churchill in the center of the front row, from the 1894 Lucky Bag. *Courtesy of Special Collections & Archives Division, Nimitz Library, U.S. Naval Academy.*

John Paul Jones ceremony at the U.S. Naval Academy, 1906. Courtesy of Special Collections & Archives Division, Nimitz Library, U.S. Naval Academy.

"Sir: It is a remarkable fact that from 1870 until this year a rowing crew of any description has not been in existence at the Naval Academy. When one considers that the latter stands alone as a school for those who are to spend their lives on the water . . ."

Churchill and several of his peers had already organized an informal crew team by the time he composed his letter. When describing its activities he said, "It requires no constant nagging here on the part of a captain to keep his crew from indulgences and excesses for the simple reason that such things are out of reach. Supper is postponed for the crew and beefsteak is added to the menu; when your crew man reflects that in case he does not row he will have to go to an early supper without beefsteak and that there will not be time enough to go see a girl, he generally decides in favor of beefsteak."[2]

Churchill's persuasive prose worked, and crew returned to the Academy. Yet despite this and other achievements there, Churchill sensed that his military career would be brief. He had already started to write sketches and short stories and, in 1892, he confessed to his uncle a strong desire to resign from the service to "let in a man below who has probably set his heart on it." Later, during his final year at Annapolis he wrote, "I have made up my mind that I would rather shovel coal than go in the Navy."[3] Then, on September 11, 1894, just three months after graduating from the Academy, he resigned from his duty station in New York City to become a writer.

Upon resigning, Churchill worked briefly for the *Army and Navy Journal* in New York, a job that thrilled him as much as military life had. Next he turned to *Cosmopolitan Magazine*, where he rose to managing editor in just nine months. Yet Churchill still wasn't satisfied. In 1895, he married the wealthy Ms. Mabel Harlakenden Hall, whose family fortune enabled him to abandon journalism and write independently.

In 1899, the couple bought 100 acres in Cornish, New Hampshire, where they built a home called "Harlakenden House." Churchill quickly became the talk of the town in Cornish—and not for positive reasons. He owned one of the area's first, perhaps the very first, cars that some called the "gray devil." Cornish resident Charles Burlingham criticized it in a chiding newspaper letter to the editor. He wrote that, "I am quite sure that all prudent people, who value their lives or property, will carry lights whenever there is a chance that they may meet the Churchill motor car!"[4]

Harlakenden House became a favorite colony for artists, writers, and even President Woodrow Wilson, who rented it as his "Summer White House" for three years. Like Wilson, Churchill also held public office. Starting in 1902, he served two terms as a Republican in the New Hampshire State Legislature. During this time, he became outraged by lobbyists' corrupt methods (and the "corrupting power of the Boston and Maine Railroad"), both of which influenced his choice to run for Governor of New Hampshire in 1906. During his campaign he said, "I can see no other way of clearing the atmosphere but to

Carvel Hall as seen from Prince George Street. Courtesy of M. E. Warren and Historic Annapolis Foundation. Copyright © [no date on photograph] by M. E. Warren.

come out plainly and squarely with what I believe to be right—with what I have always tried to set forth in my books as right."[5]

Churchill lost the gubernatorial race in 1906 and again in 1912 as a Bull Mooser, or member of the Progressive Party led by Theodore Roosevelt in the presidential campaign of 1912. Although this defeat marked the end of his political career, he continued to press for political reform through writing. "I am not merely writing a story— I am giving a solution," he said.[6]

As an author, Churchill is best known for his historical fictions, including *Richard Carvel.* The *New York Times* hailed this national bestseller as "the most extensive piece of semi-historical fiction which has yet come from an American hand," upon its release in 1899.[7] Churchill began imagining the book's plot while attending the Academy. In 1896–97, he returned to Annapolis and traveled to Baltimore and Washington, D.C. to gather additional background for the book.[8]

Richard Carvel impacted Annapolis shortly after it was published. For instance, it influenced the return of John Paul Jones's remains to the city in 1906. Jones appears as a hero in the book. He rescues its main character, Richard Carvel, from pirates who are holding him captive aboard their ship the *Black Moll.* Jones sinks the ship, saves Richard, and takes him to Scotland and London. Although Richard eventually returns to Annapolis, he later rejoins Jones as a member of his crew aboard the *Bon homme Richard.*

The real John Paul Jones died in Paris in 1789. However his grave was never marked and consequently, was lost during the chaos of the French Revolution. Its location remained a mystery for over a century until U.S. Army General Horace Porter read *Richard Carvel* in 1899. Porter was America's Ambassador to France at the time, and reading the book enticed him to search for Jones while he was in Paris.

Porter pursued Jones's grave for five years using his own financial resources; he even stayed abroad after his term as ambassador expired to complete his quest. His efforts bore fruit in 1905 when he discovered the grave beneath a building, in an abandoned Paris cemetery; officials then decided that Jones's remains should rest permanently at the Naval Academy.

They returned there in style. President Roosevelt sent the Atlantic Fleet's Third Division to return them to Annapolis, where an impressive ceremony occurred. At first, they were housed on the Yard beneath Bancroft Hall's staircase. Then in 1913, they were placed in a crypt beneath the Chapel.

Jones's return was not the only impact *Richard Carvel* had on Annapolis. It also incensed many Annapolitans. Churchill defamed their city in the book's introduction by writing, "The lively capital which once reflected the wit and fashion of Europe has fallen into decay. The silent streets no more echo with the rumble of coaches and gay chariots, and grass grows where busy merchants trod. Stately ballrooms, where beauty once reigned, are cold and empty and mildewed, and halls, where laughter rang, are silent . . . Mr. Carvel's town house in Annapolis stands . . . a mournful relic of a glory that is past."[9]

The New Hotel
—
Carvel Hall

NOW OPEN.
—
ROOMS WITH PRIVATE BATH.
—
CAFE.

Arrangements for Receptions,
Teas, Card Parties, Banquets, etc.

Advertisements for Carvel Hall from the Evening Capital *(October 12, 1903).*

While this description angered citizens, it also made them aware of their city's decaying heritage and value.[10]

Churchill's book influenced Annapolis in a final way. It inspired the name of Carvel Hall. This hotel can trace its origins to 1901, when real estate developer William Larned purchased the historic William Paca estate (c. 1763–65) on Prince George Street for approximately $15,000.[11] Richard Swann's heirs owned the mansion and were using it as a boarding house at the time.

Mr. Larned transformed the site into a luxurious 200-room hotel. It opened in October 1903, and was named Carvel Hall to benefit from *Richard Carvel*'s enormous popularity. This was a fitting name since Churchill had boarded at the Paca house while gathering background for the book.[12]

As *Richard Carvel*'s popularity soared in America, another author named Winston Churchill began receiving extraordinary amounts of fan mail in Great Britain. Initially, he thought the letters were congratulations for his novel *Savrola;* however, he soon realized that they were written in praise of *Richard Carvel* instead.

At about the time the British Churchill made this discovery, two of his recent novels had just been issued in the United States: *London to Ladysmith* and *Ian Hamilton's March,* which were based on his adventures as a war correspondent for the *London Morning Post* during the South African War. To avoid future confusion (and potential legal action) the British Churchill wrote to the American and agreed to sign his name Winston Spencer Churchill for all of his future books. In response, the American Churchill said he would gladly add his middle name as well, if he had one. He also considered adding "The American" after his name, but never did. Consider this passage, from his correspondence to the British Churchill, dated June 20, 1899:

"Mr. Winston Churchill is extremely grateful to Mr. Winston Churchill for bringing forward a subject which has given Mr. Winston Churchill much anxiety. Mr. Winston Churchill appreciates the courtesy of Mr. Winston Churchill in adapting the name of Winston Spencer Churchill in his books, articles, etc. Mr. Churchill makes haste to add that, if he had possessed any other names, he would certainly have adopted one of them . . . Mr. Winston Churchill, moreover, is about to ask the opinion of his friends and of his publishers as to the advisability of inserting the words, 'The American,' after his name on the title page of his books . . ."[13]

The two Churchills had much in common. Each graduated from his country's service academy, made his living as a young writer, became a politician, a reformer, read the others' works, and of course, had the name Winston Churchill.

Robert Campbell Recalls Prohibition and Politics in Annapolis

Robert Campbell grew up close to Carvel Hall in its heyday. Recently, this native Annapolitan reflected on his local adventures—both as child in a "smaller, simpler" Annapolis and later, as a politician.

Robert Campbell had a head start on his political competition. He began campaigning before his birth thanks to his mother, Mary France "Mamie" Campbell. It was June 1919 in Annapolis, and Mamie, who had just recovered from Spanish Influenza, was five months pregnant with him. Yet despite these facts—and the summer heat—she worked on John Levy's mayoral campaign, helping him to defeat Charles Henkel at the polls on July 14.

Mamie delivered Robert four months later at the Annapolis Emergency Hospital, on Franklin Street. She took him home to 121 Prince George Street that her husband Henry had just bought, and where Robert lives now with his wife Jane.

As a boy, Mr. Campbell walked to Annapolis Grammar School on Green Street. The school's location was ideal; it was close to his home and even closer to Dr. John Ridout's on Duke of Gloucester Street. Dr. Ridout's backyard had fruit trees that provided free after-school snacks for Mr. Campbell and his peers. "We'd sneak into his yard for pears or apples, mostly apples," he said.

Mr. Campbell worked to help support his family during grade school. He started collecting and selling bottles to bootleggers at age eight—even though Annapolis had been declared a "dry zone" in 1918, Congress had passed the National Prohibition Act in 1919, and the 18th Amendment had outlawed the sale of liquor since 1920.

Annapolis had several bootleggers then, including one on Maryland Avenue, another on Compromise Street, and one Prince George Street, where Mr. Campbell sold most of his bottles. He carried them in a wagon to the porch, where the bootlegger inspected, counted, and paid him for them. "We got 2 cents for a quart-sized bottle, a penny for a pint, and a half cent for half a pint," he said.

Mr. Campbell continued to help support his family during the Depression. He turned ten just before the stock market crashed on Black Tuesday, 1929, and eleven the year his father was forced to close his business.

"My father sold general merchandise and ship chandlery goods at 122 Dock Street," Mr. Campbell said. "But during the Depression the A&P sold cheap. The competition was horrible . . . you could buy bread and beans there for 5 cents. We couldn't meet that price." To make matters worse, locals often charged goods at his father's store. "But they couldn't pay their debts when the Depression came," he said.

Food was often scarce in Depression era Annapolis, including at Mr. Campbell's home. "There were no bread lines, but sometimes there wasn't enough to eat," he said. Nevertheless, he and his friends improvised; they snuck aboard the USS *Reina Mercedes* at the Naval Academy for meals.

Built in Spain in 1887, the 278-foot *Reina* initially served under the Spanish flag. She became the Academy's station ship in 1912 and was used for many purposes, including punishing out-of-line midshipmen. They could be confined there for up to two months and, although they attended regular classes and drills, they slept in hammocks and ate aboard the ship.

121 Prince George Street, where Robert Campbell has lived since 1919. Illustration by the author.

USS Reina Mercedes. *Courtesy of Special Collections & Archives Division, Nimitz Library, U.S. Naval Academy.*

They received two large meals aboard the *Reina* on Sundays, which is when Mr. Campbell usually went. "We went under the gangway and snuck in through the porthole to the main deck galley . . . We got in good with the cooks, and ate food, and drank black tea in heavy porcelain mugs. You could drop those mugs on the steel deck and they still wouldn't break!" he said.

Mr. Campbell also sneaked aboard to watch movies. "Towns kids had no money for movies. But a few times a week—Wednesdays and weekends—there were movies on the *Reina* for officers' families . . . They sat on the benches, but we sat on the floor," he said.

One night, in 1932 or 1933, Mr. Campbell received a surprise while aboard the ship. "I ran into Lou Robertshaw on the *Reina*'s bow. I was there to see a movie; he was there for his demerits," he recalled.

Louis "Lou" Robertshaw was a "three striper," and star athlete while a midshipman. He played baseball, basketball, and football for the Academy for four years, captained the school's 1935 football team, and was "one of the finest centers in the country," to quote the 1936 *Lucky Bag.*

Shortly after Mr. Campbell met Lou Robertshaw, he entered politics as a runner. "I was a runner and ran information from one precinct to another, like bankers who 'ran' checks from one bank to another," he said. That was just the beginning. From that point on, politics remained a crucial part of Mr. Campbell's life. Sometimes, this got him into trouble. Consider what happened in 1941. That summer, former Annapolis Mayor Louis Phipps asked Mr. Campbell to help Walter Moss defeat Jesse Fisher in the race for Ward One Alderman. Mr. Campbell agreed, which outraged Fisher's supporters.

USS Reina Mercedes. *Courtesy of Special Collections & Archives Division, Nimitz Library, U.S. Naval Academy.*

In response, a friend told Mr. Campbell that they "were going to fix me for working for Moss," and that they had a plan to do so. They were going to have him arrested for selling fish bait at his family's market house stall on Sundays (an act that violated an 18th-century Blue Law). Despite this forewarning, Mr. Campbell continued to help Moss and to do business as usual. And, as a result, Officer Frank Connell arrested him one Sunday for selling shrimp to a man who was going fishing. "The cop confiscated the shrimp and put me in a cell," he said.

Fortunately, Mr. Campbell made bail and a judge heard his case soon thereafter. During the trial, the judge asked Officer Connell "Where's the evidence?" to which he replied, "Your honor, the shrimp were stinking so bad we threw them out!" This was good news for Mr. Campbell. Since there was no proof, the judge said, "You threw out the evidence? Case dismissed!"

Mr. Campbell encountered Fisher eight years later—this time, as a candidate for Ward One Alderman. The two vied for the Democratic nomination on the June 20, 1949, primary election. Fisher was overly confident according to Mr. Campbell. "He used to say, 'That boy's not going to beat me,' while sitting with his good friend, Mayor William McCready, in front of his Main Street store," he said.

But Fisher underestimated his competition. "I hit on every door in the ward, door to door, and won by forty-five votes," Mr. Campbell said, "and when the polls closed, and Fisher saw that I won, he said, 'That ain't right—look at the machine again!'"

After defeating Fisher, Mr. Campbell won the general election on July 12. He served as alderman until 1961, and as acting mayor for nine months in 1952.[1]

Henry Campbell, the Old Fish Market, and How "Old Bay" Came to Town

Robert Campbell's grandfather, Henry Campbell, was one among the first tenants to occupy the city's Fish Market, which was built in 1890. What follows are Robert's thoughts about his grandfather, the market, and his family's longtime relationship to it.

My grandfather, Henry Campbell, had a stall in the old Fish Market. He had his own business, nets, and boats and gave people money to buy or build their own nets and boats. Then, they had to sell what they caught to repay him. He also leased oyster beds from the state, planted his own oysters, and stocked Cat Hole [Lake Ogleton] in Bay Ridge with rockfish, and hard heads, to catch once they grew . . .

He lost his stall in 1930 when the city destroyed the Fish Market—even though Walter Quenstedt had promised him a new one. Quenstedt was running against Charlie Chance for mayor in 1929. Chance developed Chance's boatyard in Eastport, where Carrol's Creek Cafe is today.

While he was campaigning, Quenstedt promised my grandfather that he was going to build him and the other merchants a new Fish Market. This enticed him to contribute $100 to his campaign—and that was a lot of money back then . . .

Now Quenstedt won by one vote—just one vote. But the next year, the city tore down the market and didn't build a new one as promised. Instead, they went across the street to the present market, put stalls on the exterior part facing the street, and rented them.

My grandfather rented one of the new stalls. But he was seventy-five, and said he wanted to retire. My father, Henry Clay Campbell, was also going out of business. The stock market had crashed, people charged goods at his store, but couldn't pay their bills . . . so he closed his store and took over grandfather's stall in the market.

Robert was already working at the market house at the time. Like many local youths, he started working in grade school to help support his family. In addition to selling bottles to bootleggers, he gathered and sold shoeboxes and newspapers to the market's merchants. "They used the newspapers to wrap seafood and the boxes to sell soft crabs," he said. Mr. Campbell recalled what the market house and its surroundings were like then:

> We used to play around the market house as kids, in what you'd call Market Square. In the summer, farmers came from the Eastern Shore and put their produce on the backs of their cars: corn, tomatoes, cherries, chickens, and turkeys. Watermelon boats also came from the Shore. So did a theatre, Adam's Floating Theatre, which traveled up and down the Bay. The boat had a stage and stayed at the head of the dock for a week or so every summer. It had big wooden casks that needed to be filled with water. I did this and got a free ticket to the shows . . .
>
> During Thanksgiving and Christmas they [the merchants] put a tablecloth over the hoods of their cars or opened the tailgates. You could get chickens, meat, kill hogs, and cattle—all at Market Square.

"Medicine Men" also came to Market Square according to Mr. Campbell. He recalled that, "The Indians came in their headwear and sold half-pints of 'cure-all,' which they claimed cured everything—cancer, flea bites, insomnia, coughs. It cost 50 cents a bottle and later, $1 a bottle. Sometimes the Indians came on horses and wagons, other times in automobiles and trucks.

Courtesy of the Maryland State Archives SPECIAL COLLECTIONS (Ruth Kean Photographs of Annapolis Collection) The Fish Market, c. 1925 MSA SC 4238-1-1.

There were umbrella men too, who could fix your umbrellas and sharpen your knives. They all ended up here—the umbrella men, the medicine men. The cynosure point of Annapolis was Market Square and its market house."

Robert worked for his father's company, Campbell's Seafood Company, in the market as a teenager, in high school, and after graduation. He recalled what the building, and his father's business were like at that point:

The market house had stalls, offices, and storage space inside, where we [the merchants] stored our goods, and supplies at night. We'd come and set up the next morning, along with Watson, Schaeffer, Brown, and Ernest Miller who had the Chesapeake Sea Food Company. Mornings were the busiest, when people bought their fish, seafood, and produce for the day.

Our company was called Campbell's Seafood Company, retail and wholesale. We sold all kinds of seafood: fish, oysters by the pint and quart, crabs, soft crabs, and peelers (crabs that hadn't shed yet) for bait, and other baits. We bought our seafood from all over the place.

We bought first from local fishermen and crabbers. Sometimes we went out to Mayo, Sandy Point, or Skidmore to get soft crabs. The crabbers went out in the morning and I left the market at around noon to pick them up. I finished at four or five then returned to the market and packed them in ice in the icebox. We put seaweed over top of them, then a layer of newspaper, and then chip ice—the ice went on last, so as not to freeze them . . . We got our ice from the Annapolis Dairy Products Company, where Loews [Annapolis Hotel] is today. We got it from Mr. Lazenby, who started the company—75 cents for 300 pounds of ice. Can you believe it?

We bought and graded about a hundred dozen crabs each day. Small ones cost 15 cents a dozen, jumbos 75 cents a dozen, and there were sizes in between. This was more than we could sell so we went to Baltimore to sell our surplus there, at the wholesale market, for $5 a dozen. Not all of this was profit though. Some died on the way, there was no refrigeration, and we had to pay for transportation to and fro . . .

We got most of our oysters locally too. There were a hundred oyster-tonging boats at the dock and dredge boats in the harbor. They came here because

Campbell's Seafood Company advertisement from the Evening Capital, *(October 10, 1940).*

the creeks and rivers froze but the dock stayed clear. We also got salt-water oysters from North Hampton and Accomack Counties in Virginia, sent to us by Marshall Express in big yellow trucks . . .

Herbie Sadler also sold us seafood. He was in Eastport at the foot of Third Street. He learned from grandfather—started working for him when he was twelve. He sold us salted eels, eels, peelers, and soft crabs. He made the best deviled-crabs . . .

We had hard shell clams shipped up on Railway Express from Ocracoke Island in North Carolina. Each heavy grass sack had 500 clams in it. We bought them for a penny a piece and sold them for 25 cents a dozen. We also got crabmeat shipped from Morgan City, Louisiana; Biloxi, Mississippi; and from Colburn and Jewett on the Eastern Shore. It came [from the Shore] in ice barrels on a ferry boat.

The Campbells sold seafood to a host of clients including residents, restaurants, the Naval Academy, hotels such as Carvel Hall and the Maryland Inn, and the Claiborne Annapolis Ferry Company. Mr. Campbell recalled how he carried fish to the ferry as a little boy in a basket or on a wood strip: "I'd strip a piece of oak and cut it into thin strips, a foot long each, then sling the fish on them and sell them for 25 cents a bunch . . . We also sold crabcakes aboard the *Emma Giles,*" he said.

And we traded too. Old Man Nutwell was the pie man in town. His wife made pies for 25 cents each and he sold them. We traded fish for pies—two pies for two bunches of fish. We never exchanged money with the Nutwells . . .

We traded with the legislators who met every other year for ninety days then. Those who came to town from Allegheny and Garrett County rented rooms and went back on the weekends. They didn't have oysters there in Western Maryland but they did have maple trees, which they tapped for syrup. No money changed hands but we traded. A gallon of maple syrup cost 50 cents and oysters sold for 50 cents a bushel. So we traded a bushel of oysters for a gallon of syrup. There was a lot of bartering in those days . . .

The market was a big affair—almost like a country fair—on weekends. People came from all over. The country people came to sell their ware and spend money. They came

The Campbells sold crabcakes aboard the Emma Giles. *The Tolchester Steamboat Company operated this steamer until the 1930s. Illustration by the author.*

to see what was being sold and who was buying it. It was a gathering place where people came to see and be seen, to buy and to sell. Orville Lee Bowen came from the country. He was three years younger than me and his father, [Joseph] Dell Bowen, had a farm on Riva Road. Orville came to the market to sell their sausages.

Women also came from all over Annapolis and the county. While the husbands sold their goods at the market, the wives would shop on Main Street, Market Space, and the first block of West Street at shoe stores, hat stores, and general merchandise stores. If they had colored servants, they'd carry their baskets or take the goods home for them.

Mr. Campbell brought the first "Old Bay Seasoning" to Annapolis and its market house in summer of 1939. As he recalled,

> The man who made Old Bay was a Jew who had fled from Hitler; he had been a spice man in Austria. He settled in Baltimore, where he started a spice store on the second story of a building on Market Space. He had bins of spices in his store . . .
>
> Now in those days, I'd go to Baltimore's fish market to sell what we, our company, had a surplus of and buy what we lacked. And the spice man was there—at Baltimore's fish market—with his slap basket. He was selling his spice mixture in pint boxes, for 25 cents a box. First he sold the spice and later it got its name.
>
> I thought we could probably sell some of his spice in the city market in Annapolis so I bought ten boxes for 25 cents each. Then I brought them back here and sold them for 50 cents each. Man, it sold like hotcakes! I sold the first Bay Seasoning spice here in Annapolis—to my knowledge . . .
>
> In the old days we—Annapolitans that is—cooked crabs in vinegar, black pepper, red pepper, and salt to season the crabs. We spread it in layers and steamed them. Or, Sam Lorea cooked his in beer . . . We started using Old Bay regularly in the '40s.[1]

The "spice man" Mr. Campbell referred to was Gustav Brunn: a German-Jewish sausage maker who fled Nazi Germany in 1938. He came to Baltimore that year with a spice grinder and "knack for using it to create mixes to spice-up bland recipes."

Upon arriving, Mr. Brunn asked grocers what spices they were buying and how much they cost. In 1939, he started his own wholesale spice business. He called it the Baltimore Spice Company, and it was located above the Southern Sea Food Company on Market Place, across from the Wholesale Fish Market.

Mr. Brunn and his wife ran the company from there for twenty-one years. And it was during this time, that he created Old Bay using more than twelve

The *Evening Capital* published a special *Historical and Industrial Edition: Portraying the Glorious Past and Future Possibilities of Annapolis, Maryland* in 1908. It featured Robert's father, Henry Clay Campbell, in this passage:

Campbell & Phipps: Groceries, Provisions and General Merchandise

"Among the energetic and enterprising men who have done much for the progress of Annapolis are the two gentlemen who comprise the firm Campbell & Phipps, dealers in groceries, provisions and general merchandise, whose place of business is located at 122 City Dock. This firm is comprised of Mr. Henry C. Campbell and Mr. James A. Phipps, who formed a co-partnership about two years ago, and have since that time worked together most admirably. There is nothing in the grocery, provisions, and general merchandise line that they cannot supply at the lowest market price and of a quality that is guaranteed to be satisfactory. Their store rooms are near the market, convenient to any part of the city and a veritable emporium of good things, and it is gratifying to know that their efforts to please have met with abundant appreciation. Both men are members of the Business Men's Association and the Junior Order of American Merchants. Mr. Phipps is a native of Anne Arundel county, while Mr. Campbell was born in Annapolis. This is the headquarters for Edison phonographs and records."[3]

herbs and spices. The product's original name was "Delicious Brand Seafood Seasoning" and it was an instant hit.

According to McCormick & Company records, Mr. Brunn "convinced a seafood wholesaler located around the corner to take five or ten pounds of his seasoning and just try it." When the customer returned, he ordered about 20 pounds of the mixture. This was just the beginning. Old Bay's popularity soared, and McCormick bought the brand in 1990.[2]

William Henry Hebron, the "Jewish" Fish Merchant

Robert Campbell's family knew William Henry Hebron, who some called the "Jewish" fish merchant because of his light complexion. Mr. Hebron's great-granddaughter, Janice Hayes-Williams, is an Annapolis-area historian—one who knows her family's heritage well. Recently, she shared these thoughts about her ancestor, his business, family, and community life.

William Henry Hebron was born into slavery on August 12, 1860 in Calvert County, Maryland. He moved in the 1870s to Annapolis, where he established a family, a seafood business, and a sound reputation.

Mr. Hebron came to town during Reconstruction, as many businesses among the area's black population began to flourish. In the 1880s for instance, large numbers of African-American men received and renewed oyster tonging licenses in Anne Arundel County.

Mr. Hebron was among those who did. At first, he sold seafood as a huckster at City Dock. *Johnson's Directory for Annapolis* listed him as an "oyster-shucker" there in 1897.[1] That July, Mr. Hebron was nominated to become the city's Market Master. Wiley H. Bates, an African-American Alderman from the Fourth Ward, nominated him when city council met to elect various city officers. Unfortunately, Mr. Hebron received just one of eight votes and lost the nomination to John Russell.

Mr. Hebron started renting a stall in the Fish Market in the late 19th or early 20th century. Some called him the "Jewish fish merchant" because of his light complexion. He received fresh catch from local watermen from the back of his stall and sold it to customers from the front, which faced the market house. *Gould & Halleron's Annapolis City Directory* noted that he sold fish, crabs, and oysters at the market in 1910. It also preceded his name with an asterisk, which it used to denote "colored persons or firms." The Fish Market's other tenants at

William Henry Hebron and his wife, Louvinia King Hebron, late 19th or early 20th century. The original black and white photographs were colorized in the 1950s or 1960s. Courtesy of Janice Hayes-Williams and The Capital. *Photographs by J. Henson.*

FISH, CRABS AND OYSTERS.

Brown Bros., Compromise st.
Gaubatz, George, Johnson place.
*Hebron, W. H., Fish Market.
Holliday, Thomas H., & Son, Fish Market.
Martin Co., The C. W., Fish Market.
Parkinson, A. M., Fish Market.
Quaid & Lowman, Fish Market.
Sanders & Co., Fish Market.

Mr. Hebron's listing in the 1910 Gould & Halleron Annapolis City Directory. The directory used an asterisk to denote "colored persons or firms."

the time were Thomas Holliday & Son, the C. W. Martin Company, A. M. Parkinson, Lowman & Quaid, and Sanders & Company.[2]

Mr. Hebron lived close to his business, with his family, on Washington Street. He was the proud father of six daughters from two marriages. He also had a son with Mrs. Williams's great-grandmother, Louvinia King Hebron. His name was Arlington Hebron, and he died at age five.

None of Mr. Hebron's daughters expressed an interest in continuing his seafood business. However, two of the three who lived in Annapolis became caterers. Both owned small restaurants on Clay Street, and one of them, Ethel Hebron Weems, was renowned for her special crab cakes.

Mr. Hebron's daughter Louisa married George Phelps, Sr., who worked at the Naval Academy after several years of military service. He became the school's head chef and fed the masses there for thirty years. *Bay Times* printed one of his menus in 1963; crab cakes were the main course, and they were made with relish, and matzoth meal among other ingredients.

Today, Mrs. Williams's mother, Virginia Hayes, lovingly refers to Mr. Hebron as "Grandfather." She remembers him as a warm pious man, who never raised his voice, and spent many hours with his grandchildren. What she recalls most about him, however, is that he always smelled of fish, and the scent of his favorite snack, "ginger snaps."

Mr. Hebron worked tirelessly in business, and in service to his family, and community, throughout his life. He was a long-time trustee of Asbury Methodist Episcopal Church in Annapolis and was among its leading fundraisers. He also donated to many organizations that helped the poor and was a lifetime member of the Masonic Order, attending Universal Lodge #14 of the Free and Accepted Masons on Clay Street. He died in 1930, the same year that the Fish Market was torn down.

Robert Campbell was very young when he knew Mr. Hebron. He recalled the location of his stall in proximity to the one occupied by his family's business.

He also said that Mr. Hebron was a distinguished, quiet man, who was fair and respected by all locals—regardless of race, both black, and white.

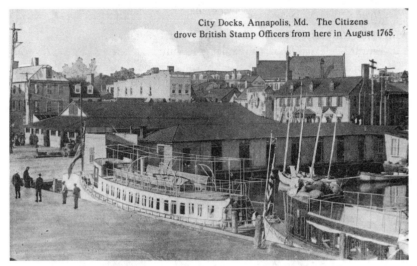

City Docks, Annapolis, Md. The Citizens drove British Stamp Officers from here in August 1765.

The city built a Fish Market (above, c. early 1900s) at the head of the dock in 1890. It opened in winter of 1891 and was torn down in 1930. From the author's collection.

Edward and Ella Burtis: Market Master, Market Mistress

Mr. Hebron surely knew Edward Burtis. After all, Edward was the city's Market Master for many of the years that he worked at the Fish Market. This is Edward's story, and that of his wife Ella, who became Market Mistress upon his death.

Edward was the oldest son of Captain William H. Burtis: one of the city's pioneer watermen, who captained a police boat in the State Oyster Navy. Capt. Burtis married Emily Hollidayoke in 1860, and they had Edward in 1861. Edward, in turn, married Ella Lee Thompson in 1888, and the couple lived at 22 Market Space.[1]

Initially, Edward worked as a "huckster" at the market house. Hucksters used the market, or any other place in the city, to sell produce, meat, fish, or other goods that were not "manufactured, produced, or raised by them or upon their farms, gardens or poultry yards." They were not butchers, fishermen, or oystermen "in the prosecution of their legitimate business," and they had to obtain a license from the city clerk, which cost $10 per year.[2]

As a huckster, Edward ran a produce and poultry stall until 1904, when city council chose him as Market Master. Councilmen had considered him for the job in 1903, along with Robert Strange, Thomas J. Linthicum, Jr., and Frank Mitchell. However, Robert Strange won by a narrow margin.

Edward defeated Robert a year later, on July 11. The next day the *Evening Capital* reported, "Everything passed off quietly and there was no unpleasant discussion or friction to mar the meeting . . . For Market Master—Messrs. Edward Burtis and Robert E. Strange were put in nomination. Mr. Burtis having received 5 votes and Mr. Strange 3, Mr. Burtis was declared elected."

Edward had to do two things before taking office. He had to give bond to the city $2,000 "conditioned for the faithful performance of his duties, and the trust reposed in him by this or any future ordinance." He also had to take this oath, which the Market Master had taken since at least 1839: "I . . . do swear

Edward Burtis in front of his home at 22 Market Space (now Griffin's Restaurant), c. 1916. He is probably holding Ella Marjorie Graefe, his granddaughter, and the daughter of Emma Burtis and George Graefe. The car pictured probably belonged to George Graefe, who helped to save the market house from destruction in 1941. Courtesy of Claire Fowler.

that I will diligently and faithfully, to the best of my skill and judgment, execute and perform all and singular the duties of market-master without favor, affection, partiality or prejudice."[3]

The council reappointed Edward annually for nineteen additional consecutive terms. During this time he earned $600 per year, and had "full power and authority to take possession, care and charge of the market-house." Some of his duties were to:

- Rent the market and Fish Market stalls annually in April. City Code prohibited him renting them to anyone in "arrears" to the city, who didn't plan to rent a stall for the entire year, or who didn't intend to use it as a "place of business";
- Collect fees from the market's tenants, and from everyone "selling during market hours anywhere in Market Space from Church to Randall Streets";
- Enforce the law limiting "the hours of holding market on Saturday night";
- Wash out the market every Saturday night and as often as necessary;
- "Cause the market house to be swept every day, and to remove all dirt, filth, and snow, from the same, as often as may be necessary";
- "Prevent all blown, stuffed, unsound, or unwholesome provisions, from being sold or being exposed for sale";
- Decide any disputes that arose between buyers and sellers in the market. Anyone who was "aggrieved by" his judgment could appeal to the mayor or aldermen, whose decision was final; and
- Report or "make arrests for violations" of city law "appertaining to his department" or the market house.[4]

Four sources reveal what the market house and Fish Market were like during Edward's tenure as Market Master. Clarence and Evangeline White wrote this account of them, in *The Years Between*:

Going around the Dock facing the City Market was our fish market; a long, narrow, shedlike building separated into stalls, which each fish vendor occupied for a small rental fee and where he could buy and sell his wares. The whole front facing the street was wide open, the back was enclosed except for a door at the end of each stall. This building partially overhung the dock or the bulkhead, and here the boats drew up to sell their catches to the vendors who placed them in their stalls, where they in turn sold them to the consumers. Each stall was equipped with a scale, a money box, often just a cigar box, a stack of newspapers for wrapping the fish, and a scaling and cleaning bench at the end. All of the refuse from cleaning the fish was dumped through the door overboard. You can imagine that over a long period of years this way of disposal began to contaminate the surrounding waters, so other means of handling our seafood, which was one of the main industries of Annapolis, had to be devised . . .

The old fish market was torn down and housed in the new big City Market house, with strict laws governing the handling of the oysters, fish, and crabs and disposing of the refuse . . . Our City Market has always occupied its present location, though it is greatly changed as to appearance and contents. In the old days it was a very small struc-

Edward Burtis at City Dock, c. 1916. Courtesy of Claire Fowler.

ture containing a few stalls; the outer ones for fruits, vegetables, and flowers; the center ones for our meat market. Here our butchers dispensed their own butchered and dressed meats, their homemade sausages, and all the delicacies obtainable at meat markets, but not prepared and packaged by the big commercial meat manufacturing companies . . .[5]

Two years after the Whites wrote this passage, Don Riley reflected on the market, c. 1900, in the article "I Remember . . . Sights and Smells of Old Annapolis Market," which the *Sunday Sun Magazine* printed in 1959. What follows are some of its most vivid excerpts:

A trip through the old Market Place at City Dock in Annapolis on Saturday night was like a crowded, jostling tour of a county fair, with a carnival thrown in for good measure. It was, that is, in the town's horse and buggy days.

Blocks before you got to the market you heard it—an excited, sustained hubble-bubble of voices, as stall operators shouted and chose from huge, colorful piles of green produce, racks of baked goods, trays of seafood. It was always a dramatic thing to see in the dusk, for the low, spreading building—little more than a shelter without walls, actually—was lit by flaring gas torches, their flames flickering in the evening breeze.

The market did business on weekdays and some weeknights, but only on a routine scale. At those times a trip there for just enough bread or vegetables or meat to 'tide' the family over until the weekend was merely an errand. It was on Saturday nights that Annapolis families did their big shopping, and the market on those nights was literally stocked to overflowing. Heavily laden farm wagons, their tailboards down and arranged prettily with piles of fruits and vegetables, lined the curb on both sides of the market place . . .

Inside the market, the fruits and vegetables made beautiful displays. John Tydings and Thomas Linthicum were always stocked with Anne Arundel county's finest green produce. Henry Boston, Sam Lorea and Macaluso's were other 'must' stops in this department. I remember ripe, sweet strawberries, huge boxes of them for 10 cents a box. Cantaloupes of superb flavor were two for 15 cents, and watermelons cost twenty cents or less. Rudolph Kaiser always had lovely flowers brought down from his beds on College avenue and in West Annapolis.

You followed your nose to the fish market. The sharp odors of it may have offended some visitors, but regular customers didn't mind. In those days I was more interested in the variety and size of fish than I was in the prices, but I remember tremendous shad (with the roe in) selling for less than 50 cents. Big oysters were less than a penny a piece.

White perch were cheap. Yellow perch (known as 'Yellow Jack' to many, and disdained by them because it was a mud-eater) were practically given away. . . .[6]

In 1917, Hildegarde Hawthorne described the Fish Market in this passage from her book, *Rambles in Old College Towns.*

Annapolis is as clean and bright as a new whistle, in spite of its dignified age . . . Close to the park is the fish market, and if there is anything more worth seeing than a fish market, why, I remarked to Sister, bring it on. There, in shining rows and heaps lay the flashing catch of the sea. Heaped in baskets were oysters—Annapolis has a big trade in oysters, packing away barrel upon barrel of the famous Chesapeakes. Salty men hung about, wearing battered hats and blue shirts, and mumbled to each other, indifferent to the rest of the world, as is the fashion of elderly sailor-and fishing-folk. Beyond extended the wharves and docks, crowded with small boats and smacks. Dogs lay in the sun, and small brown children played about.[7]

Finally, *Polk's City Directory* offered this glowing account of Annapolis and its market house in 1924:

Annapolis has superior advantages as a residential city. . . . The waters, markets and gardens in and about Annapolis furnish the best and freshest of fish and vegetables. Its market stalls afford the choicest meats, and its large and well filled stores supply provisions and groceries of the finest character. The city of Annapolis, with its healthfulness, pure air, peacefulness, order, good government, intelligence, refinement and hospitality, is a model American residential city. The stranger always receives a hearty welcome.[8]

Edward died on August 22 of the year that the *Directory* was published. His health had been failing for some time, and he had recently been taken to Spring Grove State Hospital for treatment. His obituary described him as a "well known citizen of the city."[9]

Three days after Edward's death, city council appointed his widow, Ella, as "Market Mistress." One newsman clearly approved of her, as he wrote "Mrs. Burtis is very familiar with the duties of the office, in view of the fact that she transacted practically all business of her husband during the several months of his illness."[10]

Ella served as Market Mistress for fourteen consecutive years: a remarkable feat since several politicians tried to oust her from office during this period.

Consider what happened in 1931. A new city council was elected that July, comprised of Mayor Walter Quenstedt, Counselor Roscoe Rowe, and Aldermen Jesse Fisher, Harry Leitch, Arthur Elliott, Anthony Davis, Thomas Basil,

Harry Bean, Charles Oliver, and Charles Spriggs. They met for the first time on July 20 to choose various city officers. It was a stormy session, as the *Evening Capital* reported the next day:

Hot and Heavy Meeting—Personal Attack Hot and Heavy

Not only was the temperature stifling, but the members in several instances worked themselves into a state of excitability in which defiles were issued, threats made and turmoil permitted to reach such an extent that a throng of voters were converted into a giggling audience . . . [Counselor Rowe even declared], 'I've crossed the Sahara Desert and the Equator and also have spend five years in torrid zones, but this meeting of the City Council has been the hottest spot I have ever been in.'

Part of the conflict centered on choosing a Market Master. The council's Democrats nominated Ella; yet its Republicans opposed her, and nominated Oden Stewart instead. They also rejected Katherine Linthicum, the Democrats' choice for City Clerk, and nominated Lee Kalmey for this position.

Despite the G.O.P.'s efforts, Ella and Katherine won. The newspaper reported that they "were re-elected although the Mayor, Counselor, and colored aldermen Spriggs and Oliver opposed them."[11]

Ella faced stiffer opposition in the 1930s. These were trying times to be in charge of the market. Many tenants resented the city for razing the Fish Market in 1930; many were demanding lower stall fees; and, worst of all, many weren't paying their rent. Councilmen addressed this problem on April 10, 1933. They discussed that Ella was having trouble collecting the rents and referred the matter to the Market House Committee.[12]

The council took action three months later. On July 24, it ordered that any tenant "in arrears" would lose his stall if he didn't pay $1 per month on rent in arrears, and present his rent when it was due.[13] Unfortunately, this tactic didn't work. The problem persisted. And, to make matters worse, the market house was deteriorating. The committee noted this in a chiding report, which it gave to the council on October 14, 1935. When submitting the report, Alderman Elmer Jackson said,

After careful study of conditions existing at the City Market, I as chairman of the Market House Committee have the following recommendations to make:

1. That a capable man who is both an experienced carpenter and painter be hired as market master. The man employed should be a willing worker who would keep the building clean and wash windows as well as enforce the market regulations. Mrs. Ella Burtis has served the city faithfully but the market is in a dirty condition, the moral of the occupants is

poor, and there is continued wrangling. The position of Market Master is a man's job, and no easy one at that.

2. That a floor plan be worked out and those having stalls be charged for what they use.

3. That no favoritism be shown for delinquent stall renters.

4. That the interior of the Market be given a cleaning up and then painted white.

5. That the committee be empowered to further consider some means of improving the fish market.

It is my belief that the market should either be sanitary and properly operated or discontinued. The above recommendations may improve conditions and I urge that they be tried. The market as now operated is certainly of no credit to the city nor of any financial value either.[14]

"Considerable discussion" followed Mr. Jackson's remarks. During the prolonged exchange, City Counselor William McWilliams said, "We should clean it [the market house] up and fix it up and put a capable man in charge. He can see that collections are made promptly . . . "

In Ella's defense, Alderman Fisher replied, "The market mistress has done all in her power to collect rentals but the last counselor refused to collect them."

The debate continued for some time until finally, the council referred the report back to the committee for further consideration.[15]

The committee responded in November. It submitted a new report that "urged that a man be placed in charge of the market, in view of the unsightly and unsanitary conditions there, together with improper operation." Five councilmen agreed and voted to fire Ella; the other five voted to retain her. Given this tie, they decided to revisit the issue in December.[16]

The council reappointed Ella by a majority vote when reconvened that month. Two factors influenced this result. First Counselor McWilliams, who had voted against her in November, was absent. Furthermore, since then, 365 citizens had signed a petition drafted by Alderman J. William Graham. The document urged the council to "re-appoint" Ella, and its number of signatures convinced two councilmen who had opposed her to change their minds.[17]

Ella was reelected in 1936 and in 1937, although the council delayed its choice that year. As the *Evening Capital* noted on July 20, "It was announced that appointment of a Market Master (the point of much discussion two years ago) would be held over until the next meeting. It was learned today that Mrs. Ella Burtis is not likely to be retained the council being divided between former Police Justice Louis M. Hopkins and William O. Young for the appointment. However, these names were not discussed at the council meeting."[18]

The council reappointed Ella for the last time in 1938. By then, her responsibilities had increased dramatically. Since 1935, city law had authorized the Market Master (or in this case, Market Mistress), to "perform all duties and exercise all powers heretofore vested in the wardens of the port by the City Charter." Some of her new duties were to:

- Regulate the building of wharves, piers, and improvements in Annapolis regarding how far they extended into the water, and how, and of what they were built;
- Cause any wharf, etc. that was "run out, extended, added, or erected at a greater distance from the shore than indicated by the port warden's line" to be demolished at the cost of the offender;
- Examine and report "all cases in which the proper lines of the harbor and dock have already been encroached upon by wharves, [etc.]"; and
- Keep the "harbor and dock, and the access and approaches thereto, and the access and approaches to all private and public wharves in . . . Annapolis free from obstructions of an improper character."[19]

By 1939, the council was convinced that Ella couldn't perform these tasks. It fired her on July 10 and hired Wilmer Watson (a former market house meat merchant) as Market Master and Harbor Master. It also ousted Mrs. Addie Tongue, who lost her job as bookkeeper of the City Clerk's Office to James Vansant.

Mayor George Haley tried to explain the council's decisions. He said "the two women were replaced for reasons not in any way political or as a slight to women as a group," to quote the *Evening Capital*. He also said that Ella "could not handle the added duties," and added, "It isn't a woman's job to jump on and off boats, take charge of parking meters, keep order among boat men and carry out other orders of the Council."[20]

Mrs. Edna Payne, who lived at 77 Franklin Street in Annapolis, disagreed. She said, "A woman can do almost anything a man can do." Mrs. Payne was president of the Anne Arundel County Board of Education at the time. She was also an officer of the National Woman's Party. And in July, she wrote this letter to the council protesting its choice on the Party's behalf:

As the Legislative Chairman for the local branch of the National Woman's Party, it is my duty to watch all action taken by deliberative bodies in regard to the civic welfare of women. We know there are still some men, smug in the belief of intellectual and so-called inherent superiority, who do not believe women have the same right to paid work as men: but certainly, this thought is as obsolete as an old phonograph record. Therefore, you may imagine our deep chagrin and disappointment at your action of July 10th in removing two women, Mesdames Addie Tongue and Ella Burtis from civic positions and replacing them with men. In these complex days the best interests of our city are most effectively served when men and women work together, with high purpose and intelligence to bring about a solution of the problems common to us all, and, since we are certain that Annapolis is peopled

Ella Burtis in her backyard at 22 Market Space, c. 1916. Courtesy of Claire Fowler.

almost equally by men and women only the combined judgment of both can solve its problems.

The act of losing employment is tragic to women and the National Woman's Party deplores injustice through discrimination because of sex. Surely we have the right to expect you to deal fairly and justly with women as citizens, and having that right, it is difficult to understand why, if these two women had to 'walk the plank,' other women were not named to replace them.[21]

Unfortunately, Mrs. Payne's letter didn't persuade the council to change its mind. Ella left office quietly. She died in 1945, the first—and last—woman (to date) to hold the title of Market Mistress of the city of Annapolis.

Lou Hyatt, "the King of Shoeboxes"

Lou Hyatt worked at the market house while Ella was its Mistress. What follows are his thoughts about the market he knew as a child, and how it, and Annapolis have changed since then.

Lou Hyatt was born in 1928 in Annapolis. He was raised on Cornhill Street, close to his family's shoe store, at 81 Main Street. His father Samuel founded it there in about 1915, after running similar establishments at 119 Cathedral Street, among other places.[1]

Mr. Hyatt started working at the market house at age nine. "I was on the street by the time I was nine, making deliveries for the market's merchants. This was before electric refrigerators, when people had to buy their perishables every day," he said.

Mr. Hyatt delivered goods to Market and Conduit Streets, especially to many of the World War I widows who lived there. He also went to an East Street area that he likened to "Little Italy," toting tomatoes, eggplants, and other produce in his wagon.

Being a delivery boy had its perks according to Mr. Hyatt. "The typical tip was a dime, which was good pay then," he said. "And when I worked at the market for Mr. Brown, I'd bring ripe peaches, corn, and tomatoes for mother to use at home. We lived near our store, but many people lived right above their stores in those days."

Mr. Hyatt did more than deliver the market merchants' goods; he also sold goods to them. As he recalled,

I collected shoeboxes and sold hundreds, maybe thousands, of them for half a cent each. I was the King of Shoeboxes. Merchants used them to sell soft crabs, crabs that hadn't shed yet called peelers, and bloodworms. They also sold plants—like small tomato plants—in ones for men's shoes. This was before plastics. When plastics came about during World War II, the merchants no longer needed the shoeboxes . . .

I also sold newspapers (both new and used) to the merchants. They used the old ones to wrap fish. I delivered them in my wagon, all spread out. Mr. Miller [of the Chesapeake Seafood Company] was a customer; so was Mr. Campbell.

Courtesy of the Maryland State Archives SPECIAL COLLECTIONS (Jim Hefelfinger Collection) Jim Hefelfinger, View of City Dock (Hyatt's Shoe Store detail), *c. 1935 MSA SC 1885-1-834.*

Mr. Hyatt recalled several other merchants who worked at the market at the time: "The Basil family had a meat stall and Schaefer had the main produce market. Schaefer worked for Roland Brown, who was the market's last main produce man in 1968. There was also a Mrs. Cook who had a flower and plant stand. The Sands family had a seafood stand at the corner of the market. So did the Campbells; Bob Campbell's dad had a fish stall. Mr. Lawson also had a stand outside with bananas. There was a pecking order and everyone had a certain position where they kept their stand in the market area."

Mr. Hyatt also described the market's conditions: "The market house didn't have air conditioning then, except for maybe a few of the meat and fish stalls. The exterior of the market had many open stalls, filled with fresh produce, including freshly picked watermelons delivered by horse and wagon. Mr. Feldmeyer brought the melons from his farm in Eastport, where President's Point is today."

The market house thrived on Saturdays, according to Mr. Hyatt. "That's where the action was. It stayed open much later then, and it was crowded well past dark," he said. "Market Square was also bustling on Saturdays. It was a happening. Horse-drawn wagons brought fresh goods to the dock. It wasn't unusual to see six or eight such wagons there, until about 1940. Oscar Grimes and his family came with fresh eggs, sour cream, and the like from their farm in Davidsonville. And in the summers, schooners arrived from the Eastern Shore with cantaloupe, corn, and tomatoes. An Indian medicine man came in an old Buick, wearing a headdress. He tipped his trunk stand down and sold goods from it, including a rubbing liniment. A black man called Stove Pipe also did blackface entertainment. Market Square was crowded 'til eleven at night on Saturdays. Ninety-nine percent of the people there were locals, and many came to town by boat to shop; we rarely saw tourists except for during June Week."

Mr. Hyatt offered three final thoughts about the market's history. He recalled going there as an adult,

Another Annapolitan named Sam Hyatt owned a shoe store at 52 West Street. Here is one of his advertisements, published by the Evening Capital *on March 27, 1918.*

particularly to Schley's. "Schley's Delicatessen made sandwiches galore in the '60s. They were delicious," he said.

He also recalled how the market's business suffered, due in part to competition from the A&P grocery stores. "In the market house, goods were displayed in wooden baskets. But the A&Ps displayed their stocks in nice refrigerated cases. They [the goods] were more attractive that way, which is probably what drew customers there."

Finally, Mr. Hyatt recalled when he—and five other aldermen—voted to demolish the market in 1968. He based his vote on a City Engineer claim that it was "structurally unsound and should be condemned." Others, including the "merchants and historic interests" thought something else had influenced his choice. "They got angry because they thought I wanted to transform the area into a parking lot. My brother, Mel, ran Dockside Restaurant on Dock Street, and they thought I wanted more parking for his restaurant," he said.

Mr. Hyatt eventually changed his mind about the market's future. In 1969, he voted to save the historic building. "I thought the market should stay a market. It should stay a market; it has served a very useful situation and purpose," he said.[2]

James Strange Spoils Halloween for Local Youths

Lou Hyatt and James Strange had at least three things in common: both were born in Annapolis, both of their families owned businesses on Main Street, and both served on city council. As an alderman, Mr. Hyatt angered adults when he voted to demolish the market house in 1968. And as mayor, Mr. Strange angered children when he spoiled their Halloween fun in 1918. This story describes the source of their outrage.

Planning to wear a mask on Halloween? If so, your costume might have been illegal—at least in early 20th-century Annapolis. Wearing masks became illegal for local youths in 1918, due in part, to events that occurred in 1916.

That year, the *Evening Capital* called Halloween "an occasion for much fun-making, parties, tricks, and jokes at the expense of housekeepers or pedestrians." In response, it gave "housekeepers and pedestrians" these tips for surviving the holiday:

1. Wear your old clothes when you go out; the witches are well armed with flour and beans;

2. Look out for hidden strings across the sidewalks; the witches have a sense of humor;
3. Don't answer your bell without first arming yourself with a weapon and making careful inquiries as to who is without. Ringing doorbells and running away is one of the spirits' favorite pastimes;
4. Don't call for the police when you hear a mysterious rapping on one of your back windows—it will be that familiar object known to small boys as a "tick-tack"; and
5. Don't fail to nail up your furniture, garbage boxes and gates—otherwise when morning comes you will find they have departed.[1]

Unfortunately, not everyone took tip number five seriously. And, as a result, many awoke to find that their gates, shutters, and doors were missing. The newspaper blamed children—especially boys—for these pranks. It declared that, "The small boy is in his glory when he can go along the street removing or kicking down everything moveable or engaging in other forms of racket and yet escape the watchful eye of the police."[2]

Local youths made more Halloween mischief in 1917. Wearing "costumes of the weird and grotesque, they paraded the streets from just before dusk until

Three-year-old Michelle Rowland in October 1985. Courtesy of The Capital. *Photograph by Stephanie Gross-Harvey.*

late at night." They played pranks; they played games; however, unlike years past, they didn't throw flour.[3]

The *Evening Capital* explained why. First, throwing flour had become illegal in Annapolis. It noted that, "the throwing of flour, formerly a great custom among the fun-makers . . . has been prohibited by law." Flour was also expensive. The paper claimed that World War I had increased its price, which in turn, had probably prevented people from wasting it by breaking the law.[4]

Annapolis lost another long-time Halloween tradition in 1918: the wearing of masks. City Code already prohibited "masking," yet most ignored the law until October of that year. At that point, specific events—including Halloween pranks that had occurred in 1916 and 1917, and a recent string of unsolved robberies—prompted local leaders to make public safety a priority.

Many of them thought that forbidding masks would help to curb the recent trouble. As the newspaper noted, "On former occasions the holiday, with the customary masking, gave the opportunity to those inclined to rowdyism to commit all sorts of depredations, like moving doors and shutters, taking down signs, marking buildings and the like [without being recognized]."[5]

James Strange, who served as mayor from 1909–19, led the drive to abolish masks. Initially he wanted to do more—much more: he wanted to abolish Halloween costumes completely. "It was his first intention," one newsman wrote, to prohibit "the wearing of all kinds of costumes on the streets." However, he agreed not to "interfere with the old customs to that extent," after it was pointed out that, "this practice was merely innocent fun."[6]

He called a special city council session on October 28, 1918, to consider the matter of masks. Councilmen were determined to see that "the line between fun, on the one side, and rowdyism and vandalism on the other, [was] to be distinctly drawn during the coming Halloween."[7]

Mayor Strange took a bold stance during the meeting. He insisted that, "the provisions of the City Code forbidding masking would be carried out with strictness, and that it would apply to persons who blacked or otherwise disguised their faces." The council agreed.[8]

Yet prohibiting masking was just one step the council took to improve public safety that night. It also passed a strong Juvenile Curfew Ordinance. The original ordinance had been proposed earlier that month and had three parts. The first part addressed time. It made it unlawful for girls younger than sixteen, or boys

WITCHES AND SPOOKS TO CAVORT TONIGHT

It Is HallowE'en, So Beware of the Goblins

FUN-MAKING PRANKS GALORE

'Tis Time to Learn From the Spirits Your Fate for Good Or Ill.

Evening Capital *newspaper headline regarding Halloween, October 31, 1916.*

younger than fourteen to be on any street, lane, or alley, or in any public place in Annapolis after 9:30 P.M. in the summer, or after 9 P.M. the rest of the year. There were a few exceptions. Any child accompanied by a parent, guardian, or other adult who had temporary custody of him or her, would be exempt from the curfew.

The second part addressed penalties. Youths who violated the ordinance, or adults who enabled them to, could be fined from $1 to $10. The third and final part dealt with enforcement. It declared that the ordinance would go into effect one week after it passed and would last for the duration of the war.

Many supported the ordinance; yet some felt it was too severe. As the newspaper reported, "No piece of proposed municipal legislation in years has been so generally supported as this, and there is little doubt as to its prompt passage . . . [but] If the ordinance is too drastic and in danger of inflicting an unnecessary hardship on those it is designed to protect, then it will never be enforced properly and its passage will do no good."[9]

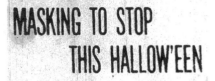

MASKING TO STOP THIS HALLOW'EEN

City Council Determines That Rowdyism And Vandalism Must Not Occur Again

CURFEW RULES APPLY

CURFEW ORDINANCE EFFECTIVE AT ONCE

Children Off Streets Last Night And Few Offenders Against New Ordinance

ALL PARENTS MUST HELP

Evening Capital headlines regarding masks and the juvenile curfew ordinance, October 29 and 30, 1916.

In response, councilmen amended the ordinance before passing it. One of their amendments impacted Halloween for local youths; they declared that the law would become effective immediately, rather than a week later. And, consequently, children would have to be in by 9 P.M. that night.

This outraged the children. However, that they wouldn't be able to wear masks upset them even more. As the paper noted, "The Mayor has been besieged by children who think it a hardship that there is to be no masking or blackening up on Hallow'een. However . . . this disguising has been the cover of much ruffianism and vandalism on previous occasions, and the children will have to content themselves with dressing up and must remember to be home by nine this year."[10]

Obviously, adults could stay out past 9 P.M. on Halloween. They could also wear masks, as the newspaper's account of a party held that night at the State

Armory reveals. Hundreds of people attended the event, which featured food, games, and fortunetellers. According to the *Evening Capital,* the guests "were partially disguised with noses, and some wore masks, while the girls were costumed in sheets and pillow slips and white muslin false faces."[11]

Peter and Helen Palaigos Recall Pete's Place

Like Mayor Strange, Peter (Pete) and Helen Palaigos lived and worked in downtown Annapolis. This is their story and that of their bygone business on Main Street.

Main Street had two-way traffic when Pete Palaigos met Helen Pappas in Annapolis. He was from New York, but was working in Washington, D.C. at the time. She was living at her family's home on Duke of Gloucester Street. They met at a mutual friend's engagement party, he proposed on Valentine's Day, 1947, and they married in June.

The newlyweds lived on Conduit Street, close to Helen's kin and their business: Brunswick Billiard Hall at 163 Main Street. Now home to ACME Bar and Grill, this site has an intriguing history. It was originally part of Lot 46, as designated on James Stoddert's map of 1718. Its first owners were Mary and Henry Woodward, who sold it and Lot 45 to Henrietta Dulany for 810 pounds in 1761.[1]

Henrietta died within five years of the sale and bequeathed both lots to her son Lloyd Dulany.[2] Sadly Lloyd, a British Loyalist, had little time to enjoy his inheritance. He died in 1782 in London—at age forty—from wounds received during an earlier Hyde Park duel with Reverend Bennett Allen, a former rector of St. Anne's Church in Annapolis.[3] Because Lloyd was a Loyalist, the state seized and sold his Annapolis property upon his death.

George Mann bought the lots from the state in 1783, and transformed what had been Lloyd's home into a tavern.[4] The tavern, later called City Hotel among other names, was one of the city's leading hostelries.[5] George Washington stayed there, as did Samuel Vaughan who praised the facility in 1787. He wrote in his diary that, "[It is] an excellent publick house, 4 rooms on a floor and one for company 66 by 21 feet—the second story Lodging Rooms, all wainscoted to the ceiling, might vie with any tavern in England."[6]

Mann expanded his tavern along Conduit Street in the 1780s, and it retained its strong reputation well into the 19th century. It became a Naval Academy preparatory school in the 1890s and was later converted into tenements.

Then, when a fire destroyed Mann's original tavern around the turn of the 20th century, Lot 46 was subdivided and sold.

Construction on the new, smaller lots—including 163 Main Street—began immediately. 167 Main Street was completed in 1903; the Colonial Theater facing Conduit Street was finished in 1904; and 163 Main Street was developed between 1903 and 1908.[7]

William (Bill) Pappas bought this particular lot from Constantine and Stamateke Cardes in 1919.[8] Bill, who had emigrated from Greece to America in the late 19th century, was a successful entrepreneur in Charlottesville, Virginia. He owned a thriving billiard hall on that city's Main Street and sought to replicate his success in Annapolis—with help from his cousin, George Pappas.

George had come to America from Greece as a seventeen-year-old in 1911. He was well-established in Annapolis by 1919, when Bill bought 163

Peter and Helen Palaigos tending to their bar at Pete's Place in March 1985. Courtesy of The Capital. *Photograph by Bob Gilbert.*

Detail of the pressed tin ceiling at 163 Main Street. Courtesy of the city of Annapolis Department of Planning and Zoning. Photograph by EHT Traceries, Inc., 1994.

Peter Palaigos, standing near his May Basket entry at 163 Main Street on May 2, 1967. Courtesy of The Capital. *Photograph by Lee Troutner.*

Main Street. Bill imagined the site as a billiard hall and convinced George to embrace his plan for it. He would own the property, offer advice, and remain in Virginia, while George oversaw its day-to-day operations.

They called their business Brunswick Billiard Hall and opened it in about 1921. At that point George's cousin, James Fotos of Utah, came to help launch the billiard as George's business partner. Three years later, George and his wife had a daughter, Helen, who was born at the Annapolis Emergency Hospital.

Helen has fond memories of Brunswick's early years. Gentlemen came there for several reasons, she said. While "many came to shoot pool, others came to get their hats cleaned, or shoes shined" at a stand near its entrance. She also recalled the billiard's beautiful tin ceiling, and its arched storefront, which she called "the original McDonald's golden arches."

Helen started working at the billiard when she married Pete. In fact, they began managing the business together once they married. Helen opened shop at 8:30 or 9 A.M. and Pete closed at night with help from others such as Frank Yates, who worked there for about twenty years. "We used to close at 11, and we were one of the last to close," Pete said. "Annapolis was a sleepier, smaller town then."

Helen agreed. "Almost everybody knew everybody—especially if you had a business on Main Street," she said.

Shortly after Pete and Helen took over the billiard, it became known as Pete's Place. And soon, it started to provide customers with delicious food, as well as recreation. Helen's homemade crab cakes, which she made for lunch, were especially popular. Served on a saltine cracker, they sold for $1 each. Pete's also made the "best kosher hot dogs in town," Pete said, which were served on "delicious rolls from Johnny's Sweet Shop."

Pete's Place Restaurant in March 1994, seven months prior to when it closed. Courtesy of the city of Annapolis Department of Planning and Zoning. Photograph by EHT Traceries, Inc.,

Midshipmen and St. Mary's High School students—including Speaker of the Maryland House of Delegates, Michael E. Busch—were among the billiard's regulars. So were former Annapolis Mayors Al Hopkins and Roger "Pip" Moyer, as well as former Anne Arundel County Executive Joseph Alton, Jr. "Women didn't start coming 'til the '60s," Helen said.

Pete's Place became Pete's Place Restaurant and Bar in 1987: the year it was renovated as a restaurant, packed away its billiard tables, and received its first phone. Until then, people had called the restaurant next door if they needed to speak with someone at Pete's.[9]

Pete's closed permanently in September 1994. Much about the site has changed since then, and even more so, since Pete and Helen started managing it in 1947. There are no pool tables or cues inside the building, and outside, traffic travels only one-way on Main Street.

Francis R. Geraci, Jr., and the City's Former "Tonsorial Saloons"

Francis Geraci was a regular at Pete's Place; so were his uncles, Angelo and Frank. These men, like their father Onofrio, were among the many barbers whose shops thrived in late 19th- and mid-20th-century Annapolis. Recently, Francis reflected on this, and other aspects of his family's history.

Francis's great-grandfather Onofrio was born in Palermo, Sicily, in 1847. He came to Baltimore in 1865, married Mary Ellen Noonan of Anne Arundel County in 1871, and was naturalized in 1883. The couple eventually settled in Annapolis, where Onofrio became an entrepreneur. He established a barbershop at 81 Conduit Street, and a fruit and confectionary store at 201 Main Street. Both ventures flourished; in fact, within two decades of moving to town, Onofrio had acquired a home on Green Street, and several boats. His will also suggests that he owned a boathouse. It states "Boats and boathouse to be sold immediately after my death. Inasmuch as my boathouse is located on ground of the Redemptive Fathers of St. Mary's Roman Catholic Church."[1]

Onofrio died in Annapolis in 1906, leaving behind his wife, three sons, and a daughter. He left his wife their home, his daughter Mary Katherine or "Mamie" his gold watch, but was far less generous with his sons. As his will noted, "All my sons are self-supporting and shall get nothing."[2]

Two of Onofrio's sons were barbers, having learned the art from their father. Frank, the oldest (and Francis's grandfather), lived in Eastport. He worked as a barber on West Street before moving his business across Spa Creek. Angelo lived downtown. He ran his father's barbershop for many years, before becoming a "tonsorial artist" on Main Street.

Angelo's shop was open from 8 A.M. to 8 P.M. on weekdays, from 8 A.M. to 10 P.M. on Saturdays, and was incredibly successful. As he said in 1920, "The work now is so much harder than it used to be . . . in that there is no letting up from Monday morning when we open and Saturday night when we close—a constant grind—and it is simply impossible for us to endure it . . ."[3]

Mamie managed the family's fruit and confectionary store after Onofrio's death. She later changed professions. She became a nurse and was Superintendent of Nurses at the Annapolis Emergency Hospital. Francis's mother Naomi was also a nurse there, as was his sister Donna. Francis even worked at the hospital, where he was born in 1947.

Francis with his mother, Naomi Minnix Geraci, at the home of his uncle Alvin Geraci in Ferry Farms in Annapolis, c. 1953. Courtesy of Francis R. Geraci, Jr.

Francis lived at 144 Charles Street until his mother passed away in 1953. He then lived with his maternal grandmother, Ada Minnix, on Conduit Street, before joining Mamie on Green Street. Francis helped with the family's shopping at the time.

He recalled that, "They [his grandmother and aunt] sent me to Rookie's Market to shop. Rookie was the best butcher in town—not just for meat, but for milk, and other staples." Francis recalled two facts about walking to Rookie's from Conduit and Green Streets: that an Amoco Service Station stood at the base of Main Street, and that the station's adjacent bathrooms were segregated.

The Geracis were devout Catholics and sent Francis to St. Mary's Elementary School. He'll never forget one of his teachers, Sister Mary Gerard Muth, who started teaching there in 1906. "She tossed chalk at students and cleaned erasers by sailing them over our heads toward the chalkboards," he said.

When not in school, Francis enjoyed exploring Annapolis. Many of his old haunts have changed since then. Take City Dock for instance. "Back then, during the winter oyster season, you could walk from workboat to workboat all across the harbor . . . There were oyster tongers, skipjacks, and watermen everywhere," he recalled.

The city's streetscape is also different. "The streets were quieter and there wasn't as much traffic," Francis said. "By nine o'clock at night the streets rolled up—even Main Street." Some of his bygone favorites on this street were the Playhouse Theatre; the La Rosa Restaurant; Read's Drug Store, "a teen

Hack's hobby shop and Chris' Submarines. Courtesy of Historic Annapolis Foundation.

hotspot"; Hack's, "the best hobby shop in town"; Murphy's 5 and Dime, "a general merchandise store with creaky floors"; and Chris' Sub Haven, a "greasy spoon, with paying pinball machines."

While Francis usually went to Chris' with friends, he dined with his father at the Annapolis Yacht Club. "The club had the best terrapin soup. It was creamy with a lot of sherry," he said. "We ate in the long, narrow, elegant dining room where black waiters wore tuxedo jackets. It was downstairs and overlooked Spa Creek."

Francis often crossed Spa Creek to Eastport—an area that's also changed. As he recalled, "What's now the Chart House had a marine railway, and Sadler's Crab House was nearby. We'd walk onto Sadler's pier, where black ladies were picking crabs as fast as they could for packing and shipping . . ."

Sometimes, the Geracis bought their seafood in Eastport or at the market house. Other times they

Francis's father, Col. Francis Geraci, Sr., USMC, (nicknamed "The Colonel" or "Reg") with his children, Donald and Donna Marie, c. 1945. Courtesy of Francis R. Geraci, Jr.

caught their own. "We'd take our boat to Greenbury Point, where the water was crystal clear. We'd just leap in. There were grasses and fish everywhere. We'd go fishing and catch baskets of rockfish—good-sized rockfish . . . It was a gentle, happy life growing up in Annapolis. It was a kind place," Francis said.

Today, Francis has a unique reminder of his hometown's past: a two-hour video. Filmed by his uncle Alvin of Ferry Farms, it's more than a home movie; it's also a documentary, which depicts Annapolis in the 1940s–50s.

The film starts in black and white. Its early footage shows the old Severn River Bridge, the Severn River, swimmers wearing old-fashioned bathing suits and caps, and countless sailboats—there's not a motorboat in sight. Several scenes later, the film becomes color. It shows the Severn again, and again sailboats fill its waters. Next, it features Ritchie Highway—although it's hardly recognizable. Traffic is sparse and from the cameraman's viewpoint, there appear to be no homes along it—only large, healthy trees.

The film's final footage features these and other city scenes: parades, including one that appears to be from Annapolis's Tercentenary celebration, a red

Regal Laundry truck approaching Church Circle from West Street, the Water-witch Hook & Ladder Co. No. 1 on East Street, and a City Dock overflowing with workboats.[4]

Carolyn Martin's Sandwiches

Francis Geraci and Joseph (Joe) Martin, Jr. have much in common. Both are native Annapolitans, both frequented Pete's Place, and both of their families owned small businesses in town. This story celebrates the one that Joe's mother started in 1949.

Joe Martin is an expert when it comes to sandwiches. He's been making them since 1949, the year his mother Carolyn launched a sandwich business at her home in Annapolis. Carolyn started the business to supplement her family's income. Her husband Joseph already had a good job as an electrician at the Naval Academy's North Severn Station; however, she wanted to help with expenses, such as their new house at 11 Steele Avenue in Murray Hill.

Starting the business was a family-wide effort. Carolyn's mother, Inez Mann, actually had the idea while visiting from South Carolina. Mrs. Mann knew her daughter could cook, and therefore, thought she should make and sell sandwiches on consignment. Next, Mr. Martin converted their basement into a preparatory kitchen. He removed its upright piano and Wurlitzer Jukebox to make room for workspace and supplies. Once the kitchen was ready, he also made sandwiches with his wife and sons, Joe and Bobby. Joe, who was eight years old at the time, recalled their routine:

"Mom and Dad—who still had his regular job—started the night before doing basic prep work—slicing produce, meat, and cheese, and making salads. They got up the next morning at 5 and Bobby and I joined them at 6. Mom went back upstairs at 7 to make breakfast while we worked. We ate, loaded the car, and then delivered the sandwiches—all before school!" he said.

Carolyn launched her business at an ideal moment. Construction on the Chesapeake Bay Bridge had just begun and its builders provided a large, hungry customer base. She delivered their sandwiches—sometimes as early as 6:30 A.M.—and sold them for 50 cents each. They didn't last long. "We could sell the whole car full in twenty or thirty minutes—ham and cheese, tuna salad, pimento cheese and olives. The workmen liked the heavy beef sandwiches but they bought the cheese ones too," Joe said.

Workmen weren't Mrs. Martin's only customers. In fact by 1950, her consignment route had about forty daily stops. As Joe recalled, "We stopped at service stations and shops with restaurant counters throughout Annapolis. Kitchin's Drug Store on West Street was one of the first on the route. The guys who worked at Henry B. Myers walked across the street to get our sandwiches there." They also delivered to Phil Richman's Drug Store, Levy's Groceries, the Old Town Inn, G. C. Murphy's, and Winegardner's Gulf Station, which kept their Crosley station wagon running for deliveries, among other downtown spots.

The Martins also delivered to sites beyond downtown such as the J. F. Johnson Lumber Co., Tubby's Drive-In, the roller-skating rink, and Finkelstein's Furniture. Their western-most stop was Jewell's gas station at 2043 West Street, an area "that was considered the country back then," according to Joe.

In addition to making and delivering sandwiches, Joe bought groceries for the business, which was trademarked as Mrs. Mann's in 1950. He patronized small, independent grocery stores including Rookie's Market, Earle's Food Market, and the Cohen's on Franklin Street. "Mom was a stickler for giving business to local shops," he said. "The A&P and Safeway were last resorts. Since we only went for two or three celery stalks or a can of pimentos, we didn't need to use them, or a wholesale supplier."

Joe worked for Mrs. Mann's until he entered the U.S. Army in 1958. That was a momentous year for his mother; she won a contract to supply sandwiches to 7-Eleven stores throughout Anne Arundel, and in parts of Prince George's, and Baltimore Counties. By then, she had hired ten women to keep up with the demand. As Joe recalled, "Mother had ten women working with her in the 'sandwich room.' My sister Candy joined in the making when she was about eight. They made the sandwiches then dad, Bobby, and our former bread deliveryman delivered them in two refrigerated trucks.".

Carolyn wasn't the only woman who ran a business from her home in Murray Hill at the time. So did Florence Leddy, a furrier, at 2 Steele Avenue. Mrs. Leddy made mink muffs, bowties, repairs and alterations. "She and mother were grand-fathered into the city's modern zoning laws. They were licensed to make and sell goods from their basements, as were other entrepreneurs," Joe said.

Carolyn wasn't the Martin family's only entrepreneur, either. Her husband's great-grandfather, Benjamin Martin, owned a successful livery at the corner of Lafayette and West Streets during the Civil War era. His son, John Benjamin Martin, also had a tavern at 102 West Street

Mrs. Martin began making her sandwiches at home at 11 Steele Avenue (above) in 1949. Photograph by David Hartcorn, 2005.

in the late 19th century. "Women weren't allowed in the tavern," according to Joe. "Instead, they came through a side alley to a sliding door behind the bar. They pulled a chain to let the bartender know they were there, and he filled their pails with beer." Finally, John's son, John Francis Martin, started Martin's Music Store in 1929 that sold instruments and sheet music at 55 Maryland Avenue. "Most of his customers were midshipmen, who brought their instruments to be repaired. Then in 1933 he started J. F. Martin & Sons, American Beer Distributorship," Joe said.

Carolyn's business thrived in the late 1950s, '60s, and early '70s. Its success prompted her to take a bold step in 1972. She and Joseph became tenants in the city's newly renovated market house. Joe and his wife Jo Ann joined them full-time in 1973, and the business incorporated under Martin's Quality Foods, Inc., trading as Mrs. Mann's.

The couple recalled the market and its tenants when it reopened: "Alvin Kaufman was there, so was Mann's, Machoian's, Salzinger's imported sausage and cheese, Curran's deli, George Hannon's seafood, coffee and then ice cream, and Muhly's Bakery. Rausch also had the cheese stall.

The market house was one big space when it reopened. There were height restrictions. None of the equipment could be over 5 or 6 feet tall. You used to be able to look around the whole market, and see from one end to another . . . "

Joe went to the Eastport Democratic Club after many a day's work at the market. One of his favorite pastimes there was a game—one that delivering

Joseph Francis Martin, Sr. at Mrs. Mann's inside the market house, 1974. Courtesy of Joseph Francis Martin, Jr.

Joe and Jo Ann Martin at Mrs. Mann's, 2004. Courtesy of Joseph Francis Martin, Jr.

sandwiches as a child prepared him for. As he recalled, "After work, I used to go the Eastport Democratic Club, where we played a game. We'd take a piece of blank paper, draw a line across it, name a street, and challenge each other to re-construct that street building by building during a specific time frame—say right after World War II to 1950. Equally as good was my longtime friend Huck Winegardner—I miss him. It [the game] awakened things people forgot about . . . and that's important."

Jo Ann attributes much of her husband's success at the game to his early work experience. "Joe did well on streets on this side of the [Eastport] bridge because he worked here, and used to deliver sandwiches along the streets. I understand Teddy Christensen was Joe's counterpart—Eastport's street histo-rian—and a good one," she said.

The Martins operated Mann's for thirty-one years before leaving the market house in November 2004. Of course, they had a lot of help over this period. "We've hired brothers and sisters, and children of children of children who have worked for us," Jo Ann said. "High schoolers, who started in high school, would continue to work for us in college . . . We feel like we've raised half the city of Annapolis."[1]

Dr. Faye Allen Reflects on Practicing Medicine and Marrying Dr. Aris T. Allen

The Martins launched their business just before Dr. Faye Allen moved to Annapolis. Recently, Dr. Allen reflected on living and working there with her husband, Dr. Aris T. Allen.

Faye Watson never imagined herself as a doctor. "I wanted to be Florence Nightingale since the beginning. My ambition was to become a nurse," she said. Yet Faye became a doctor, Dr. Faye Watson Allen, and as such, served the greater Annapolis area for over forty years.

Born in 1921 in Springfield, Ohio, Faye was the oldest of five children. She left high school to attend Ohio State University, and later, transferred to Freedman's Hospital Nursing School in Washington, D.C. Faye made two crucial choices at Freedman's. First, she chose to continue onto medical school after her teacher, Dr. Moses Young, encouraged her to. He asked Faye to stay after class one day, at which point he spoke frankly to the aspiring nurse. "Miss Watson, I've decided you should be a doctor," he said, as he tried to convince her of her potential.

Initially, Faye dismissed the idea. But Dr. Young persisted, and eventually, his persuasion worked. She graduated in 1944 as a registered nurse—with the school's highest examination score in twenty-five years—and began pursuing her new goal with zeal. She attended Howard University and finished her pre-medical studies in a year—while working a forty-eight hour week on night duty at Freedman's as an R.N.

Faye also chose to date the handsome Aris T. Allen while at Freedman's. He was a third-year Howard medical student whose clinical work brought him into contact with nursing students, including Faye.

"I admired him and he was fun," she said. "But I had no thoughts at the time of marrying him. He was eleven years older . . . he wanted a wife to be there for him and I told him 'I don't fit your job description!' "

The two dated off and on before taking a six-month break. Then suddenly, out of the blue, Aris surprised Faye as she was leaving class. He expressed a desire to marry her and, although she still had two years left of medical school, they wed immediately.

Faye continued studying at Howard, while Dr. Allen built his medical practice in Annapolis, which he had started in 1945. He lived in a small "efficiency" above his office on Carroll Street, near the post office at Church Circle, and she rented a humble apartment in Washington.

Faye's mother joined her there in 1948: the year she shocked her peers by giving birth to her first son, Aris T. Allen, Jr. "No one [at Howard] noticed I was pregnant because of my big white lab coat," she said.

Dr. Allen graduated from Howard in 1949 and joined her husband's practice in 1950. Yet her race, gender—and the fact that she had two young boys—made it difficult for her to establish herself professionally in town. "I was introduced to Annapolis under difficult circumstances," she said. "Some of the male physicians were not cooperative. They'd say, 'She's just a woman.' And patients, both black and white, they didn't want a woman. It was a double whammy."

Unlike their local white colleagues, Dr. Allen and her husband could not belong to the Anne Arundel County Medical Society. Nor could they attend its meetings that offered physicians opportunities to further their education. This forced them to travel to Chicago, and other cities "to keep up with everything," Dr. Allen said.

The Allens were also barred from joining the Anne Arundel General Hospital staff in Annapolis. Instead, they delivered babies at patients' homes, or at Dr. T. H. Johnson's hospital on Northwest Street; they referred sick patients to Freedman's or Johns Hopkins; and they referred surgical patients to local surgeons. They received hate mail after one such surgeon invited Aris to "stand in the O.R. (operating room)" while operating on one of their patients.

The Allens belonged to an informal social club in Annapolis called the Weekenders that met regularly in the early 1950s. Its members (including the Allens, Hynsons, Badens, Williams, Wisemans, and Browns) met at each other's homes on Saturday nights. Dr. Aris T. Allen is standing in the back row, second from the left, and Dr. Faye Allen is seated in the second row, fourth from the left. Courtesy of the Maryland State Archives SPECIAL COLLECTIONS (The Annapolis I Remember Collection) Thomas Baden, Jr., The Weekenders, c. 1953 MSA SC 2140-1-449.

Aris was drafted into the Air Force shortly after Faye joined him in practice. She maintained their office while he served as a Captain at Vance Air Base, Oklahoma. She saw patients in town and made house calls throughout Anne Arundel County—including what she calls "late-night calls way back in South County."

Dr. Allen remembers navigating through its dark, rural landscape, falling asleep at the wheel, being jolted awake by the bumpy roads, and arriving at patients' homes to find them "waiting with lanterns at the ends of their lanes."

Many of the Allens' patients, especially those in rural areas, couldn't afford their medical services. Those who lacked money or insurance traded crops, baked goods, meals, livestock, or other goods for treatment.

Dr. Allen recalled one particularly amusing incident involving live chickens that her husband received for treating a farmer's family. Dr. Allen's biography, *Achieving the American Dream,* includes his account of the event. As he recalled,

> I received a call late one night from a man out on a farm who explained that his wife was ill. I went out and treated her . . . When I finished the husband was very apologetic. 'Doctor, I can't pay you. I haven't any money. But I have some vegetables and three live chickens.' I said, 'That will be fine.' We tied up the chickens and with the vegetables, put them in the back seat of my car. I then drove back to Annapolis perfectly happy. . . .

Dr. Allen's elation was short-lived. Upon returning to town, he discovered that the chickens had destroyed his new car's upholstery.[1]

"My husband had just bought the first new car he ever had in his life," Dr. Allen said. "He had to pay more to clean it up than the bill would have cost!"

Five years after Dr. Allen joined her husband's office, segregation's stronghold on Annapolis began to wane. They both joined the hospital's staff in 1955: the same year that it opened its delivery room to African-American mothers. And, although Dr. Allen is now retired, her son continues the family's tradition of service to the hospital and community. Aris T. Allen Jr., who was once concealed by his mother's "big white lab coat," has served on the hospital's Board of Trustees since 2001.[2]

Harry Klasmeier Recalls a "Quiet and Reserved" Annapolis

Harry Klasmeier worked close to the hospital, and the Allens' medical practice, for many years. What follows are his thoughts about the Annapolis he knew when he started working there in 1954.

Annapolis, Maryland: June 14, 1954

Today was the day. Harry Klasmeier couldn't help but smile as he donned his suit, picked up his briefcase, and left for work. Driving south from Lombardie Beach, he reached the old Severn River drawbridge and beheld the Annapolis city skyline.

He found the view to be especially beautiful that morning—his first morning as Anne Arundel County's first Fire Marshall. After crossing the bridge, he continued into town, parked his car, and walked briskly to his new office on Church Circle.

Annapolis was "fairly provincial" then, Mr. Klasmeier said. "It was quiet and reserved . . . a very small town . . . The big things were the legislature and the Naval Academy, and the stores were oriented towards shoppers, not tourists."

Mr. Klasmeier was right. Annapolis was certainly smaller in 1954. It had only 26,500 residents (about 10,000 less than today), and 11,000 telephones in service. Its amusements, according to *Polk's Annapolis City Directory* for that year, included water sports, golf, tennis, horseback riding, and three motion picture theaters with a total seating capacity of 2,000.

Annapolis also had fewer restaurants in the 1950s, according to Mr. Klasmeier. Of course there was Elmo's Lunch, the Hitching Post, Alsop's Restaurant, Jim's Corner, the Sanitary Restaurant, and others. Yet his favorite was the Royal Restaurant and Cocktail Lounge at 23 West Street. Mr. Klasmeier was a regular at "the Royal," which was owned by the Pantelides family. He walked there most days for lunch, since it was just paces from his office in the Anne Arundel County Circuit Courthouse. Many remember the bygone Royal's home-style food, including one retired Naval officer and his wife, who savored its deli sandwiches, mashed potatoes, and gravy.

In addition to the Royal Mr. Klasmeier frequented Wagon Wheels at the corner of Jones

The Royal Restaurant Cocktail Lounge and Club Room introduced shish kebabs to its menu in spring of 1956, when patrons could enjoy "full course dinners" for $1.25 at the restuarant. The Royal announced the new kebabs in a series of Evening Capital *ads in March. One, dated March 27, included this photograph, described the Royal's new "ultra-modern rotisserie," and noted that the restaurant had been "famous for fine foods since 1913."*

Mr. Harry Klasmeier, 1963. Courtesy of Harry Klasmeier. Photograph by William E. Clark.

Station Road and Ritchie Highway. He and Annapolis's Fire Chief, Mr. Charles Steele, typically met there for lunch on Tuesdays. Former Maryland Governor Marvin Mandel also dined there from time to time.

But there was little time for leisurely lunches in 1954. There was work to be done, and Mr. Klasmeier was the ideal person to do it. Fire safety was a natural career choice for the Baltimore native, many of whose relatives served as firemen. He grew up in a home located between two fire stations, at a time when memories of the city's devastating fire of 1904 were still fresh. Mr. Klasmeier even recalled rushing to fire scenes as a child to observe how they were fought.

Mr. Klasmeier's interest in firefighting continued through his military service and college years. Upon graduating from Johns Hopkins University in 1949, he worked for the Maryland Fire Underwriters Rating Bureau that set fire insurance rates for fire insurance companies. The Bureau used specific standards to determine a rate, such as a town's water supply, type of fire department and zoning, and distance between fire stations.

Mr. Klasmeier's focus shifted in 1954, shortly after Anne Arundel County adopted its fire prevention code. His job as the county's first Fire Marshall was to enforce this code and direct the Fire Prevention Bureau. Twenty-three volunteer fire companies served the area at the time, although the county did

The Anne Arundel County Circuit Courthouse, where Mr. Klasmeier worked for many years. Illustration by the author.

Mr. Klasmeier during his tenure as Fire Administrator, February 1977. Courtesy of The Capital. *Photograph by Darryl F. Wilson.*

supply one or two paid employees per station. Many firefighters slept at the stations—although this wasn't required.

Centralizing communications among the stations and supplying each with communications equipment was crucial when Mr. Klasmeier took office. There was no centralized fire alarm system at that point, and a person could only hope that he called the station closest to him during an emergency.

Ten years after Mr. Klasmeier took office, the county adopted its Charter. The Charter created an Anne Arundel County fire department and outlined the responsibilities of its Fire Administrator or Chief. Mr. Klasmeier was appointed to this position in 1964 and held it until he retired in 1983.

During his tenure as Fire Chief, Mr. Klasmeier oversaw sweeping changes to fire safety in the county. To name just a few, he developed a training program to ensure that firefighters were well—and consistently—prepared. Under his leadership, the number of county fire stations increased, the department's headquarters moved to Millersville in 1966, and the government hired its first paid firefighters two years later. He also helped to establish an advanced medical help program for the county's Paramedic Service, which he called a "first class system, one of the best in the country." In addition, he integrated the county Fire Service and hired its first female and African-American firefighters.

Mr. Klasmeier never imagined that he would witness these, and other improvements, when he started working at the courthouse. Let's rejoin him as he finished his first day of work there. The thought of staying in town to see the movie *The Command* at the Circle Theater was tempting. Yet so was the prospect of returning home to relax and read the *Evening Capital* over a hot meal, which is exactly what he did.[1]

Part 2: Places

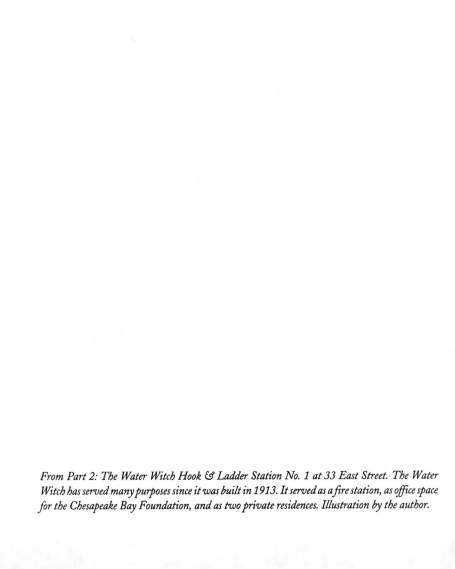

From Part 2: The Water Witch Hook & Ladder Station No. 1 at 33 East Street. The Water Witch has served many purposes since it was built in 1913. It served as a fire station, as office space for the Chesapeake Bay Foundation, and as two private residences. Illustration by the author.

Market House on the Move (1698–1775)

The year 2004 marked for the Annapolis market house a turning point. That year, the last of its local tenants left as the city prepared to lease the entire building to one entity. When *Annapolis Vignettes* was published, many assumed that the building's new occupant would be Dean & DeLuca, a New York–based gourmet and specialty food retailer. The next two vignettes celebrate the old market house and trace its history as it moved (many times) from the 1690s to when it settled at its current location in 1857.

I

Annapolis had five different market houses—at four different sites—from 1698–1775. This chapter features them all, starting with the first, which stood at the intersection of Market and High (now Duke of Gloucester) Streets.

The city's current market house is actually its eighth identified to date. The first resulted from an act passed by Maryland's General Assembly in 1683. That year, Annapolis was still a small 20-acre port called Arundelton. And, as a port, it was "one giant market," which eliminated the need for a "specific market area."[1]

This changed when the act established port Arundelton as the town Ann Arundell Town. Titled an "Act for the Advancement of Trade," it named and authorized commissioners to buy 100 acres of land on the Severn River, survey the site, and lay it out in "convenient streets, lanes & alleys, with open space places to be left" for a church, market house, or other public buildings.[2] Unlike ports, towns such as new Anne Arundell Town needed these permanent features to sustain their residents.

Richard Beard, Jr., surveyed the new town. Beard came to Maryland from Virginia as a youth with his family in 1650. He became an Anne Arundel County justice in 1679, and the county's Deputy Surveyor in 1684, the same year he completed his survey.

The task had posed a challenge for Beard, who had mainly surveyed plantations until then. Unlike this type of work, surveying the new town required him to "lay out a grid over an area already settled upon."[3]

Even so, he succeeded. He laid out a simple grid for the area, by creating streets based on existing rough paths such as Market, Shipwright, and High Streets. However, he did not designate an open market space—at least not yet.

The Assembly passed further legislation regarding Anne Arundel Town in 1694. It appointed Beard to resurvey the land, this time under the guidance of two parties: Royal Governor Francis Nicholson and the Council of Maryland. Nicholson proposed an ambitious baroque plan for the site—one that was far more complex than Beard's basic grid.

Perhaps this is one reason why Beard failed to finish his new survey on time. It remained incomplete when the Lower House called for him to present

Courtesy of the Maryland State Archives SPECIAL COLLECTIONS (Maryland State Archives Map Collection) James Stoddert, A Ground Plat of the City and Port of Annapolis, *1718 MSA SC 1427-1-6. Stoddert's plat shows Market Square, as laid out by Richard Beard, Jr., in 1695.*

it in March 1695. As the Speaker of the Lower House explained, "the said Beard saith that for want of some Large Paper to draw the same on, it is not yet done." Beard finally unveiled his design (eight months late) on October 11 to the Assembly, which was pleased with it.[4]

Unlike his initial plan, it created an open Market Square at the corner of Market and Duke of Gloucester Streets. This site made sense, since that area was a thriving commercial center: There was a wharf near the end of Charles Street, a gunpowder magazine on Shipwright Street near today's Upton Scott House, and goods could be moved easily between Acton's Cove and Market Square via Market Street.

The square became home to the city's first market house between 1695 and 1698. We know this, thanks in part to a conflict that occurred in 1698: one between the town's needs and property owners' rights—specifically those of Captain John Perry.

> The city's first market house caused what was "probably the first zoning battle fought in Annapolis over the rights of property owners versus those of the city."
>
> —Anthony Lindauer, 1997.[5]

II

Life in late 17th-century Annapolis was good for John Perry, also called "Perry the Postman." In 1695, he was the Province of Maryland's official mailman: a lucrative, demanding job that required him to ride a lengthy mail circuit eight times per year. He began at the Potomac River then traveled in order to Leonardtown, Annapolis, Kent Island, Oxford, New Castle, and Philadelphia.

When not traveling, Perry lived in Annapolis in a small brick house that he built sometime before spring of 1698. It stood on Market Square, at the southeast corner of Market and Duke of Gloucester Streets, and had a garden that overlooked the city, Weathering Cove (the current harbor area), and Acton (now called Spa) Creek.

Perry's view didn't last long; the city's first market house blocked it when it emerged at Market Square. Perry complained about the eyesore to the Assembly on March 28, 1698. He lamented to the Lower House "that whereas he has been att great charges in building a brick house in the porte of Annapolis a certaine Small Market House was since so incommodiously erected that it deprived him of his sight and prospect. . . ."

The Assembly sympathized with Perry. It also agreed to move the market under two conditions: that it would be rebuilt at a site approved by several commissioners, and that Perry would pay for its relocation. As it declared, "Upon considering of the said petition the house do consent that the Markett House be removed at the petitioners charge and placed in such place as the Com[rs] [commissioners] of the port of Annapolis shall direct."[6]

Perry agreed to pay for the market's removal. And, as a result, a new market house was built at the intersection of State Circle and Northeast Street (now Maryland Avenue). We don't know exactly when this happened. We do know, however, that it was sometime after 1717 thanks to sources such as Ebenezer Cook's *Sot-Weed Factor* (1708) and David Ridgely's *Annals of Annapolis* (1841).

These lines from Cook's poem suggests that Annapolis lacked a market house in 1708:

> Up to Annapolis I went,
> A City situate on a Plain,
> Where scarce a House will keep out Rain;
> The buildings fram'd with Cyprus rare,
> Resembles much our Southwark Fair:
> But Stranger here will scarcely meet
> With Market-place, Exchange, or Street;[7]

Annapolis still lacked a market house in 1716, according to Ridgely. Using now-missing Corporation of Annapolis records he wrote, "In 1716, the corporation took into consideration 'whether a market-house was requisite or not, and resolved, nemine contradicente, that it is very requisite,' and determined it should be built on or near the state-house hill."[8]

One year later, the market still hadn't been rebuilt. Again, we know this thanks to Ridgely and Corporation records. In 1717, the Corporation passed an act to regulate the market and limit door-to-door food sales. It forbade Annapolitans to buy "any flesh or fish, living or dead, eggs, butter or cheese (oysters excepted) at their own houses." Instead, they had to "repair to and buy at the flagge staffe, on the state-house hill, until such a time as there shall be a market house built . . . ." Anyone who violated the act could be fined 16 s. 8 d (about $140 in today's currency).[9]

It's not clear if the Corporation's restriction worked in 1717. Nor is it clear why officials tried to regulate food sales on the streets then. Anne Yentsch addresses this question in her book, *A Chesapeake Family and Their Slaves.*

She speculates that they did because "appropriate people had encroached into inappropriate space." In other words, middlemen (the appropriate people) were buying goods from producers on the roadside (an inappropriate space) before they passed through the city gates. The laws against forestalling would have curbed this problem, by making "the market house a sanctioned zone for trade, and commerce by the side of the road an illegal activity."[10]

III

An open-air market stood at "state-house hill" for some time; goods were bought and sold there, but not in a permanent building. The market was open

In 1718, Stoddert described the site set aside for the public market place as: "All that parcel of ground within the city and port of Annapolis lying between South East street, market street, and Duke of Gloucester street, Beginning at the north east corner of the shade of a brick house belonging to Charles Carroll, esq. and running thence south east thirty three feet to a locust post then north east one hundred and sixteen feet to another locust post then north west one hundred and sixteen feet to another locust post then south west one hundred and sixteen feet to another locust post then with a straight line to the beginning containing thirteen thousand four hundred fifty six square feet more or less."[11]

Dr. Morris Radoff believed that, "We have every reason to assume that this was the original market place surveyed and set aside by Richard Beard in 1694."[12]

weekly on Wednesdays and Saturdays, starting at "8 or 9 o'clock in the fore-noon." Someone beat a drum at "half quarter of an hour" to announce its open-ing, and patrons couldn't buy anything there until the beating stopped.

The city eventually built an actual market house near the intersection of State Circle and Northeast Street. This happened shortly after 1717; however, it's missing from a plat of Annapolis that was made at the time. Here's why:

Several years prior, great confusion had arisen over the ownership, bound-aries, and numbering of lots in Annapolis. To clarify matters—and to resolve a massive sea of property disputes—the Assembly ordered the city to be re-surveyed in 1718. This was crucial since Beard's second survey had burned in the State House fire of 1704. Moreover, since Beard had died by 1718, the As-sembly appointed James Stoddert to do the work.

Stoddert barely made his deadline. His plat was due sometime before Au-gust 1, 1718, and he completed it in late July. One would expect it to show the market house at State Circle and Northeast Street. Yet it doesn't. Instead, it shows Market Square at the place that Beard drew it in 1695: at the intersection of Market and Duke of Gloucester Streets.

Why did Stoddert draw it there, rather than at its true 1718 location? Be-cause he was hired to clarify real estate disputes by recreating Beard's plan or, simply put, to draw what should be, instead of what was.

The city's second market house stayed at State Circle for about a decade. Then, shortly after 1728, a new one emerged closer to the water—although it would move several more times before settling at its current spot.

IV

Before exploring the city's third market house, it's important to mention this: The market wasn't the only place where goods (and gossip) were exchanged in 18th-century Annapolis. Fairs offered further opportunities for commerce, fel-lowship, and fun.

> "In early 18th century Annapolis, "market-trading was done primarily by pro-
> ducer-traders (i.e., those who made/grew/raised the foods were the ones who sold it)."
> —Anne Yentsch, 1994.[13]

The Assembly authorized Annapolis to hold fairs after it became Maryland's capital in 1694. (Annapolis was called Anne Arundel Town at that point;
it was renamed Annapolis in 1695.) Fairs had occurred at the former capital, St.
Mary's City, as well. That city's charter, which was granted in 1686, permitted
officials to hold one fair there per year.

In October 1696, the Assembly passed "An Act for keeping good Rules
and Orders" in Annapolis. The act did several things. It made Governor
Nicholson, Thomas Lawrence, Nicholas Greenbury, Thomas Tench, John
Hammond, Edward Dorsey, James Sanders, and Richard Hill (or any five of
them) the town's "body corporate," trustees, and commissioners.

It also gave them considerable power. For instance, it authorized them to
preserve "peaceable & quiett liveing and resideing" in town; to "restreine and
prevent all disorders and distur-bances . . . that may Cause Annoyance or incon-
veniency" to its residents; to "Erect and Constitute" a market every week, and to
hold an annual fair.[14]

The commissioners could choose the fair's time and place. However, they
were supposed to choose venues that would be "Convenient for the Vending,
selling, buying and purchasing all or any Sorte of Lawfull, Goods, Chattells,
Wares, or Merchandizes whatsoever." No one who came to the fairs could be
arrested—except for murder, treason, or felony.[15]

About ten years after this law passed, Maryland's Royal Governor, John
Seymour, granted Annapolis its charter. Dated August 10, 1708, it proposed
four changes to the city's fair policy. First, it doubled their frequency. It authorized the mayor, recorder, aldermen, and common council (the Corporation) to
hold two annually. It also established the fairs' dates. One was to occur on "St.
Phillip and Jacobs Day" (May 1), and the other on the "feast of St. Michaell, the
Archangell" (September 29). If these dates fell on Sundays, then the fairs were
to occur on the following Monday.

The charter also offered greater protection for the fairs' attendants. It exempted them "from any arrest, attachments, or executions," during, and two
days before or after they occurred.

Lastly, the charter gave city officials two types of control over the fairs: financial and judicial. Financially, it empowered them to set tolls on any
"goods, cattle, merchandizes and other comodities" to be sold there. The tolls
were to be "reasonable," which according to the charter, meant they couldn't
exceed "sixpence on every beast sold" or the "twentieth parte of the value of
any comodity."

Judicially, it empowered them to hold a "courte of Pypowdry" at the fairs. The court would resolve any "controversies and quarrels" that arose, and officials could keep "all profitts and perquisits due, incident and belonging" to it.[16]

William Blackstone defined this type of court (also spelled Pipowder, Pie Powder, Py-Powder, Piepoudre, etc.) in the 18th century. In short, it was the lowest—yet most expeditious—court of justice in old English law. It was held at fairs and markets for a reason: many traveled long distances to these events and needed to have their cases decided quickly, rather than deal with the delays and hassles of regular law.[17]

Legislators amended Annapolis's charter before confirming it. One of their changes involved local fairs. They set strict guidelines for how officials could toll goods brought there for sale: they could only toll items worth 20 shillings or more, charging 6 pence for every item worth between 20 shillings and 5 pounds, and 12 pence for everything worth more than 5 pounds.[18]

Several sources reveal what fairs were like in 18th-century Annapolis including Elihu Riley's *The Ancient City* (1887). It states that:

"The two fair days of the annual fairs were the gala days of the people, as the high days and holidays of the gentry were the birth-days of Prince and Proprietary. May-day, Whitsuntide, Michaelmas, and Christmas, Militia Trainings, and muster-days also broke the monotony of daily duty."

Riley noted what happened at the fairs. He claimed that horseracing was a main attraction, and that "in one [fair] advertised for 'Baltimoretown,' a bounty was offered of forty shillings to any person that produces 'the best piece of yard wide country made white linnen, the piece to contain twenty yards. On Saturday, the third day, a hat and ribbon will be cudgelled for; a pair of pumps wrestled for; and a white shirt to be run for by two negro girls.' "[19]

Unfortunately, Riley didn't indicate how often fairs occurred in Annapolis. Nor did he provide a date for the one that occurred at "Baltimoretown."

The *Maryland Gazette* also mentioned fairs. Consider these announcements, which it published on October 25, 1745; October 14 and 28, 1747; April 16, 1752; and June 14, 1753:

On Wednesday the 30th day of this Instant October, and Thursday the 31st of the same month, a Fair will be kept in the old fields near John Conner's in Anne Arundel County. On the fifth day of the Fair will be Run for by any Horse, Mare, or Gelding Twelve Pounds current money, to run three Heats, Two Males each Heat, and to carry one hundred and twelve pounds . . . On the day following, will be run for on the same course Eight pounds current money, to run three Heats, and to carry the same weight; the winning horse in the first day, to be excepted on the second . . . . "

The subscriber hath obtained a Patent for keeping a Fair at Frederick-Town, near Monocacy, on the 31st day of October and the 10th day May next, each fair to continue Three Days, and for a Market to be held there every Saturday after the 1st of November next. All persons who will bring any goods, merchandise, cattle, or any thing else to the said Fairs, or Markets, to sell, shall be free and exempt from the payment of any Toll, Stallage, —, or any other charges for the term of five years next — this last day of August 1747.—D. Dulany

Lost during the last FAIR, a woman's side saddle, without any covering, the Seat Buck-skin almost new, A horse strayed away with it on his back, but was taken up without it. Whoever finds and brings it to the subscriber, shall have 10 shillings reward. —James Barnes.

To be Sold by Public Venue On Friday the 8th Day of May next, being the Second Day of the Fair, at Baltimore Town . . . About thirteen hundred Acres of Land, near Soldier's Delight, in Baltimore County; whereon are two Plantations, well improved . . . . Also, to be Sold at Annapolis, the Second Day of May Fair next, at the House of Soumaen, A Parcel of likely young NEGROES, for Bills of Exchange, Gold, or Paper Currency. The Sale to begin, at Eleven o'Clock.—Sarah Hammond.

ANNAPOLIS . . . On Monday last was held on the North Side of the Severn, for the first Time in the Memory of Man, A FAIR, where were run several Horse Races, for sundry good Prizes; and a fine SMOCK was Run for, by certain Persons, who were not all of the Female Sex, which was won by a well legged Girl. The Day was concluded by two sumptuous Balls, at two Several Places.

Annapolis wasn't the only place that held fairs in colonial Maryland. So did Baltimoretown, St. Mary's City, and others including "Charles-Town." This town's residents made a bold move in 1744: they hosted a fair without authorization, or "of their own Accord" on May 10.[20]

Shortly thereafter, the Assembly made fairs at Charles-Town regular occasions for two reasons. First, the fair had been very well attended. And second, lawmakers noted that the country around Charles-Town produced "many useful Commodities, which . . . might be of Benefit and Advantage to the Trade and People of this Province, if the Time and Manor of keeping such fair . . . were under due regulations . . . ."[21]

The Assembly authorized Charles-Town's commissioners to host two fairs per year: one in April, the other in October. Each could last up to three days, excluding Sundays. Everyone who lived in town was exempt from arrest during the fairs. Visitors enjoyed an even greater privilege: Not only were they exempt from arrest during the fairs, they were also exempt from the same, one day before and after they occurred. Of course, as in Annapolis, there were exceptions; locals and visitors could be arrested for "felony or breach of peace."[22]

V

From butchers "blowing wind into dead calves to make them seem alive," to brawls between farmers, market house life in early 18th-century Annapolis was lively to say the least. And, it was during this time that the city's third market house emerged. It was built in about 1730 on Church Street just below Francis Street.

The Assembly made the new market possible. In 1728, it passed an act that appropriated part of the land designated for a Custom House in Annapolis for the building of a market house.[24] Locating a market there made sense. It was a large site whose dimensions, "210 feet in breadth on the water, and 360 feet in length, and 82 feet in breadth on the head of the said land," could easily support the building. Of this area, the Assembly gave the Corporation "60 feet on breadth in the water, 360 feet in length, and 25 feet on the head of said land," on which to build the market.

Second, the land that was originally meant for a market house, Market Square, was also unsuitable at the time. Since the square was laid out, the city's center of population and activity had shifted from Acton's Cove to the dock area. As the act's preamble declared, "Whereas the Land design'd for a Market-place, in the said City, is not so convenient for the same, as Part of the Land design'd and allotted for a Custom-house; and which, at present, lies useless and unimproved . . . ."[25]

To fund the market's construction, the act authorized the Corporation to sell "all the land formerly laid out, allotted and left vacant for a Market House." This had to happen soon, since the act also contained this provision: the Corporation had to build "or cause to be built" a market within two years after it was "surveyed, marked and laid out."[26]

Fortunately, this process went smoothly. Henry Ridgely and John Welch surveyed the site in 1729. The same year, Charles Daniel bought the old Market Space land for 22 pounds 15 shillings. The Corporation then used these profits to build the market.

We don't know what the new building looked like. However we do know several shocking practices that occurred within it. Its butchers sometimes tried to trick customers into buying second-rate goods, according to Anne Yentsch. She wrote that, "The town's lower-ranking butchers—the ones who sold meat in market stalls—were contentious, and not above sly practices such as 'blowing wind' into dead calves to make them seem alive."[27]

" . . . food was central in the daily life of the pre-industrial town, and, for many people, the workaday world revolved around activities associated with food."
—Anne Yentsch, 1994.[23]

The market could also be a dangerous place for out-of-town venders. According to Yentsch, "when country farmers brought animals or meat to sell, things got nasty." Disputes between them and local farmers "escalated from insults and threats to blows, gouging, assault and battery."[28]

One farmer experienced such violence when he came to town on September 12, 1730. This outraged city officials, who responded by publishing the following notice in the *Maryland Gazette* on October 20:

Whereas, We the Mayor, Recorder, and some of the Aldermen . . . have heard, That a Person who came into Town on Saturday the 12th of September last, to sell some Beef, was Insulted, Threatened, and Hindered from useing any of the stalls in the Publick Market House by some of the Town Butchers. These are to certify and afford all the Persons, who will bring Provisions to Market, that they shall have all the Encouragement we can give them, and shall be effectually protected from any ill treatment, that any person within our jurisdiction, who shall presume to insult or abuse them, shall be punished according to law: And that if any person residing out of our jurisdiction, shall treat anyone ill, who brings Provisions to our Market, we think ourselves obliged to use our utmost Endeavors to bring every such offender to condign Punishment and that we will act accordingly given under our Hands at Annapolis . . .

> Robert Alexander, Mayor
> Daniel Dulany, Recorder
> Benjamin Tasker
> John Beale
> Vachel Denton
> Robert Gordon[29]

The city's third market house operated for about twenty years until locals became dissatisfied with its service. In response, Annapolitans—including Mayor Benjamin Tasker—complained to the Assembly in 1751 that the building was "of very little use to the inhabitants." The Assembly agreed and passed "An Act for erecting a new Market-House in the City of Annapolis."[30]

The act empowered the Corporation to sell the current market and the land it occupied, use the profits from the sale to buy a new site within the city,

---

"Any Workman or Workmen, who will undertake to compleat the said Building; in a Workmanlike Manner, may apply to the said Corporation, on Thursday the 13th of August next, who will then meet at the Court-House in Annapolis for the Purpose, at 6 o'Clock in the Afternoon."
—Call for bids placed by the Corporation in the *Maryland Gazette,* July 30, 1752.

Benedict Calvert lived near the city's fourth market house at his home on State Circle. He moved to Prince George's County in the early 1760s, and his residence was used for many purposes after that. For instance, he let his business partners (Wallace, Davidson, and Johnson) sell British cargo onsite in 1772. According to Anne Yentsch, "Its proximity to the market house on the Circle made it a natural choice, and one can readily envision the brick-paved courtyard area as a display area for merchandise."[37]

and rebuild the market there. About a year later, Lancelott Jacques bought the old building and lot for 155 pounds, and work on the city's fourth market house began shortly thereafter.[31]

We know a lot about this building. First, a call for bids placed by the Corporation in the *Maryland Gazette* on July 30, 1752, reveals what it probably looked like. Assuming that what the call requested was built, the market was 40 feet long and 20 feet wide. It was "underpinn'd, with four Courses of Brick above the Level of Ground, with a Brick floor below and Loft above." The loft was accessible via a trap door and ladder, and it contained windows to ventilate the space.

Painted "red with Oil Colour," the market had three doors on each side and one at each end, with each door measuring 8 feet high by 6 feet wide. Its posts and rafters were made of yellow poplar, and its weather boarding of "feather-edged yellow Poplar Plank." The market's roof was made of "Galloping Rafters, and had a small "Turret for a Bell" in the middle of it. The roof and turret were shingled with cypress.

The building stood at the base of State Circle, to the right of the Old Treasury Building, at a spot Rebecca Key described as "just below the present Gun House." According to Mrs. Key, who lived in Annapolis from 1754–1840, it "was about half the size of our present market, but very commodious."[32]

Unfortunately, locals began complaining about the market soon after it was built. Even the Corporation labeled it as very "irregularly kept" in 1754. In response, it passed "A Bye law to regulate the Market, in the City of Annapolis." The law appeared in the *Maryland Gazette* on February 7, 1754. It began "Whereas the Market . . . is irregularly kept, whereby the inhabitants of said city, are held under several inconveniences," and offered several solutions to the problem.

It established Wednesdays and Saturdays as regular market days. Although locals probably appreciated this regularity, that it was open just two days per week presented a challenge. According to author and historian Jane McWilliams, "winter would afford natural refrigeration, but the two-or three-day interval between market days must have posed quite a storage problem in the summer."[33]

The law also established regular market hours. It ordered that "all Victuals brought to this City for sale, upon these or any other Days, shall be carried to the Corporation's Market House, there to be sold to the Inhabitants at the stated Market Hours, to wit, from any Time in the morning 'til Twelve at Noon." There was one exception: "Any Person or Persons bringing Fish, or

In 1776, Maryland's Council of Safety passed the following order, which affected the city's butchers. It's possible that it affected those who sold meat at the market house.

"Whereas it hath been represented to the Council of Safety by physicians and others that the intolerable Stench arising from Slaughter Houses and spreading green Hides to dry in the City of Annapolis may be productive of pestilential Disorders and ill Consequences to the Troops and others residing in the said City, Therefore Ordered that no Butcher or other person shall, after the twenty sixth Day of this Instant, presume to slaughter Bullocks, Mutton or any kind of meat, or put up green Hides to cure within the Limits of said City for and during the Term of three months thence next ensuing."[38]

Oysters, brought by Water to the Said City" could sell their goods at other times or days of the week.

The market's new schedule benefited out-of-town farmers. It allowed them to compete with local ones, since the law forbade anyone to buy "victuals" brought into town except at the specified days and times. Anyone who did could be fined 20 shillings, half of which went to the Corporation, and the other half to the informer.[34]

Tragedy struck the market two decades after the Corporation regulated its schedule. A violent windstorm hit Annapolis on September 2, 1775. It stripped most of the new copper roof from the State House, and blew the market down, as the *Maryland Gazette* reported:

On Saturday night last we had a most violent storm from the northeast, which for several hours blew a mere hurricane, with heavy rain; the water rose three feet perpendicular above the common tide; a great quantity of the corner of the State House was torn up and the market-house blown down; the damage sustained in different parts of the province we are told is very considerable.[35]

Historians such as Dr. Morris Radoff believed that, "it is probable, but not certain," that the market was rebuilt at the same site after the storm.[36]

Eight Generous Gentlemen

After moving three times in less than a century, the market house found a permanent home, at the head of the dock, in 1784. This vignette explores what—or rather who—made this possible, and the market's early history there.

I

Four years after a windstorm destroyed the Annapolis market house, officials planned to build a new one elsewhere in town. In 1779, the Assembly authorized the mayor and common council to sell Temple and Dean Streets and to use 80 percent of the profit for this purpose. Yet when the sale finally occurred in September 1784, its profits were no longer needed; the Corporation had already appropriated 260 pounds for the building.[1]

Once funded, the new market was built at today's Market Space, thanks to eight local businessmen: Nicholas Carroll, James Maccubbin, Jacob Hurst, Charles Wallace, John Davidson, Thomas Harwood, and Joseph and James Williams.

Carroll was born in 1751 to Nicholas and Mary Carroll Maccubbin. He changed his last name, however, when his uncle, Charles Carroll the Barrister, willed his estate to him, and another brother on the condition that they take the name Carroll.

Nicholas Carroll was an active, prominent citizen. He served several terms as mayor of Annapolis and was a common councilman, alderman, and justice of the peace. He also represented Anne Arundel County in the Assembly's Lower House, and was a member of the Constitutional Ratification Convention, which met in Annapolis in 1788. He lived on Green Street with his wife Ann Jennings, whom he married in 1783, and their five children.

Courtesy of the Maryland State Archives SPECIAL COLLECTIONS (Historic Annapolis Collection of Sachse Lithographs) Edward Sachse, Bird's Eye View of the City of Annapolis, *1858 MSA SC 2449-1-1.*

Carroll's second cousin, James Maccubbin, also made the new market possible. Born in 1759, he lived at the corner of Cornhill Street and Market Space. He served as Secretary of the Senate, a common councilman, and chief judge of the Orphans' Court. He was also a successful merchant whose first store, a three-story building, stood at 24 Market Space.

Like Maccubbin, Jacob Hurst was an accomplished merchant who owned property on Market Space and Church Street. He was a contemporary of Annapolis silversmith William Faris who kept a meticulous diary. In it, Faris called Hurst a "Pedler," and noted his death in this excerpt dated October 7, 1792: "Old Mr. Husk, commonly call'd the Pedler died Last night & was Buried this evening."[2]

Faris also mentioned Charles Wallace, who outlived Hurst by twenty years. Born locally in 1727, Wallace was a staymaker, tavern keeper, merchant, and politician, whose positions included alderman, common councilman, and Executive Council member. He was also a developer. In 1769, he bought the land between Francis and East Streets from the Bordley family, laid out Fleet and Cornhill Streets there, and subdivided the area into lots. He later became builder or "undertaker" of the present State House, yet failed to complete the job.

As an entrepreneur, Wallace formed a mercantile partnership with Joshua Johnson and John Davidson in 1771. Their firm, "Wallace, Davidson, and Johnson," built and occupied one of four connected, identical, three-story offices called "Factor's Row" at 28–34 Market Space.

Davidson was born in Scotland in 1737. He was a patriot and was an officer in one of Anne Arundel County's three militia battalions during the Revolutionary War (the Provincial Convention established the battalions in 1776). As an officer, he was authorized to seize the firearms (except pistols) of any eligible man who failed to enroll in the militia by March 1, 1776.

While in the militia, Davidson served as Collector of Customs starting in 1777. He held this position until 1794: the year he purchased the Reynolds-Trueman property on Church Circle between West and Franklin Streets, and the year of his death. The *Maryland Gazette* described the deceased as "a tender husband, a good father, the uniform patriot, and an honest man."[3]

Davidson had much in common with Thomas Harwood, another well-to-do merchant whose three-story brick home fronted City Dock. Harwood ran a thriving import business with his brother Benjamin in the 1770s–80s. He also held public office; he became Treasurer of the Western Shore in 1775, sheriff in 1783, and Commissioner of Loans in 1791. He also co-managed a lottery to raise funds to complete St. Anne's Church in 1790.

Like Harwood, James Williams was a public servant. Born in 1741, he served three terms as mayor of Annapolis, and as an alderman, common councilman, and county sheriff. He and his brother Joseph ran a prosperous store that they took over from their uncle, Thomas Williams. James's success enabled him to own a two-story building on the dock with a kitchen, and milk and smoke houses. He also owned a racing stable that housed stallions such as "Pitt," named for the British Statesman William Pitt.[4]

II

These eight men made a crucial choice in 1784—one that redefined the city's waterfront for centuries to come. On July 28, they deeded 1.43 acres (approximately today's Market Space) to the "Mayor, Recorder, Aldermen and Common Council of the City of Annapolis." (See appendix 1 for the deed.) The deed contained a few conditions. First, it required the recipients to pay "five Shillings sterling" for the land (This was the customary price for a transfer intended as a gift.). More importantly, the deed would be "void and of no Effect" if the Corporation failed to build a market house on the lot within three years.

Not just any market house, either. The deed set strict guidelines for its appearance and location. It instructed officials to build "a good Substantial Brick Stone or framed Market House well fitted with the Accommodations necessary for the Reception and Sale of Provisions. . . ." It was to be 60 feet long, 40 feet wide, and built at the westernmost part of the parcel, near Church Street. Its western side was to oppose this street, and its front was to parallel the "large brick building" occupied by Wallace, Harwood, Davidson, and Joseph Williams.

The deed set further guidelines for the land around the market. Two "publick streets," 80 feet wide each, were to separate it from the "large brick building" on one side, an d the water's edge on the other. Another 80-foot space in front of Gilbert Middleton's home was to connect the two streets. Aside from these spaces, the remaining land was reserved for possible additions to the market house.[5]

Officials reacted immediately to the deed. On the same day it was made, the Corporation ordered a "framed house" to be built onsite. Five days later, it secured funds to erect a market there; on August 2, it appropriated 260 pounds "out of the first money received by the Treasurer" for the new building and appointed a committee to oversee its construction.

Four men, each a sound choice for the job, comprised the committee: Wallace, Davidson, James Brice, and Isaac Harris. Wallace and Davidson have already been mentioned. Brice, who lived at the corner of East and Prince George Streets, was equally successful. He was a lawyer, planter, and public servant who had been two-term mayor of Annapolis, and acting governor of Maryland. Harris had also held public office and was a respected blacksmith. He did "smith's work for the Assembly rooms during their construction" and had "advertised for workmen to make weapons" during the Revolutionary War. An August 1786 court record later called him a "gentleman."[6]

Under their leadership, construction began on the new market—the city's sixth in less than a century. Workers forged its foundation using lime, sand, and stone raised out of the city's old wharf. Other materials purchased for the building included bricks, brads, and oil for paint; spikes, shingles, scaffold

> "To be sold, by the subscriber being in Annapolis, at Public Sale, on the 20th day of March, at 11 o'clock, for ready money, A House in Annapolis, which stands upon a leased ground, a pleasant situation, near where the new market-house will stand. At the same time will be sold, some cabinet work . . ."
>
> —William Sefton.[7]

poles, and a saw; and nails, lathing nails, white lead, laths for plaster, and poplar plank for arches.

Once finished, workmen furnished the new structure with these essentials: benches, butcher blocks, stalls, hooks, and a tin plate to weigh butter. It also had scales, two measures, a horse rack, weighing house, and a hay machine, or one used to weigh hay.[8]

A city bylaw established the market's schedule, soon after it opened. It was open only on Wednesdays and Saturdays, which again made keeping food fresh a challenge in the summer. Its hours were from early morning until 10 A.M. from May 1 through September 30, and until 11 A.M. the rest of the year. Buying or selling market goods anywhere else in town was forbidden with the following exceptions: oysters, beef, dry fish, pork, and fish in barrels or large casks, cattle, sheep and live hogs, flour, wheat, Indian corn in barrels, dried peas and beans, oats, rye, and bran.[9]

Isaac McHard was the new market's first clerk, or master, and held that job until he resigned in November 1793. He oversaw the market's activities, collected the tenants' rents, and provided an account of them to the Corporation. Prior to becoming market master, McHard had been a tavern keeper. He ran the Indian King Tavern at 10–12 Francis Street, which he leased from 1774–82; and in 1783, the Corporation paid him to house members of Congress who were meeting in town that winter.[10]

McHard knew the silversmith Faris. They were among a group of Annapolitans described as "requisitioning" scarce supplies from local plantations during the Revolutionary War.[11] Faris noted him in this diary excerpt dated September 9, 1792:

> a cloudey day. in the after noon rain. this after noon, Richard Beard was buried aged 72 and Mr. Thomas Hyde told me that he should be 71 in January next and Mr. Charles Wallace said he should be 66 in May next. Cloudey dull evening. Blows Hard and looks as if wee should have a Harrican. The pall Bearers to Mr. Beard's Burial, Messrs. Thomas Hyde, Charles Wallace, A. Quynn, Isaac McHeard, and Jubb Fowler & William Faris Senr [short for senior].[12]

Faris also wrote about John Wells, one of the new market's first tenants. He applied for and received Stall No. 1, for which he paid 6 shillings 8 pence to the sheriff in February 1787.[13] Wells was a butcher, as were other members of his family. He supplied lamb, mutton, veal, and beef to Faris, who mentioned him in these diary entries:

February 3, 1799: "snow'd in the night. a clear cold day. in the evening Mr. John Wells's daughter was married to Mr. Sherred—who lives on the Eastern Shore."[14]

April 11, 1803: "a fine morning. about 9 oclock Mrs. Faris and Marriah pitt went of in the Packett for Baltimore. this fore noon I sow'd the ocoro, or coffe, Silve's watering the Flower Beds. I have put more simlin seeds in the Hills. a fine day. in the evening about sun sett John Wells's wife died."[15]

April 13, 1803: "Sylve's dug the Border for the nutmegs I sow'd 48 rows of seed, she then went to sticking the 4 rows of Peas in the Bigg Bed. this afternoon Mrs. John Wells was Buried, a dull Heavey cloudey day."[16]

May 23, 1803: "a cloudey morning. last night Mr. John Wells (the Butcher) died and I sow'd a row of Peas in the lott this morning and Isac mow'd the grass in the garden, in the after noon Mr. John Wells was Buried. a cloudey drisley afternoon."[17]

Market tenants such as Wells could rent stalls on a daily, monthly, quarterly, or annual basis for $7 or $ 8 per year. They sold fresh fish, meat, produce, dairy products, and possibly horses, according to a special fee collected in 1811.[18]

Lucy Smith, a free black, was another of the market's early tenants. She rented Stall No. 9, in the early 1800s, for at least seven consecutive years, for $7 per year. Later, she operated a bakeshop near the corner of Main and Green Streets. She lived at 160 Prince George Street (the Patrick Creagh House) with her husband John, who bought the property in about 1820. The house was built c. 1735–47 and became known as "Aunt Lucy's Bake Shop."[19]

Faris was among the market's early customers. He described one of his trips there on August 2, 1794: "Phillis went off with her self this morning before Mrs. Faris got up and while I was at market . . ."[20] He also referenced the building on January 11, 1793 when he wrote, " . . . In the afternoon thay got the Way House to the place intended by the Market House."[21]

Faris made his most startling entry about the market on August 3, 1795—one that could have easily been written after Tropical Storm Isabel hit Annapolis in 2003. He wrote that it, "rained very hard last night and Blow'd a Harrican . . . the tide was so high this morning that one could not get to the Market House with out a Boat."[22]

Faris probably did more than shop at the market house; he most likely obtained his news there too. For going to market meant more than a trip to the store, because the market was more than a store; it was also a meeting place and forum where people exchanged ideas. Thus, in addition to being an economic asset, the building was a social and political factor in the city.

III

The city's sixth market house operated for about thirty years before it was razed and replaced. In 1819, the Corporation paid Andrew Shein to build a new one on the same site. Made of brick, like its predecessor, it measured 40-by-60 feet.

Although the building resembled the old one, its management, policies, and layout were different. In terms of management, the Market Master assumed greater responsibilities at the new market house. On June 29, 1818, the Corporation had ordered that, "the offices of Sheriff and Collector, Hay-weigher, and Clerk of the Market, shall be vested in one person, who shall perform all the duties pertaining to those offices." "On motion by Mr. Sands," it appointed George Duvall to the new position.[23]

By 1839, the Corporation appointed the Market Master annually; he earned $60 per year paid quarterly and had to do two things before taking office. First, he had to give $200 bond to the city "conditioned for the faithful performance of his duties, and the trust reposed in him by this or any future ordinance."

He also had to take this oath: "I, A.B., do swear that I will diligently and faithfully, to the best of my skill and judgment, execute and perform all and singular the duties of market-master without favour, affection, partiality or prejudice."

Once in office, the Market Master "had full power and authority to take possession, care and charge of the market-house." Some of his duties were to:

- Rent the market stalls on the first Monday in January, for one-year terms. He could rent them for shorter terms, but not for less than three months, nor at a less rate than 50 percent of the annual rent. He could also rent the center stalls for 50 cents per day, the east side's eave benches for 25 cents per day, and the other benches, stalls, or stands for 12 ½ cents per day;
- Collect the tenants' rents;
- Attend the market house daily during normal market hours and "enforce obedience" to its rules and regulations;
- Attend the weigh-house daily from 6 A.M. to 9 A.M. from November through February, 5 A.M. to 9 A.M. in March, April, September, and October, and 4 A.M. to 9 A.M. from May through August. He also had to weigh items in the large scales as needed, but could keep the profits if he had to do so during non-market hours;[24]
- "Prevent all blown, stuffed, unsound, or unwholesome provisions, from being sold or being exposed for sale";
- "Weigh, try and examine, all butter, lard, and other articles of provision, sold at a given weight," to make sure it weighed what merchants claimed it did. If it didn't, the Market Master could seize and dispose of it to the highest bidder. Anyone who brought an item to the market for sale, but refused to let the Market Master "examine, weigh, or ascertain its quality," could be fined up to $10;

- Decide all disputes that arose between buyers and sellers in the market. Anyone who was "aggrieved by" his judgment could appeal to the Mayor, Recorder, or Aldermen, whose decision was final;
- "Cause the market house to be swept every day, and to remove all dirt, filth, and snow, from the same, as often as may be necessary"; and
- Report all violations of city law regarding the market and Market Master.

The new market's policies were also different. First, every day was a "market day," except Sunday. Any goods brought to town for sale "at market" had to be "carried to the market-house," and sold during "stated market hours." These were from "anytime in the morning" until 9 A.M. in May, June, July, August, and September, and until 10 A.M. the rest of the year.

The market was the only place where people could buy goods that were brought to town for sale "at market." Anyone who bought them elsewhere could be fined $5 or $10 per offense. Free men and women paid $10 per offense, and the master or mistress of any "apprentice, servant, or slave" caught doing so paid $5 per offense. In both cases, half of the fine went to the informer and half went to the Corporation.

It was also unlawful to buy and resell goods that were en route to or at the market. Anyone who did paid $10 per offense. There were a few exceptions. Citizens could buy and resell "fish at the public wharves or . . . hay, fodder, straw, oysters, beef in barrels or larger casks, fish and pork in ditto, dry fish, live stock, such as cattle, sheep and hogs, wheat, Indian corn, dried peas and beans, oats, rye, bran and fruit, at any time or place."

Officials set strict guidelines regarding butter sales at the new market. Any butter brought there for sale, in lumps or prints of less than 2 pounds, had to be in lumps of 1 or ½ pound each. Anyone caught trying to sell butter (weighing less than 2 pounds) in other amounts had to forfeit it "to the use of the corporation."

Two key policy changes occurred in 1832, when after-hours loitering became a problem at the market. Alderman Jeremiah Hughes responded to the problem. He made a motion at the June 1 Corporation meeting, ordering the Market Master and city constables "to prevent the frequent assembling of negroes and others in the public Market House in other than Market hours."

Hughes addressed another problem for the market in 1832: people sleeping on its benches. In response, he called for such people to be "arrested and taken before the proper authority to receive a suitable punishment to be had."[25]

The city's *Revised By-Laws* defined "suitable punishment" in 1839. It stated that, "Anyone laying or sleeping upon the benches or in any way demeaning themselves indecently in said market at any time shall, if free, pay $2 for every offense. And, any slave so offending shall be punished for each offence by any number not exceeding twenty stripes, in the discretion of the Mayor, Recorder, or Alderman, before whom the case may be tried."[26]

The market changed to meet the needs of new merchants in 1838. That year, two of its benches—the first two on its northeast side—were "fitted out" to accommodate merchants who sold meal. The market also received several scales for this purpose.[27]

The new market's layout was highly defined. Its east side was reserved for "sellers of fish." It had "eave benches," which rented for at least $5 per year, and other "benches, stands, and divisions," which rented for at least $3 per year.

The center of the market, within its pillars, was used for butchers' stands and stalls, which rented for at least $12 per year. City law held that no one was to "keep or occupy any bench, shamble, or other apparatus, whereon to expose butchers' meat for sale, except under the roof of the market-house, and within the brick pillars thereof." Anyone who did paid $3 per offense.[28] There was one exception: country merchants "not in the usual practice of selling butchers' meat," were exempt from the rule.

Country merchants occupied most of the market's west side. Its eave stands were "declared and directed to be appropriated exclusively to the use of persons from the country having articles for sale." They were rented on a first come, first serve basis, or, as the *Revised By-Laws* noted, "the person first occupying the same having the right to the space necessary for his or her use." If a dispute arose over the stands, the Market Master was to "settle" it, by "assigning to persons thus disputing, their respective stands, and his decision [was to] be obeyed and enforced."[29]

IV

City council ordered the construction of a new market house (the city's seventh) in 1857. It was to be built at a different spot on the same land deeded to the city in 1784: just northeast of the old market, this time at its current location.

Again, as in 1784, officials moved swiftly. On April 1, 1857 the council authorized the mayor to contract with John Davis to build a new "Markett House." Next, it appointed a committee comprised of William Bryan, Daniel Hyde, and Benjamin Linthicum to oversee the work. They received $3,000 for the project, which was borrowed from Farmers National Bank of Annapolis. Costs, however, escalated to $4,461 by the time the final payment was made on April 10, 1858.[30]

The new market was finished in less than a year, as these proceedings from the council's April 2, 1858 meeting reveal:

Report of the Committee of the Market House

Undersigned a committee appointed by your Honorable boddy to manage and Superintend the building of the new Market House, beg leave to report that they have diligently carried out the duties imposed upon them . . . the House is now entirely completed and accepted by the Committee and they take pleasure in saying that it has been completed to their entire satisfaction; the balance now due to John M. Davis for all extra work done once all extra materials furnished is one thousand sixty one dollars and fifty cents which amount the committee recommend that he be paid all of which is [his?] respectfully.[31]

Once finished, the new market was vastly different from the former one. Measuring about 60-by-120 feet, it was nearly twice as large. It was also built with cast iron columns: "a rather sophisticated form of construction in 1857," to quote Annapolis architect James Wood Burch, who added, "Annapolis can be proud of having such a market house dating from that early period of cast iron construction."[32]

The columns stood in two parallel rows around the building's four open sides. Those along the perimeter were about 8 feet tall, those on the interior row were about 14 feet tall, and they supported a "shingled hipped-roof." Perhaps the market's strong, iron columns help to explain its longevity. For prior to being restored in the early 1970s, it survived the Civil War, two World Wars, and several "parking lot wars" in the mid-20th century.

Save the Library!

The market house is a crucial part of the city's fabric. So is its public library on West Street. This story celebrates the library's past; it is a timely one, since its future is uncertain. When *Annapolis Vignettes* went to press, officials were considering several options for the building—options such as augmenting it with a larger, central library somewhere else (possibly the Annapolis Towne Centre at Parole), or even (as rumor had it) eliminating it completely.

The library's story starts in 1919. That fall, locals who had been discussing founding a Community House in town reached an important conclusion. What Annapolis needed most, they thought, was "public library service."[1] A committee formed to see if others agreed, and its members were Nettie Mace, Agnes Quinn, James Saunders, Naval Academy Professor Horace Fenton, and the Academy's Librarian, Richard Duvall.

The committee also tried to raise awareness and gain support for its cause. Pro-library articles appeared in the newspaper; Professor Fenton addressed civic groups such as the University Club at Carvel Hall; and non-committee members, such as Dr. Silas Persons, appealed to others including his Presbyterian Church

The library used this label to identify books belonging to its collection. It shows Reynolds Tavern, which was the library's home from 1936 to 1965. From the author's collection.

parishioners on February 22, 1920. Citing scripture that advised citizens to "give attention to reading," he said, "If we are to give attention to reading as a community, we must have a public library."

Dr. Persons had a crisp vision for the library. He imagined it as a "museum filled with art treasures, antique articles that should be preserved, records of historic value and a thousand things which would be of public interest." These items, along with books would provide "the gold and frankincense and myrrh of wisdom . . . " he said.[2]

Public support grew for the library, and soon, Professor Fenton and Dr. Persons asked city council to establish one. Their petition worked and had two results. First, the council agreed to provide a free home for the library: a small, second-story room in the Municipal Building, also called City Hall, on Duke of Gloucester Street. It also appointed a Library Commission to oversee the library's development and operations once it opened.

Yet there was much to do before then. Most importantly, the library needed books. The committee asked locals to donate books from their own collections, and they responded with zeal. Nearly 2,000 books were collected in less than a year, thanks in part to Professor Fenton and Bishop G. M. Williams, who offered their automobiles to transport them.

Citizens also donated tables, chairs, bookcases, and shelves. George Sterling, an Eastport carpenter, supervised a group of men who built additional shelves in the library, while another group sorted, catalogued, and organized the books.

The library was finished in midwinter 1921. It opened Saturday, January 8 to an eager crowd, many of who probably saw this announcement in that day's *Evening Capital:* "Everybody is wanted and welcome at the new public library which is to be thrown open this afternoon from 3 to 5 o'clock in the upper room of the Municipal Building . . . "

Initially, the library was open three days per week: Tuesday, Thursday, and Saturday from 2:30 to 5:30 P.M. It had adult and children's books, which patrons could borrow for free for two weeks. To do so, however, required a registration card, which cost 10 cents. Patrons could also buy books at the library. It

Patrons outside of the library at Reynolds Tavern, c. 1950s. Courtesy of the Anne Arundel County Public Library.

had a "pay shelf," which contained new publications such as *All Men are Enemies*. And, as of December 1923, it had an "old book store." It was located on a stand behind the librarian's desk and contained used books on a variety of subjects.

The library operated without a paid librarian at first, since no money was appropriated for a "custodian of books." Instead, volunteers took turns manning the room including Beatrice Gunn, Marjorie Bartlett, and Eliza Suydam, among others.

Miss Suydam eventually became the library's first paid librarian. She started on October 11, 1921, earned $25 per month, and enjoyed a short commute to work since she lived at 144 Charles Street at the time.

Barrett McKown described Miss Suydam in his book, *The Annapolis and Anne Arundel County Public Library: a History*. He quoted old library minutes, which praised her efficiency, hard work, and personal zeal. Yet he also labeled her as "a cantankerous old maid who was easily annoyed," and who got patrons' attention "by pounding her cane on the floor." When things got too noisy she even told young people to "Take your books and get out of here!"[3]

Miss Suydam hired Marian Sherman as an assistant shortly after she began. Miss Sherman earned 50 cents per week from 1921–24 and, during that period, the library flourished. Its collection grew; its circulation increased; it was mailing books to over thirty locations outside of the city; over 500 patrons from thirty-seven out-of-town locations were coming to use its services; others, including a librarian and high school volunteers, started helping Miss Suydam, and the library extended its hours.

The library continued to serve Annapolis for another decade at its first home. Then, in early January 1934, city council named a committee to help it search for new quarters. This was crucial because the Municipal Building's Assembly Room was going to be moved upstairs.

The committee's members were Mayor Walter Quenstedt, and Aldermen Arthur Elliott, Elmer Jackson, Jr., and Charles Springs. They worked quickly and by mid-January they had secured a new, temporary site for the library: the old Annapolis High School building on Green Street.

The library closed for one week to move and reopened on January 22, 1934. That day, locals checked out 223 books—the largest daily circulation in its thirteen-year history. Shortly thereafter, the Library Association began to look for a larger, permanent home for the library. It looked across town and saw the perfect opportunity: the historic Reynolds Tavern building on Church Circle was for sale.

Farmers National Bank owned the building at the time. And while the bank's former president, L. Dorsey Gassaway, had lived there for many years, it was vacant. Although the building was for sale, its future as a library seemed doubtful for three reasons. First, it cost $22,000. Second, an oil company was prepared to pay that price in order to develop it into a filling station. And finally, not all of the Library Association's Board members thought the purchase was a good idea.

Those who did planned to use the tavern's first floor as a library and to rent its second floor as county government office space. Opponents, on the other hand, said they lacked the funds to buy, repair, and maintain the building. In addition to the asking price, it would cost about $1,500 to improve its interior, and $1,000 to maintain it annually.

Despite this disaccord, the board agreed unanimously on one point. If the tavern became a library, and if its second floor became county government office space, the Anne Arundel County State's Attorney's Office should not be located there. As the board declared, "Too many undesirables call upon a State's Attorney to allow his office to be situated in a library where young children would come in contact with persons in difficulty with the law."[4]

Finally, after much debate, the board approved the purchase in early January 1936 by a vote of twelve to five. By then, the bank had reduced its asking price—thanks to a committee who had negotiated with its officials, and locals who had protested the oil company's plans. The Association bought the tavern for approximately $20,000, with funds borrowed from the Female Orphan Society at a 3 percent interest rate; it obtained a 5-year lease on the remaining 40 feet of the lot for $2,000; and planned to use city and county funds to maintain the site.

The sale was finalized in late January 1936, and the library opened in February. Mrs. Clara Palmer earned $50 per month as its librarian, Miss Suydam earned $25 per month as her assistant, and together, they oversaw the library and its 5,000 books.

Unfortunately, not everyone could access its collection. The branch was segregated, and the city's black population couldn't use its resources until a Clay Street branch opened in September 1940. This branch was located in the College Creek Terrace Community Hall. It was furnished with new bookshelves, tables, chairs and reading lamps, and was open to people from across the city. Three black women, trained by the main branch's librarian and paid by the National Youth Administration, were in charge of the library, which was an instant success. Sixty patrons joined immediately, and each paid 10 cents for a card that enabled him or her to borrow books.

The city's black population was not the only group that lacked access to the main library. Many Anne Arundel County residents had difficulty reaching it—especially those without transportation, or gasoline when it was rationed during World War II.

Consider the residents of Green Haven, located north of Annapolis. In May 1943, the *Evening Sun* reported that "250 bored residents of the Green Haven section, many of them defense workers," had "no gasoline to go anyplace." This prompted them to tell Emil Krueger, a member of the Anne

Miss Esther King, above, was among the Bookmobile's drivers. When describing her role the Baltimore American *said, "The work of a librarian, once considered a most ladylike occupation, now entails the talents of a truck driver, but Miss Esther King likes it."[11] Courtesy of the Anne Arundel County Public Library.*

Patrons inside and outside of the Bookmobile. Courtesy of the Anne Arundel County Public Library. In 1947, the Anne Arundel County Public Library system had roughly 8,900 registered borrowers, and a total circulation of 78,000 books. Both figures had nearly doubled by 1948. The Baltimore Sun *attributed "this astonishing increase in a single year largely . . . to the operation of a bookmobile, which accounts for 50 percent of the circulation."[12]*

Arundel County Board of Education, that they wanted a library in their community. In response, he consulted with Miss Esther King, who the main branch's librarian at the time. She worked with Mrs. B. F. Treat, of the county Civilian War Services, to collect and take 100 books to Green Haven.[5]

The new Green Haven library was located in Mrs. Joseph Truffer's home. She converted her dining room into a reading room, and posted its hours on a flagpole in her front yard, as well as at the local grocery store. She also volunteered as its librarian. By August 10, her library had become immensely popular. It had almost as many registered patrons as it had books: 88—including 31 children. Mrs. Truffer's daughter, Rita, even started a Saturday afternoon children's story hour.[6]

Four years after the Green Haven branch opened, the Annapolis library received a modern marvel: its first Bookmobile. County funds, as well as funds raised by the Pan Hellenic Society of Annapolis, the Galesville Improvement Association, other groups, and individuals made the $2,600 vehicle possible.[7]

The Bookmobile was painted a light grayish-blue, carried roughly 1,000 books, and delivered them throughout Anne Arundel County. During its first year in operation, it stopped regularly at eight schools, fifty-five neighborhoods, a church, the Crownsville State Hospital, and the homes of two individual patrons.[8] The Bookmobile service did not charge patrons for library cards or overdue books.

The vehicle made three or four trips per week, reaching each of its stops about once every two weeks. It began its journey "jaunty, neat and shining" at 9 A.M. in front of the city's library, where "a cross section of books—carefully selected" were placed on its shelves, and returned at 6 P.M. "to unload, looking as though it . . . had a hard day."[9]

When describing its operation one newsman wrote, "Once the 'Bookmobile' has stopped and the people begin to climb on, the truck ceases to be a truck and immediately becomes a library. The unmistakable hushed air of all libraries prevails although there is more comfortable chit-chat here than the forbidding atmosphere of a city library."[10]

Shortly after the library received its Bookmobile, it began to outgrow its home at Reynolds Tavern. While the library had a book stock of 5,000 when it opened in 1936, this figure had tripled by 1961. Shelf space was scarce, lighting was dim, parking was limited, and on some days, its staff carried up to 2,000 books up and down four flights of stairs.[13]

These and other conditions forced the library to move again. In November 1965, the new Annapolis Area Library opened on West Street, and Reynolds Tavern became the county library system's central headquarters. Of course, a lot happened to make this transition possible—but that's another story. Its details can be found in *The Annapolis and Anne Arundel County Public Library: A History,* and the library's vertical file on the topic. Both are waiting for you there.

Save the Post Office!

Like the library, the future of the city's historic post office was also unclear when *Annapolis Vignettes* went to press. In 2005, officials considered razing and replacing part of it with a mixed-use development. This chapter features this cherished landmark's story, which starts in the 1870s.

Annapolis needed a new post office in the late 19th century. Locals had lobbied Congress for one since 1872, when it occupied a small part of Temperance Hall (now Johnson's on the Avenue) on Maryland Avenue. The office moved down the street to Masonic Hall sometime before 1878. Yet this site was also inadequate. The *Evening Capital* even complained that Annapolis had "to uphold the dignity of the capital of the State with a country store for a post office."[1]

Congress finally granted the city's request in 1899, thanks in large part to Sydney Mudd, a U.S. Congressman from Maryland's Fifth Congressional District. As the paper noted, "It [the post office] is a monument to the efforts of Congressman Sydney E. Mudd, who had the bill passed enabling Annapolis to have in her midst the handsomest Federal building south of the city of Philadelphia."[2]

Once the bill passed, officials searched for a site for the office. They found one in spring of 1899, when two Annapolitans offered their land for that purpose: Amelia Owen Iglehart and Joseph Harris Forbes.

Mrs. Iglehart was born in 1832 to James and Mary Kent. She married Howard Iglehart in 1866, and they had three children: James, Waddell, and Eugene. Mr. Forbes was a native of St. Mary's County. He graduated from Princeton, enlisted in the Confederate Army when the Civil War began, and rose from private to captain during the conflict. After the war he settled in Baltimore, where he worked at N. H. Hill & Co., and the Bank of Commerce. He came to Annapolis in about 1876 with his new bride, Fannie Lightfoot Fowle Tayloe, whose father was the Chesapeake and Ohio Canal's first president. He worked in the State's Executive Department, became president of the Annapolis Savings Institution in 1887, and later, served as chief bookkeeper for Farmers National Bank. In 1899, he and Mrs. Iglehart wrote this letter, which hit the *Evening Capital*'s front page on April 10:

To the Citizens of Annapolis:

We respectfully offer for your consideration and approval as a site for the new Post Office and Custom House, the properties Nos. 5 and 7 Church Circle Cor. of Northwest Street, now occupied respectively by Mr. J. Harris Forbes and Mrs. A. Owen Iglehart, and beg leave to suggest the following reasons for its location at this point:[3]

    1. Because the property is a corner lot

2. Because the territory is ample . . .
3. Because the location is high—45 feet above water level
4. Because the location of the building here will probably occasion the laying of good streets around it—a thing much needed in this section of the city
5. Because eight streets radiate from this Circle . . .
6. Because its location here will beautify the city—[the] lot being large enough to locate building in center with lawn all around it, thus continuing the plan of locating buildings in center of grass plots, which has been adopted in this section . . .
7. Because it can be purchased for an amount within the appropriation
8. Because as [the] city grows, which it must with several million dollars to be spent at the Naval Academy and the extension of the Academy line to include King George Street, it must of necessity grow towards Murray Hill, Germantown, and West Annapolis—other sections of city being surrounded by water

For these and other reasons too numerous to mention, we respectfully offer this site for the consideration of the public, believing that the disinterested and unbiased citizens will agree with us that from a practical and aesthetic point of view no site in the city will equal or compare with it.

The U.S. Post office at Annapolis, Maryland, early 1900s. Postcard postmarked October 9, 1908. From the author's collection.

Locals agreed that the site was ideal. So did the federal government. It bought Mrs. Iglehart's land for $15,000 in February 1900, and Mr. Forbes's for $5000 that March.

The lots were then cleared to make room for the new office designed by James Knox Taylor. Trained in architecture at the Massachusetts Institute of Technology, Taylor was appointed as Supervising Architect of the U.S. Treasury Department in 1897. During his twelve-year tenure, he oversaw the design and construction of post offices in New Jersey; Connecticut; Annapolis and Carrollton, Maryland, as well as other government buildings.

The Charles McCall Company of Philadelphia built Taylor's design. By 1899, the company had already built a post office in Camden, New Jersey, the Reading Terminal and Mint in Philadelphia, and the Continental Trust Company building in Baltimore. It was also about to break ground on the Naval Academy's new Marine barracks.

The McCall Co. won the contract on October 31, 1900, and its engineer, Marshall Pugh, arrived two weeks later. He surveyed the site, and construction began under Edgar Klemroth's supervision. Mr. Klemroth and what the newspaper called his "able corps of artisans" faced several challenges. Miserable weather caused delays. So did the project's budget. Mr. Taylor had to stop to alter his design when costs began to exceed his initial $64,000 contract agreement. For instance, he substituted cheaper limestone for many details that were supposed to be granite or marble.

Despite these setbacks, Mr. Klemroth's crew completed the office in less than a year. They finished in fall of 1901, and on November 1 the *Evening Capital* announced that Annapolis was "at last to have a post office building more in keeping with its dignity as the capital of an important and flourishing State." The building was turned over to federal authorities in December and opened on January 1, 1902.

It was a sight to behold. The *Evening Capital* declared that, "The building is beautiful in design and construction, and an ornament to the city . . . [It] is a thing of beauty and no doubt will be a joy forever." The paper praised the building. On the outside, it lauded its "very fine" approaches, staircases, two "handsomely wrought cast iron standard lights, with large white globes," airtight Van Kennel revolving front door, and landscaping. The site had new shrubs, a row of Lombardy poplars, other trees, and a rear seeded lot.

The building's interior was equally impressive according to the paper. It complemented its "flying stairway," vaulted ceiling with "attractive cornice ornamentations," terazzo and red Champlain marble floor, three large fireproof vaults, 477 post office boxes (there are now 750), and even its toilets, which had "the latest sanitary plumbing."

The paper also described the building's basement. It contained the mail "carriers' swing room" where they stayed while off duty, as well their lavatories, and a coal, furnace, and bicycle room.[4]

Washington Tuck was the city's postmaster when the new office opened. He became postmaster in 1890, was replaced by Abram Claude in 1895, and returned to serve from 1899 to 1909. The *Evening Capital* wished him "keen enjoyment in the new post office; more clerks and less worry about the delivery of mail from the depot," upon the building's completion.

Dennis Mullan (USNA 1863) mailed the first letter there on opening day. Written and sent to the *Evening Capital* it read,

> A very happy, prosperous New Year to you . . . May heaven's choice blessings be given to you, yours and the tried *Evening Capital*. May she always abide with us, to give us the daily news. Ever to enlighten us, and always be the banner paper in our now growing Capital city. This greeting to you on this New Year's Day, 1902, will be the first epistle to be mailed in the new postoffice in this city, and I believe I am the first citizen of this old, colonial, historic town to purchase stamps, etc., in this our new edifice. With many happy returns of today and kind regards, I am
>
> Your sincere friend,
Dennis W. Mullan.[5]

Twenty-four years after Mr. Mullan mailed his letter, the post office expanded. It received a one-story brick service wing and loading dock in 1926. A larger service wing visible from Northwest Street replaced both in 1939. It is this wing that officials considered razing and replacing with housing and retail space in 2005.

Gil Crandall Recalls the Opening of the "New" Severn River Drawbridge

Gilbert (Gil) Crandall was raised near the post office in downtown Annapolis. One of his favorite childhood memories there involves the old Severn River drawbridge, which was replaced in 1994. This story includes his recollections of the bygone bridge's opening day.

Gil Crandall will never forget June 14, 1924. It was hot. He was eight. Yet he and his mother Lillian walked several miles from his father's pharmacy at 50 State Circle to the Naval Academy Golf Course. There, near today's Perry Circle apartments, they joined 10,000 others for a special event: the grand opening of the "new" Severn River drawbridge.

Gilbert A. Crandall, 1922. Courtesy of Gilbert A. Crandall. Photograph by E. H. Pickering.

Many had made the impressive bridge possible. State Roads Commission engineers designed it under Chairman John Mackall's direction. Joseph Strauss—who built the Golden Gate Bridge—designed its "articulated counterweight," which enabled its moveable span. The state even hired John Greiner as a "special consulting engineer" to ensure the bridge's "perfection."[1]

Like Strauss, Greiner was among the nation's foremost bridge engineers at the time. He began his career in 1880 with Edgemoor Bridgeworks in Delaware, joined Keystone Bridge Works three years later, started with the Baltimore & Ohio Railroad Company in 1885, and remained there until he established his own practice in 1908 in Baltimore. When describing him, his contemporaries in the American Society of Civil Engineers said, "He has been a pioneer and contributor to the practices, methods and standards of bridge building. His life work has run parallel with the advancement of modern bridge building and he has been such a part of that record that it is difficult to emphasize what are his important milestones in bridge design."[2]

Naval Academy officials advised the bridge's designers. They became involved with the project as early as 1912 and were very concerned about its appearance. In October 1921, when the bridge was about to become a reality, Superintendent Admiral Henry B. Wilson wrote the following to Governor Albert T. Ritchie:

"The general description from newspaper accounts shows that the structure will be of a permanent character. The Naval Academy is naturally very much interested in this construction . . . , not only for ease of access to visitors but also the structure is on one of the main fronts of the Naval Academy, and to a certain extent, will be more or less associated with the general impression gained of this institution. For that reason I am particularly interested in hoping that the structure will not only be of a substantial character, but pleasing in appearance . . ."[3]

One month later, the Admiral stressed to Mr. Mackall that the Navy wouldn't permit the bridge's approach to occupy the Academy's property unless it was "pleasing in appearance."[4]

Once a final design was agreed upon, T. L. Eyre, a Philadelphia contractor, built the 1,827-foot long, $800,000 bridge. Unfortunately, he got off to a slow start. His pile driver arrived late due to ice jams along the Bay and Chesapeake and Delaware Canal. Therefore, his team couldn't begin work until March 4, 1922. Even then, stormy weather forced him to drive test piles close to shore, rather than risk operating the drivers midstream.

Mr. Eyre received some good fortune in spring of 1922. Annapolis adopted daylight savings for the first time on April 30, which enabled his team to work longer hours. City council passed the daylight-savings ordinance, "as a result of Baltimore's adopting the change in time. It was necessary to do the same here as otherwise it would have taken two hours to get to Baltimore," according to the *Evening Capital.*[5]

The city celebrated when Mr. Eyre finally finished the bridge. It held a grand opening ceremony on Saturday, June 14, which drew a crowd of 10,000 from across the state.

A pageant called "The Spirit of Transportation," launched the event at 2 P.M. Organized by the Annapolis Rotary Club, it starred locals and traced the evolution of transportation along the Severn River. Its script noted that "Spectators will witness the progress of 'transportation.' They will see the changes, in chronological order, from the days of the Indian, when he was lone sovereign of the Severn, up to the present moment, when progressive Marylanders will cross that picturesque river over a modern concrete bridge in the most approved of up to date conveyances."

The pageant occurred on the new bridge, nearby roads, and the Severn River. It had nineteen historic episodes, each of which had two parts: an explanation and an act. Take episode 1 for instance. First, an actor read this explanation aloud: "Maryland's first highways were her noble waters. The broad Chesapeake, the proud Potomac, the beauteous Severn—Along their banks the followers of Calvert settled, and piled their trade and intercourse in pungy and canoe."

Next, locals performed the episode's act. In this case, an actor called the "Spirit of Transportation" instructed spectators to "look toward the river where you will see Indians in canoes followed by early colonists in pungies and canoes."

Wagon traveling over the old Severn River Bridge, after 1904. From the author's collection.

125

Episodes 2 through 8 featured these transportation-related scenes: explorers blazing trails through the wilderness; colonists building backwoods settlements and trading posts; pioneers on horses and afoot; pack horses bearing pelts, calico, and other goods; widening roads, Conestoga wagons, and high-wheeled carts; public stage coaches, two-wheeled gigs, and bicycles; ferries and the Severn's first "homely bridge of wood," which "robbed the ferryman of his toll."

Then, in episodes 9 through 17, actors performed scenes with farm wagons, horseless carriages, and automobiles along real and makeshift paths, dirt roads, and paved highways. The pageant's climax, episode 18, bid farewell to the old bridge with this explanation, "Ah homely bridge you served your builders well . . . Know then, old bridge . . . another bridge is here. A bridge of graceful lines and strength to meet the greater burdens of the present hour."

With that word, the Spirit pointed to the new bridge and said, "Let transportation's wheel revolve. The old bridge dies—the new is born today." He then cut a ribbon at the end of the bridge, and Governor Ritchie and his mother rode in the first vehicle to cross it. A string of decorated automobile floats followed, representing different aspects of Maryland history. Each county created a float for the parade, and the Peggy Stewart Chapter of the Daughters of the American Revolution designed Anne Arundel County's entry.[6]

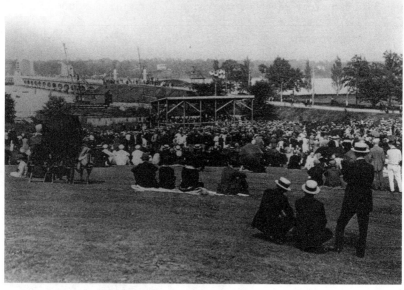

Courtesy of the Maryland State Archives SPECIAL COLLECTIONS (Robert G. Merrick Archives of Maryland Historical Photographs) Hughes Co. The Severn River Bridge, [June 14], 1924 *MSA SC 1477-5596. Gil Crandall and his mother were among those in the crowd that day.*

While the floats and Governor Ritchie's car crossed the Severn, another vehicle was less fortunate. Louis Phipps—who later became mayor of Annapolis, a state senator and Clerk of the Court for Anne Arundel County—owned and sold automobiles at Annapolis Buick on Cathedral Street at the time. According to Mr. Crandall, "He supplied an old car for the occasion, which was driven off the end of the old wooden bridge, where it had been cut off, and everyone cheered." That was over eighty years ago. And, while Mr. Crandall remembers the day well, he can't recall if Mr. Phipps's car was ever removed.[7]

Captain Roy Smith III, USN (Ret.) was also at the bridge that day. He participated in the opening ceremony as an eleven-year-old Boy Scout. In 1994 he recalled that, "I was holding the damn ribbon across the bridge while the governor's speech was made . . . When all the hullabaloo was over, he cut the ribbon and the bridge was open . . . It was a lovely day."

Capt. Smith remembered one part of the ceremony differently than Mr. Crandall. He said that the Naval Academy tried to run a decrepit truck off of the bridge. "It was an old truck. They didn't have anything to do with it so they just thought they'd get rid of it," he said. Unfortunately, the truck never made it off of the bridge; it got caught because it was moving too slowly. According to Capt. Smith, "It hung at a 45 degree angle . . . Admiral Wilson seemed a little shocked at what was happening to the truck and the failure of the expedition."[8]

Oscar and Jean Grimes Lament the Loss of Local Farmland

Unlike Gil Crandall, Oscar Grimes grew up outside of Annapolis, in nearby rural Davidsonville, on Hilldale Farm. Recently, Mr. Grimes reflected on Hilldale's history, and on how it and the local agricultural landscape have changed.

Oscar Grimes was born in Sudley, Maryland, in 1924. He moved two years later, when his father, Oscar Grimes, Sr., bought the land now called Hilldale Farm. Oscar and his four older siblings worked on the 107-acre property as children. Some of his chores included tending sheep, filling the wood box with kindling, and stocking the icehouse in the winter.

"We didn't have a pond, but we cut ice from one nearby. We put it in a two-horse wagon, and hauled it back to our place. The ice usually kept 'til about July," he said.

The Grimes raised crops and livestock. However, they didn't run a dairy like many other local farmers. As Mr. Grimes recalled, "Most nearby farmers—in the 1920s, '30s, and '40s— were dairy farmers with twenty-five or

Southern Anne Arundel County farmland near Muddy Creek Rd., 1989. Courtesy of The Capital. *Photograph by Bob Gilbert.*

thirty milk cows. They put the milk in 5- or 10-gallon cans, and put them roadside for the dairy companies to pick up. We only kept five or six milk cows to raise our calves."

Farm life wasn't easy. The Grimes's home lacked electricity until 1938, and receiving health care was difficult. "We didn't have a doctor for many years. In fact, the first doctor I remember was Dr. Hayes, who was a friend of Buffalo Bill out west," Mr. Grimes said.

Transportation was also limited. Just one school bus served the area. "It picked up the old and young kids. It took the young kids to the three-room schoolhouse on [Route] 214, where punishment was to walk around the school's circular driveway. Then, it took the older kids to Annapolis High," according to Mr. Grimes.

Mr. Grimes worked at Hilldale while attending Annapolis High School. He graduated in 1942; yet, in contrast to many of his peers, he didn't serve in World War II after graduation. His wife Jean explained why: "Labor was scarce at the time. They didn't take the farm boys away because they needed to stay and work on the farms."

Hilldale changed in two ways after the war. Two displaced Ukrainian families lived and worked there after

Oscar F. Grimes, Sr., 1979. Courtesy of The Capital. *Photograph by Keith E. Harvey.*

the conflict. One family stayed for a year before moving to Baltimore, and the other stayed for two-and-a-half years. The farm also received more modern equipment, including its first tractor in 1948, as well as better seed, herbicides, pesticides, and chemicals. "These were positive changes but they also meant higher prices and more and more regulations," Mr. Grimes said.

Mr. Grimes met Jean Wilkerson, a self-described "non-farm girl," shortly after the war, and they married in 1950. As she recalled, "We didn't expect to start at the top like young people do today . . . We lived with his parents on the farm. We worked there from five in the morning—or as soon as we had light—'til seven or eight at night. Oscar milked the cows before breakfast, while his mother cooked potato rolls over a wood stove. The rolls were so good—I gained 15 pounds the first year we were married!"

Jean married Oscar when the Grimes still came to Annapolis every Friday to sell Hilldale's goods. They brought eggs and 5 gallons of cream to Wiegard's confectionery on State Circle, as well as eggs, cream, vegetables, and 100 pounds of potatoes to other stores. "We also had Jewish customers in town, including several women, and the Cohens on Murray Avenue" Mrs. Grimes said. "We tied the chickens' legs and put them in a basket, but the Rabbi had to kill them so that the meat was kosher."

The Grimes didn't sell their goods at the city's market house. However, they recall its atmosphere with clarity. Mr. Grimes recalled that it "was a very busy, vibrant place, with people bustling and carrying food in and out to be sold . . . Mr. Bowen brought sausage and scrapple to the market house every week."

Annapolis merchants also went to Hilldale to buy goods. For instance Mr. Basil, of Basil's Meats, bought live calves and lambs there. "He paid $5 for a calf and $3 for a lamb. He'd put them in the backseat of his car and took them back to town. And cars weren't that big then!" Mr. Grimes said.

The Grimes stopped coming to Annapolis on Fridays in the late 1950s. They agree that the city and its surroundings have changed since then. For one, "neighbors don't know their neighbors like they used to. Years ago, when anyone moved here we'd take a dish to greet them . . . Now we couldn't keep up even if we tried!" Mrs. Grimes lamented.

Local roads and traffic patterns have also changed. "The county road was still gravel when we were married," she said. "But today, most of the hardships we face involve traffic. It's hard moving farm equipment from one farm to another. People blow their horns and ask you to get out of the way. They like to drive and look at the pretty land, but not what makes it possible."

Blaring horns have replaced some of the pleasant sounds that once graced Hilldale. As Mrs. Grimes recalled, "We used to hear whippoorwills and bobwhites on the farm—I haven't heard them in ten years."

Yet Hilldale has done what many local farms have failed to do: it's survived. Today, the Grimes grow corn to grind feed for their forty beef cattle—especially the steers that they "try to fatten for market." They also raise hay. "New people have pleasure horses so there's a good market for hay," Mrs. Grimes said.

Oscar Grimes still grows tobacco at Hilldale. He's shown here tending his crop with his son, Bill Grimes, in 1982. Courtesy of The Capital. *Photograph by Keith E. Harvey.*

Oscar and Jean Grimes at home at Hilldale. Photograph by John R. Bieberich, 2005.

Finally, Hilldale still makes delicious hams. "We cure about twelve hams a year, although this is much less than we used to," Mrs. Grimes said. She then explained the process: "First we buy fresh hams from the Amish Market, then rub them with sugar, salt, pepper, and saltpeter to bring out the meat's redness. Then, we lay them on plastic on a shelf for six weeks, then clean them off, and hang them in a smoke house for a few days. They lose 4 or 5 pounds from start to finish—dropping from 20 to about 16."[1]

Annapolis High School Becomes Maryland Hall for the Creative Arts

Oscar Grimes graduated from Annapolis High School in 1942. This is the story of how the school became Maryland Hall for the Creative Arts nearly forty years later.

By the time I was eleven, I had moved seven times, including across the Atlantic Ocean and back. This lifestyle made it difficult for me—a shy, late blooming, non-athlete to make friends. Yet I loved art, which made spending time alone easier—and fun too.

My family finally settled in Annapolis in 1991. Much had changed since my parents, Roger and Michele, left their hometown in the 1970s—including that their alma mater, Annapolis High School, had moved. However they were delighted by what had replaced it: Maryland Hall for the Creative Arts, commonly called Maryland Hall. They enrolled me in a class there, where I made pottery, and friends who later nurtured my gifts as a writer, as well as an artist.

This story is just one example of how Maryland Hall has enriched Annapolis, and the lives of its residents, for over twenty-five years. And, while many know about the Hall, few probably know the surprising details of its history—including that it was nearly built on College Creek, near the current Bloomsbury Square Annapolis Housing Authority complex.

Bringing a cultural arts center to town became a priority in the early 1960s, when "everybody in the arts community wanted a home of their own," according to Annapolis Mayor Ellen O. Moyer.[1] At first, the Annapolis Fine Arts Foundation, the Anne Arundel Arts Association, and other groups and individuals explored the idea. Later, the Committee to Bring a Cultural/Educational Centre to Annapolis formed to focus these efforts.

Moyer chaired this committee that researched options for the center's funding, use, and architecture. It also explored potential sites for it, including Green Street. Committee members thought that the Anne Arundel County Board of Education's Green Street property, along with the adjoining city-owned land, would be an ideal spot. They assumed that the board would vacate the property in

Maryland Hall for the Creative Arts, 2003. Illustration by the author.

the near future. And, in 1972, they produced a brochure to gain support for this concept.

Local government officials embraced the idea. In November 1972, city council, and then-Mayor Roger Moyer voted to support a feasibility study of the Green Street property.[2] Next, the Anne Arundel County Council passed a similar resolution calling for a "comprehensive study" of the same. County councilman Warren Duckett, Jr., a member of the committee, introduced this resolution.[3]

Clearly, Green Street never became the center's home. Nor did a second site that was considered, near today's Bloomsbury Square.

In 1976, Maryland Governor Marvin Mandel appointed a com-

Linnell Bowen, Director of Maryland Hall (1996–), November 1999. Courtesy of M. E. Warren and The Capital. *Copyright © 1999 by M. E. Warren.*

mission to study the feasibility of an "All-Purpose Performing Arts Facility" in Annapolis. Chaired by U.S. Senator Roy Staten, its members included Martha Wright, Ellen Moyer, Warren Duckett, Jr., Joseph Sachs, Elizabeth Whaley, and others.[4]

Staten formed an architectural subcommittee, comprised of representatives from mostly performing arts groups. This concerned visual artists who "were not organized" at the time to quote Melissa Moss, one of Maryland Hall's founders. When this fact was brought to Staten's attention, he engaged a visual arts representative: watercolorist Joanne Scott from the Maryland Federation of Arts.[5]

Under Staten's leadership, the commission explored building a cultural center on College Creek. This plan hinged on a $1.75 million state matching grant to St. John's College for the college to renovate three of its campus buildings. In exchange for the grant, St. John's would give the state 3.5 acres of land to the right of Bladen Street exiting Annapolis along College Creek. The center would then be built on that site, pending approval by the legislature and governor.[6]

The initial College Creek concept called for mostly performing arts participation. This prompted visual artists to form the Visual Arts Association of Maryland to protect their interests. Soon, over one thousand members joined the group, who advocated including gallery and classroom space in the center.

They lobbied legislators. They wrote them letters. They visited them in person. When these efforts failed, a "separate-but-equal" facility for visual artists, one to complement the College Creek center, became their goal.[7]

"Then suddenly, 'a knight in shining armor' made this 'separate-but-equal' center possible," according to Ms. Moss.[8] The knight, Anne Arundel County School Superintendent Dr. Edward Anderson, approached Staten with an idea. He knew that Annapolis High School was about to move and suggested converting a part of it called Maryland Hall into an all-purpose arts center. Earlier, Dr. Anderson had challenged Annapolis Symphony Orchestra President Joseph Sachs to explore long-term uses for the building. Mr. Sachs took Dr. Anderson's prompt to Staten's committee, of which he was a member.

Maryland Hall became the perfect fit. In August 1978, the Board of Education, and a consortium of about thirty arts groups chaired by Ms. Scott began negotiations. The consortium drafted a proposal for financing Maryland Hall, which held that the board would maintain the building and retain its title. In return, Maryland Hall would offer free admission to its classes for a select number of gifted and talented students.[9]

Dr. Anderson had faith in the proposed program. In February 1979 he said, "[The Maryland Hall proposal] has some merit. I honestly believe that with the proper management, it could be a going thing."[10]

He was right. Maryland Hall opened several months later—with a few complications. Ms. Moss recalled one of the building's early electric glitches: When she turned on the kiln, the elevator would stop and vice versa.

Maryland Hall has undergone many renovations since then, yet one item remains unchanged: the quote written above its stage when Annapolis High opened there in 1932, which states that, "The measure of a man is the depth of his convictions, the breadth of his interest and the height of his ideals."

It is appropriate that this quote remains. For Maryland Hall, as its Executive Director Linnell Bowen said, "gives our community depth by teaching the creative arts . . . breadth by providing a home for the visual and performing arts . . . and height by producing our next generation of great artists."

The Carroll Family—Buried Beneath a Shopping Center?

Robert and Norma Worden live close to Maryland Hall in Murray Hill. This story describes the remarkable discovery they made—thanks to persistence, help from fellow history enthusiasts, and a little luck—in 2003.

Have you been to the Annapolis Harbour Center? If so, you've probably seen the site of the oldest known Catholic burial ground in the area—at least where it was, until developers leveled it in 1961.

The Carroll family established the burial ground in about 1695, when Charles Carroll the Settler moved from St. Mary's City to Annapolis after it became Maryland's capital. Although the Carrolls lived on Duke of Gloucester Street in the city, they buried their dead southwest of town, on a private plot atop Beaver Dam Hill. The hill belonged to the family's 822-acre plantation called the Farm, which was part of the Annapolis Quarter: a larger property that the Carrolls acquired from the late 17th to mid-18th century.[1]

The graveyard's location had never been a secret; several of its headstones were visible in 1961 and many had recorded its presence before then. To cite just three examples, John Brewer mentioned it in a letter to Richard Caton in 1825, the St. Mary's parish history noted the "cemetery on the South River" in 1904, and Elihu Riley discussed "the old graveyard in the Priests' Farm, near the South River Bridge," in his 1905 book, *A History of Anne Arundel County.* The Daughters of the American Revolution also documented the site in 1940, while conducting an inventory of local tombstones.[2]

Yet while the graveyard's location had always been clear, its exact relationship to modern roads, and the Harbour Center was unknown until 2003. That year, local historian Robert Worden, and his land-researcher wife Norma solved the mystery. "We always knew where it [the graveyard] was in general. But we

The Charles Carroll House and Gardens, 107 Duke of Gloucester Street. Charles Carroll (the Settler) purchased the house and property when he moved to Annapolis in 1695. Courtesy of M. E. Warren and Historic Annapolis Foundation. Copyright © [no date on photograph] by M. E. Warren.

Robert and Norma Worden examine the plat that depicts the old graveyard site at the Annapolis Harbour Center. Photograph by David Hartcorn, 2005.

wanted to pinpoint its exact location in relation to today's roadwork and the center," Mr. Worden said.

The Wordens became interested in the site in the late 1970s, while Mr. Worden, archivist of St. Mary's Parish, was researching the church's history. "At first we went driving around thinking we could find it," he said. This was ineffective. Twenty years had passed since the site was leveled, and Maryland Route 2 was widened. "By then, nothing was recognizable . . . everything had changed," he said.

This prompted the Wordens to try other approaches. For two decades, they researched the burial ground using these and other methods: they searched for and read accounts of it in old letters and newspapers; studied surveys, plats, deeds, and tax maps; consulted with other local historians, and more—all to no avail; not one source showed the graveyard's relationship to modern landmarks.

Finally, Norma, a land researcher for Anne Arundel County, made a breakthrough discovery in summer of 2003. She found a plat drafted in 1961, which showed the "old graveyard site 0.16 AC [acres] +" in relation to old Route 2, with its exact geographical coordinates. The Wordens then used this plat and its coordinates to determine the graveyard's spot. It was located directly beneath the exit ramp from Route 2 onto westbound Aris T. Allen Boulevard (Maryland Route 665), about one-tenth of a mile past the shopping center entrance—if it was only .16 acres, as the plat stated.[3]

However, the original burial ground was probably much larger than that. Consider, for instance, a letter Charles Carroll of Carrollton wrote to Archbishop James Whitfield in 1832. In it, Carroll expressed his intent to "convey to the Archbishop of Baltimore the grave yard on the farm at Annapolis, where lie the remains of many of our family;" he also described the site as "two acres more or less." If this were true, then the burial ground would have also occupied the center's southern section, including the land behind Tower Records, as well as most of the land beneath the Aris T. Allen/ Route 2 interchange.[4]

Much is known about the Carroll burial ground in addition to its location. For one, we know it contained at least twenty graves. Over a 150-year period, it became the final resting place for at least one Redemptorist, fifteen Carroll family members, and possibly many of their slaves, according to Mr. Worden. We also know the names of several Catholics who were buried onsite. The Redemptorists interred one of their novices, George Reichert, there in 1855: one year before Dr. Albert Welch deeded them the burial ground, and "as much land as [they] may choose to annex to it, as a graveyard." Michael Curran and his nine-year-old daughter Catherine were also interred there, as was Mary Brewer, "the Amiable Consort of George G. Brewer," who died on December 5, 1824 at age twenty-one.[5]

Charles Carroll of Homewood, who died in 1825, was the last Carroll buried atop Beaver Dam Hill. Born in Annapolis in 1775, he was Charles Carroll of Carrollton's only son. He lived in Baltimore in an estate called Homewood, which his father bought for him at the time of his marriage. The building is now part of Johns Hopkins University campus and was, for many years, the president of the university's house.

The Annapolis Harbour Center, December 1990. Courtesy of The Capital. Photograph by George N. Lundskow.

Carroll of Homewood's gravesite was excavated in 1961, just before Beaver Dam Hill was leveled as part of a plan to expand Route 2 and develop the shopping center. And, while some thought his remains would be intact, all that was found was a casket handle, and several wooden fragments.

Carroll's casket fragments, Mary Brewer's headstone, and the Curran stones were removed on September 12, 1961. Shortly thereafter, the fragments were reinterred in a full-sized grave with the headstone in the Carroll Gardens behind St. Mary's Church. The Curran stones were moved to Woodfield Cemetery, at the intersection of Muddy Creek and Galesville Roads, in Galesville.[6]

And what about Mary Brewer's headstone? No one knows. Well, perhaps no one. Shortly after *The Capital* published this column, I received a call from Julie Fife of Historic Annapolis Foundation. She said that a gentleman had called her several years ago, seeking information about a stone he had found in his backyard. She recalled that he said "something about the words 'George Brewer' being on the stone." Unfortunately, Ms. Fife did not have any information to offer him at the time, nor can she recall his name.[7]

The J. F. Johnson Lumber Company Leaves Town

Harold Slanker, Jr., remembers when the land near the Annapolis Harbour Center was considered "the boondocks." He often went there, to the 1900 block of West Street, to visit his family's business: the J. F. Johnson Lumber Company. This story celebrates the company's history, and its founders, the Johnsons.

The company's story starts with George Johnson, who left London for America in 1635. The eighteen-year-old Kent County native came aboard the ship *Transport*, which brought him to a small island in the Chesapeake Bay. He settled in Somerset County, Maryland, where he became a farmer and, like many colonists, was probably active in timbering or woodworking.[1]

The first specific reference to lumber in the Johnson family's records appeared several generations later in 1791. They've been active in the trade since then. Joshua Johnson built a water-powered sawmill near Salisbury just after the Civil War. Known as Johnson's Mill Pond, it was the first of many that he and his son Wilmer established on the Eastern Shore, and in Virginia.

In 1894, Wilmer moved his family to Kingston where his sons—the current company's founders—J. F. (Joshua Fred) and J. P. (Josiah Purnell) Johnson, were raised. Although Wilmer lived on the Eastern Shore, he bought a tract of chestnut timber across the Bay in Anne Arundel County in 1902. He then built his first sawmill on the Western Shore near Marley and placed it in J. F.'s care. J. F. was only nineteen at the time; even so, the mill flourished under his leadership, as he made the Marley area his home. In 1904, he married Mabel Virginia Jubb, whose family owned a large farm on Mountain Road, and they started a family.

J. F.'s father died in 1905, at which point he bought the family's mill, lumber, and equipment and started producing lumber-related goods under his own name. He expanded his business nine years later; he bought a sizeable tract of chestnut near Glen Burnie, built a sawmill nearby, and moved his family close to it.[2]

J. F.'s new mill thrived, thanks in part to its location. Because it stood near the center of town, between the Baltimore and Annapolis Railroad, and Old Annapolis Road (now Baltimore & Annapolis Boulevard), he could ship and receive goods by rail, mule-drawn wagons, or water from Marley Creek. The mill's success prompted J. F. to expand again—this time, at the heart of Glen Burnie. He envisioned and built a complete retail lumber company that had a millwork manufacturing shop.[3]

Meanwhile, J. F.'s brother, J. P., was enjoying equal success. He graduated in 1910 from Washington College in Chestertown, Maryland, studied law at the University of Maryland, and then worked with the Maryland Casualty Insurance Company. His work took him to Johnson City, Tennessee, where he met and married Lois Peoples in 1916.[4]

Five years later, with each brother prospering, J. F. asked J. P. to become his business partner. J. P. agreed, and they incorporated the company under its present name on August 25, 1921. As Johnson Lumber grew, it needed other executives to oversee its activities; attorney H. Melvin Bull became its first corporate secretary in 1922, and Clarence E. Eason became its treasurer in 1923. Wilmer Burgabe, and Franklin Maddox—J. P.'s college friend and an experienced businessman—also joined that year.

Business was good for the Johnsons and their associates in the 1920s; so good, that they took a risk in 1926. They expanded and bought

Courtesy of the Maryland State Archives SPECIAL COLLECTIONS *(The Annapolis I Remember Collection) T. C. Worthington,* J. F. Johnson Lumber Company, King George Street entrance, *1941 MSA SC 2140-1-212.*

out the much larger Meredith Lumber Company in Annapolis. Located near the Naval Academy at the foot of King George Street, this company received much of its lumber by sea. Formerly the Farinholt-Meredith Lumber Company, it had acquired the Henry B. Myers Lumber Yard in 1905 and was one of several lumberyards in early 20th-century Annapolis. Its competitors included the Gardiner Lumber and Supply Company at 2nd Street, the C. W. Martin Co. at City Dock, and Parlett & Parlett at the foot of Main Street.

Johnson Lumber's management grew again after it acquired the Meredith Company and it continued to prosper. Its annual sales soared from $100,000 in 1921 to over $1 million in 1929 as its yards—one at Glen Burnie, the other at Annapolis—thrived.[5]

Each yard had its own woodworking shop and planing mill, furnished with ripsaws, resaws, and high-speed planers. Each also had a large brick incinerator to dispose of sawdust and wood shavings. Not all of the shavings were burned, however. Some were used as bedding for farmers' livestock, while others helped to keep dust down at Glen Burnie's carnival grounds.

Johnson Lumber also prospered in the 1930s. *Who's Who* recognized it as a leader in the lumber industry in 1939; it attracted clients such as the Naval Academy and St. John's College; and it supplied them, and others, with more than raw lumber. It also offered hardware, millwork, and metal lath; doors, frames, moldings, and roofing; as well as sheet rock, cement, lime, paint, and brushes.

Johnson Lumber Company advertisement from the Evening Capital *(May 2, 1939).*

Harold Slanker, Jr., J. F.'s grandson, remembers visiting the Annapolis yard at the time. Although he lived in Glen Burnie, and later Bodkin Creek, his family came to town to take a ferry to Ocean City, where they vacationed.

"Everybody knew everybody in Annapolis then," Mr. Slanker said. "It was very tight and so was Glen Burnie." Mr. Slanker also remembered his grandfather, who established the company's first yard there. "He was an outdoors kind of guy . . . an avid hunter and loved the racetrack," he said.

Mr. Slanker was age ten when the Naval Academy forced Johnson Lumber to move its Annapolis branch in 1941. The school expanded that year, adding Holland Field, 22 acres to Hospital Point

Courtesy of the Maryland State Archives SPECIAL COLLECTIONS (The Annapolis I Remember Collection) J. F. Johnson Lumber Company, 1901 West Street at Chinquapin Round Road, *1945 MSA SC 2140-1-262.*

with silt from the Severn River, and 7.5 acres behind Thompson Stadium to its grounds. It also annexed Hell Point: an ethnically and economically diverse area between Prince George and King George Streets, which included private homes, packing houses, wharves, and the Johnson Lumber property.[6]

Fortunately, the company was ready to leave when federal authorities notified it that it had thirty days to vacate. "We knew we'd have to move eventually," Mr. Slanker said. "We'd been considering it even before the Navy gave notice . . . The land in the city had grown too valuable to store lumber."

This fact had prompted the company to buy 1901 West Street in November 1941. Historically, the site was a part of Daniel Hart's 188-acre estate. Alexander Randall and Frank Stockett were appointed to sell the property in 1870, after Hart defaulted on a mortgage held by Farmers National Bank. Several families owned it in the years that followed, including the Linthicums, Carlings, and Thomas and Maggie (Margaret) McGuckian, who purchased it in December 1919.

Mr. McGuckian was a general contractor, who was born in Scotland in 1865. He died in 1921; yet his wife, also of Scotland, continued to live onsite until 1933. That year, real estate agent Charles Lee was appointed trustee and became responsible for subdividing and selling the property. He sold 10.77 acres of it to Johnson Lumber for $7,500.

Initially, the company thought moving to West Street would harm its business; after all, the site was several miles from downtown, and was surrounded by woods, farmland, and modest single-family homes, most of which dated to the early 1900s. "We were out in the boondocks and thought no one would come out to see us," Mr. Slanker said.

Yet moving proved to be a boon for the company. "It was the best thing that could have happened," he said. Not only was the new site much larger, it was also perfectly positioned. Its location prompted many builders to choose Johnson Lumber as they developed property west of the city's core.

Federal authorities also chose Johnson Lumber in the early 1940s. It was one of thirty-five companies nationwide, which supplied building materials to the government at the time. During World War II, it delivered goods to the Naval Academy, Fort Meade, Aberdeen Proving Grounds, the barracks around the Smithsonian in Washington, D.C., Ford Tank Works in Chester, Pennsylvania, the Manhattan Project at Oak Ridge, Tennessee, and other military bases, and hospitals. It also sent lumber and supplies to ports, which were shipped to the nation's armed forces overseas.[7]

"Johnson Lumber did well during the war," Mr. Slanker said. "We had a wide distribution range, not just in Anne Arundel County. We traveled far distances to deliver supplies. We were big enough to have the equipment necessary to move the lumber. But we couldn't profiteer and were monitored pretty well." The company also improved its West Street property during the war. By 1945, it had built a two-story paint store, a two-story planing mill, two lumber storage sheds, and a brick incinerator onsite.

Soon thereafter, Mr. Slanker began working for Johnson Lumber while on summer break from Severn High School. He "did whatever was needed" at the Glen Burnie yard, taking orders, working behind the counter, loading trucks, lifting and selling lumber and other goods, and meeting with clients. He continued to work there while attending Yale University and later, after serving two years in the U.S. Army, he joined the company full time in 1956.

The lumber industry has changed considerably since then according to Mr. Slanker. "Lumber's gotten so expensive. It's like it's gold now," he said. "Annapolis has also changed like Glen Burnie's changed . . . When I was a kid Glen Burnie was a very close-knit town. I don't know of any town like that nearby anymore."[8]

Part 3: St. John's College and the U.S. Naval Academy

From Part 3: The U.S. Naval Academy coat of arms and the Great Seal of St. John's College. The Naval Academy acquired its coat of arms in 1898. St. John's College adopted its Great Seal in 1793. Illustrations by the author.

Admiral Dewey Lays the Chapel Cornerstone

A golden terra cotta dome enhanced Annapolis's skyline in the early 1900s. It belonged to the Naval Academy's new Chapel, and this is its story.

Annapolis, Maryland: June 2, 1904

Much to everyone's dismay, the isolated storms that had soaked the city for days still hadn't cleared by morning. Rain continued to fall, flooding the Naval Academy, and spoiling many of its June Week events.

Conditions were equally wet in Washington, D.C. as Admiral George Dewey boarded a train for Annapolis. He was traveling there for an important reason: to lay the cornerstone of his alma mater's new Chapel, the architectural summit of Ernest Flagg's design for a "new Naval Academy."

Exactly fifty years had passed since the Admiral first saw Annapolis in 1854: the year he was appointed to the Academy from Vermont. He graduated in 1858 as a midshipman, and now, he was returning as an admiral and national hero. His brilliant victory at Manila Bay in 1898 had inspired a "Dewey-for-president" boom; over 3 million Dewey commemorative medals had been distributed; and many citizens had named their children—as well as cocktails, cufflinks, soap, spoons, and more after him.[1]

But that wasn't all; Congress had also honored then-Commodore Dewey's victory. It created the rank of Admiral of the Navy expressly for him in 1899, and he received his commission shortly before traveling to Annapolis on June 2, 1904.[2]

It's impossible to know what the Admiral's thoughts were that day. Perhaps he reflected on his "high-spirited" student years at the Academy: how he earned the reputation of being a pugnacious rabble rouser; how his midshipman's conduct record was far from perfect; how during the first year alone he received 113 demerits (200 meant dismissal) for hissing at mess, smoking in his room, and other offenses; how at the end of that year he stood thirty-third in a class of fifty-five; and how he eventually buckled down, graduating fifth of its fifteen survivors.[3]

The Academy had changed drastically since then, and perhaps the Admiral considered its most recent changes as his train sped to town. On May 4, 1898, Congress had appropriated $1 million to begin rebuilding the entire school according to Flagg's plan. Construction started in 1899 and had progressed with swift precision. The new armory and gymnasium were finished in 1903; part of Bancroft Hall, the new dormitory, was almost ready; and tomorrow, he would lay the cornerstone of what Flagg envisioned as the Cathedral of the Navy.

Admiral George Dewey (USNA 1858). Courtesy of Special Collections & Archives Division, Nimitz Library, U.S. Naval Academy.

First, however, there were other formalities to attend to. Although Admiral Dewey told the media that he wished "his visit to be a quiet one," a whirlwind of activity awaited him at Annapolis. Lieutenant Arthur Bainbridge Hoff (USNA 1889) greeted him at the station; officials fired a 19-gun salute in his honor as he approached the Yard; and he attended the Graduates' Association dinner in the gymnasium before retiring to bed.[4]

The Admiral awoke the next day to a welcomed surprise: sunshine. He watched the midshipman perform a battle drill at 9 A.M., then went to the Chapel site, where a platform had been erected around the cornerstone. Draped with flags and festive bunting, the platform's décor was "unique and attracted much attention," according to the *Evening Capital*. "The old Navy" was represented on one of its sides, and the "new Navy" was represented on the other. As the paper noted, "One side contained old guns, old swords and old implements of war, and the old sailors were stationed there, together with models of old warships. The other side had new guns, new weapons of warfare and the latest models of warships and young sailors of the new Navy."[5]

Only naval officers, their wives, and the school's Board of Visitors could sit around the platform. Everyone else, including the Brigade, which contained future distinguished officers such as Chester Nimitz and Aubrey Fitch, stood for the hour-long ceremony.

Chaplain H. H. Clark opened the event in prayer at 11:30. Next, Superintendent Captain Willard Brownson presented Admiral Dewey who "laid the first trowel of mortar, applied the square and striking the stone with a mallet, pronounced the words which declared it to be truly laid."[6] Finally, Secretary of the Navy William Moody addressed the crowd. His speech was brief, as he feared "marring the beauty and simplicity" of the ceremony with "any utterance of [his] own . . ." He did, however, make two points. First, he stressed the day's importance.

"This is a day full of significance to the navy and the country," he said. "It is worthy to stand by the side of that other day, fifty-nine years ago, come October

Chapel under construction, early 1900s. Courtesy of Special Collections & Archives Division, Nimitz Library, U.S. Naval Academy.

Chapel, early 1900s. Courtesy of Special Collections & Archives Division, Nimitz Library, U.S. Naval Academy. The Chapel's original golden terra cotta dome with ornate decorations began cracking as early as 1913. A copper-sheathed dome replaced it there in 1929.

10, when the Naval Academy was declared open at Annapolis. The days will ever be associated together."

He also described the new Chapel's purpose. "The primary purpose of this building," he said, "is to afford a place for Christian worship for upon our adherence to those principles the power of our nation depends."[7]

Secretary Moody's remarks ended the occasion, which was followed by a special "breakfast" at the superintendent's quarters. Admiral Dewey probably attended the event, the last social affair hosted by the superintendent during June Week, before taking the afternoon train back to Washington.

One month later, Alfred Schanze entered the Naval Academy as a plebe. Like Admiral Dewey, Alfred was a zealous writer; he wrote approximately 400 letters home while at Annapolis, some of which mention the Chapel. For instance on October 22, 1905, he wrote, "The chapel is being covered over with large stone tiles and looks great." Six months later he noted that, "The chapel is almost ready for unveiling. It does not looks as bad as I thought it would."[8]

Alfred attended one of the first services held in the Chapel upon its completion. And, while he probably saw its cornerstone, he probably didn't know that these items had been placed in it on June 3, 1904: a copy of the Naval Academy's regulations; a list of officers on duty at the time; copies of three newspapers, including the *Evening Capital*; and autographed photographs of President Theodore Roosevelt, Secretary Moody, Superintendent Brownson, Ernest Flagg—and, of course, Admiral Dewey.[9]

Alfred Schanze Records His Naval Academy Adventures

Alfred Schanze wrote approximately 400 letters home while at Annapolis. This chapter features some of the most amusing—and informative—that he wrote during his first year there.[1]

I

Take a moment and try to answer these questions:

1. When it is 1:00 P.M. at Greenwich, what time is it at Shanghai, in Longitude 120 degrees East?
2. Give a brief account of the Second Punic War, including its causes, dates, duration, opposing generals, important battles, and final results.

3. Find the square root of 187.364 to six decimal places (without a calculator).

Are you stumped? If so, you would have probably failed the Naval Academy's admissions test in 1904. The test was brutal; it covered Reading, Writing, and Spelling; Grammar, Geography, and Geometry; Algebra, Arithmetic, U.S. History, World History, and more.[2] And, given its rigor, many candidates came to Annapolis to prepare for it well in advance.

Alfred was among those who did. He came from Newark, New Jersey, in January 1904 to attend Wilmer's U.S. Naval Academy Preparatory School: one of several local schools that prepared young men for the exam at the time. Joseph Ringgold Wilmer was its founder and main instructor. He graduated from the Naval Academy in 1878 (forty-seventh in a class of fifty) and retired from the Navy in 1892.

The *Evening Capital* praised Wilmer's establishment in 1908 in this passage:

Midshipman 1/C Alfred Schanze (USNA 1908). Courtesy of Special Collections & Archives Division, Nimitz Library, U.S. Naval Academy.

After a careful survey of the field and knowing what we do concerning the various preparatory schools here, we unhesitatingly pronounce the United States Naval Academy Preparatory School, conducted by Wilmer and Chew, to be the very best, both as regards to accommodations, scope and character of education . . . The percentage of successful candidates from this school is far greater than that from all the other so-called "preparatory" schools combined. We live here and know what we are talking about . . . Parents note this! Candidates patronizing Wilmer and Chew's . . . stand the best chance of passing the exams, for [the] Naval Academy.[3]

Alfred joined Professor Wilmer at his school on Cathedral Street, four months before the April test. During this period, he went to class, studied, exercised, and somehow, found time to write home to his family almost daily. His letters are priceless, as they reveal much about him and early 20th-century Annapolis.

Alfred generally liked Maryland's capital. Shortly after arriving he wrote, "I find Annapolis to be a very tolerable village." Yet certain parts of the city bothered him—especially its postal service. As he wrote on April 9, "I am not at all surprised about the delay of letters . . . as the post office clerks here in Annapolis are not worth the rope to hang them."

Alfred also criticized local domestic help. He told his mother on January 7 that she was not the only one having "trouble with servant girls." So was Miss Ida Roget: the single, attractive fifty-one-year-old Frenchwoman, with whom he boarded at 252 King George Street. Alfred complained that her servants "do not sleep here and consequently have to come every morning. This morning they did not show up until 8 o'clock and every fire in the house went out through the night . . . "

Miss Roget was a contemporary of William Oliver Stevens. Stevens, who taught English at the Naval Academy from 1903–24, was also an author and artist. He described Miss Roget and her "little frame boarding-house on King George Street, snuggled up cozily to a corner saloon" in this passage from his book *Annapolis*:

> [252 King George Street] was not a very prepossessing house from the outside, and inside the rooms were small and cut up on account of the difficulties of making the building do what it never was intended to do, take "paying guests." There was no furnace, because there was no cellar. Heat in winter came from hideous, iron "Latrobe" stoves, messy with coal dust and ashes, and gassy of breath. But the first place one sought for board was "Miss Ida's." That was because her table was so generous, and because she was so charming. Her rooms were usually crowded. "Candidates" [such as Alfred] studying for the entrance examinations to the Academy, Naval officers and their wives, mothers with marriageable daughters—or at least daughters who it was hoped would be marriageable—civilian professors, mothers of midshipmen determined to keep a loving eye on them; they all came and stayed and, after a time, went.
>
> Since Miss Ida Roget was a lady, she was often imposed upon. Some of her grandest and snootiest boarders would make some excuse and slip out of town without paying their bill. Some of the others did likewise, and her colored servants, though they adored their "Miss Ida," did not scruple to carry off large quantities of provisions in the pockets of their billowy skirts—what they considered their perquisites . . .[4]

Alfred arrived at Miss Roget's confident that he would pass the admissions test. After just one day at Wilmer's he wrote, "Things look promising for a successful career . . . " One week later, he told his younger brother Edwin, "I would very much rather you would not use my compass as I will need it when I get into the Academy . . . and then it must be in first rate condition."

Alfred remained optimistic. In early February he wrote, "I feel that if I were called upon at this moment to take the exams for entrance to the Naval Academy, that I could pass them with good marks."

Yet while he was confident, two subjects worried him: Geography and Algebra. He knew the test

WILMER'S

U. S. NAVAL ACADEMY

Preparatory School

ANNAPOLIS, MD.

J. R. WILMER, Class '78, U. S. N. A.   J. L. CHEW, A.B., A.M.

Advertisement for Wilmer's U.S. Naval Academy Preparatory School, from the 1904 Lucky Bag. *Courtesy of Special Collections & Archives Division, Nimitz Library, U.S. Naval Academy.*

would include Geography questions such as "Make a voyage from Yokohama to St. Louis via Hong Kong and the Suez Canal, naming in the proper order the waters passed through. Name and locate exactly seven important ports that might be visited."

He also knew that Algebra was not his forte. And, in late February, he feared that it would be his downfall. As he wrote on February 24, "I feel perfectly sure of making high marks in everything except Algebra . . . "

Alfred's concern prompted him to seek special help in Algebra from Professor Wilmer in early March. Later that month, Alfred received a special letter from the Naval Academy, one that invited him to the Superintendent's Office at 9 A.M. on March 24.

Alfred accepted the invitation. He went to the office, where he met the superintendent's aid, Lieutenant Commander John M. Poyer (USNA 1882). He asked Alfred to call on his family in the near future, which he did on March 27. Alfred received a surprise that day. During his visit, Poyer disclosed important information about the exam. "He said that he had seen the 'question papers' and that they were 'not harder than the average,'" Alfred wrote on March 28.

Although this news must have eased Alfred's mind, he continued to study with diligence. On April 7, he told his mother that, "time passes by like lightening and I hardly get a chance to think of anything else but studies."

Alfred's efforts bore fruit. He took and passed the test in Washington, D.C. on April 19. Lt. Cdr. Poyer relayed the good news the next week. He wrote that although the test reports would not be in for several days, "I have learned however that you passed an excellent examination" and received "records above 3 [out of a possible 4] in every subject." He also added that, "You will understand that this information is for you and members of your immediate family and that you are not to make it public in advance of the regular official notice."

Unfortunately, Poyer was wrong. Although Alfred passed the test, he didn't do as well he had claimed. In late May, J. E. Pillsbury of the Navy Department informed him that he had received a 3.5 in Algebra, 3 in English, 2.9 in both History and Arithmetic, 2.8 in Geometry, and 2.5 in Geography. Nevertheless, these scores secured Alfred a position as a member of the Class of 1908.

II

Alfred entered the Academy in July as sweeping changes were occurring on and off the Yard. On the Yard, Ernest Flagg's design was replacing what had been an unsightly hodgepodge of 19th-century buildings. Work on Bancroft Hall, the midshipmen's dormitory, was well under way, the officer's club was almost finished, and Admiral Dewey had just laid the Chapel's cornerstone to cite three examples.

Outside the gates, Annapolis was also booming. New city, state, and federal buildings were transforming what the midshipmen called "Crabtown," as were paved streets, a sewer system, and other modern marvels. This progress had prompted the *Maryland Republican* newspaper to declare, "Probably no city in the country, certainly no city of the size of Annapolis has changed so much in the past two years . . . there is no question that the people are beginning to realize that the twentieth century is opening a new future for their city . . . "[5]

It is this sense of potential that greeted Alfred at the Academy. He arrived there as a well-prepared young man; he had intelligence, athleticism, good manners, and even better penmanship, which he used to write many letters home during Plebe Summer. While some are entertaining, including those that feature his attempt to woo the city's ex-mayor's daughter, others are more informative and reveal key differences and similarities between a plebe's life then, and now.

For instance, unlike the Academy's recent newcomers, Alfred and his 300 peers were inducted at different times. While some came as early as June or as late as August, he arrived on July 6. And, at the end of the day, he wrote his first letter as a plebe. "Dear Papa," it began,

> I am now a midshipman in a sailor suit. My suit case is being expressed to you at Jersey City and the key is herewith enclosed. My deposit amounted to $255 and I wrote up the entire amount on one check, so I am herewith returning the other check, also my pass. My room is all settled now and I begin work tomorrow . . .
>
> Remember me to everybody at home.
>
> Very sincerely,
> Alfred K.

Remarkably, Alfred wrote home almost daily during Plebe Summer, including Saturdays. In contrast to modern plebes, he had town liberty that day (during the summer). Yet there wasn't much for Alfred to do there, as he complained to his mother:

> The town of Annapolis is extremely dull at present. When we go out on Saturdays there is absolutely nothing for us to do but call on some of the people we know. Most of the people go away during the summer or during a good part of it.

Alfred could do more than go into town on weekends; he could also receive visitors on the Yard during Plebe Summer. He entertained visitors from New Jersey, and locals such as the lovely Miss Charlotte Steele. Charlotte belonged to a prominent Annapolitan family; they lived in Murray Hill and her father, Nevett Steele, had been mayor of Annapolis, and the prestigious Annapolitan Club's first president.

On weekdays, however, Alfred's schedule was as intense as a modern plebe's. Consider this letter, which he wrote in early July. "My dear Mamma," it started,

> . . . I have settled down to hard steady work and am always tired when evening comes. At 6:00 A.M. we get up and at 6:30 breakfast begins after the formation. From 7:20 until 8:00 we must sweep our rooms and make our beds. After this drills begin . . .

Later, he described his rigorous schedule in a letter that began, "Dear Papa,

> . . . You very likely remember that before I came here we had a talk about my doing some studying during my spare moments. There are, however, no spare moments in this place as every hour from 6 A.M. until 10 P.M. is taken up in some form of work, especially since we are studying French . . .

Alfred's tight schedule isn't the only similarity between his Plebe Summer, and that of modern midshipmen. It also took him a while to adjust to military attire. In July he complained that, "The only clothes I have at present are white working suits and I feel very sloppy in these."

Like today, summer in Annapolis was also stifling a century ago. It was "too hot for [the] Middies," according to the *Evening Capital,* which reported that, "the heat . . . has been too great for the youngsters at the Naval Academy, from five to six of whom drop in a faint during drill or exercises nearly every day."

To beat the heat, Alfred and his classmates sought relief in the Severn River. As he wrote to his mother,

> The water of the Severn is not salty enough to suit me but I swim in it every day. We are allowed to swim only at a certain time when there is a swimming master and six or eight sailors in attendance to prevent accident. Our bath house is the *U.S.S. Terror* and my private clothes hook is the star-board bow "six pounder."[6]

The *Terror* was not the only ship stationed at the Naval Academy at the time; so was USS *Santee*. She was used to discipline midshipmen for offenses such as "frenching" (going into town without permission), which is still taboo. Alfred "frenched" from time to time, and although he was never caught, his friend was. As he noted,

> . . . One unfortunate fellow was reported for doing just as I did . . . and is now spending his spare moments aboard the U.S.S. Santee. He is not alone, however, as one of our smokers was also Santeed.

Alfred received very few demerits during Plebe Summer; however he received many of something that plebes still cherish: care packages. His supporters—including several female admirers—sent him cakes, cookies, crackers, and chocolate; running shorts, shoes, and money; a dictionary, pens, and stamps for his letters. Sometimes the packages surprised Alfred; other times he knew they were coming—because he had asked for them.

On August 17, for instance, he wrote to his mother about being "midshipman in charge" of his floor. "My duties as M. C. began on Monday evening at 7:30 and continued for twenty four hours," he wrote. " . . . This is what they call being 'on duty.' It's lots of fun but gets to be monotonous and tiresome toward the end." Then, at the end of his letter, he added, "P.S. If there is any candy left after the party, put it in a box and *mail* it to me."

Unfortunately, Alfred couldn't always enjoy what he received. Consider this letter, which he wrote to his father. "Dear Papa," he began,

> Received the package containing dictionary, Soyodout [a dental paste], and chocolate, all in good condition. I had to report to the officer in charge, the contents of the packages and he told me to get rid of the chocolate before supper or else bring it to mess. I did the get rid act . . .

At that point, Alfred improvised; he paid a local boy to "get him some crackers" from town. This wasn't the only time Alfred hired the young man. In fact, he and his peers often paid him and others to "smuggle" them oranges, bananas, desserts, and other goods. This system, however, wasn't foolproof. As Alfred relayed to his mother,

> Your letter came here yesterday. I have not yet spent my dollar but last night my room-mate and I gave [him] some money to get us ice cream and cake. He got them but when he was coming in the officer-in-charge chased him, so we got left. Some other fellows tried to get a water mellon but their [boy] was captured and the O.C. had a good water mellon free of charge. Do not think that these are hardships, they are good jokes and we laugh over them.

Alfred wrote this letter in August, shortly before tragedy struck the Academy.

Watchman Daniel O'Lone was making his usual rounds on the Yard that night. All was calm until 7:30 P.M., when suddenly, the new midshipmen's quarters caught his eye: Smoke and flames coming from Bancroft Hall's northern wing! He sounded the alarm, and although citizens rushed from the town to the scene, no one was admitted inside the Academy's gates.

Meanwhile, the midshipmen and others fought to save the building. As the *Evening Capital* reported the next day, "The handsome new quarters were in danger of being destroyed and every effort was made to save them . . . During the fire the midshipmen were in grave danger. The cables that supported the tower are covered with graphite, which caught fire and the grease burned off. It was feared that the heat would be enough to melt the cables and cause the tower to fall over on the midshipmen at work on the fire."[7]

Alfred was among the firefighters. Later that night he described the ordeal in a letter that began, "My dear Mamma,

> It is now eight thirty P.M. and we have all returned dirty, wet and tired from a fire which may have cost the government five million dollars and three years of labor if we had not been right on hand to extinguish it. At seven P.M. we came out of the mess hall and scattered all over the grounds. I came up to my room to change my clothes for the working suit. Scarcely had I made the change when the fire whistle blew most frantically. Everyone at once ran and in two minutes we had every piece of fire apparatus manned and were heading for the scene of action.
>
> The fire chanced to be in the northern wing of the new main quarters so all went to work in a most vigorous fashion to save the fine structure. A number of barrels of tar in the open court of the building were blazing away at a furious rate, setting fire to a large mass of wood killed nearby. The blaze was high, giving the impression that the building was burning from cellar to garret. Every branch of the naval service was there, midshipmen, sailors, watchmen, and marines. The excitement which prevailed for the first few moments soon disappeared and within a half an hour the flames were under control and soon extinguished...

Alfred hoped that he and his classmates would be rewarded for their efforts. As his letter concluded, "We should all get leather medals for this but I do not suppose we shall."

III

From fighting flames in Bancroft Hall to studying French and seamanship, Alfred had an extraordinary Plebe Summer. At first, he and his peers practically had the Yard to themselves. Yet this changed in August, which brought unseasonably cool weather and the upperclassmen back to town.

The upperclassmen returned August 27, when their training ships reached the Severn River, marking the end of summer cruise. While some left to enjoy a month's vacation, many remained to help instruct the Class of 1908. Here's what Alfred wrote about them to his mother on September 2:

The upperclassmen are here now and are keeping us strictly up to all requirements and formalities such as, turning square corners, walking along the edge of the walks, and keeping off the benches, and a number of other stunts of a similar nature. They jolly us along upon all occasions and on all sorts of subjects. The other day they got one of the "plebes" and made him roll a match across the floor of the corridor, with his nose before allowing him to pass. He had to get on his hands and knees to do the trick and he looked pretty ridiculous.

Two days later, Alfred shared this anecdote with his father:

Last evening my roommate and I were quietly reading in our room when suddenly the door was opened by one of our classmates, who announced 'The chief muc-a-muc of the Fiji Islands. Three bows.' At the same moment an upperclassman walked in and said, 'Well, get busy.' We started to bow and he yelled at us, 'Keep stroke there!' He then asked us our names and went out . . . They're not troubling us much you can easily see for yourself. I think it is really comical to have them putting us through some of these stunts.

Many upperclassmen had returned on the USS *Chesapeake*, which was then used to train plebes at Santee Wharf. The newcomers went aboard the ship three times per week to learn practical seamanship, including making and furling sail, and climbing the rigging, which Alfred was asked to demonstrate. As he wrote in early September,

As is always my luck, I was picked out to do the most nerve trying job on the ship. They sent me aloft to the fore royal yard which is 115 feet above the deck. The officer in charge was kind enough to tell me not to go aloft if I felt that there was any danger of my becoming dizzy and falling. I took my nerve with me and skipped aloft . . . This job suited me to perfection and I succeeded without, at any time, becoming nervous or shaky.

While Alfred scaled the ship's rigging with ease, he found other tasks more daunting. "What made my head swim most" he confessed, "was when I was trying to learn the name and use of every room and stay on the spar deck . . . There are at least thirty six ropes belayed on each side of the ship and ten at the foot of both main and mizzen masts also eighteen at the foot of the foremast and about twenty just aft of the bowsprit."

Surprisingly, the plebes trained aboard the *Chesapeake* on September 15— just one day after a hurricane devastated Annapolis. As Alfred noted, "All day yesterday it blew from the northeast and rained considerably . . . It was the hardest blow I have witnessed in some time. The wind roared and the atmosphere which had been rather heavy, seemed perfectly white with dust."

The gale persisted the next morning, yet this didn't impact his training schedule. He still went aboard the *Chesapeake* where, as he recalled, "it was a job for us to stick fast to the masts . . . as the wind simply howled through the rigging."

The storm was among the worst in local memory. It destroyed 1,000 feet of the Severn River Bridge and lodged much of it against Santee Wharf, blew down a flagpole in the city's square, scattered tree limbs about its landscape, flooded crop fields, and more. It also spoiled Alfred's plans to walk with Charlotte Steele, who he courted throughout his years as a midshipman.

The focus of Alfred's Plebe Summer changed after the hurricane. As September drew to a close, the Class of 1908 began preparing for the academic year. First, they received their books, which Alfred described in this passage:

> On Wednesday I drew my books for use during this coming academic year. There are eighteen text books on the various subjects I am to study. Algebra, geometry, trigonometry, two or three rhetorics, mechanical drawing, and French are the subjects covered . . . That mathematics is the principal study here is evident from the fact that eight out of the eighteen books are on the subject of math in some form or other.

USS Chesapeake *(renamed USS* Severn*), c. 1901. Courtesy of Special Collections & Archives Division, Nimitz Library, U.S. Naval Academy.*

Unfortunately, math wasn't Alfred's strong suit; he did poorly in Geometry and Arithmetic on his Academy admissions test. Yet he looked forward to school—even though math would dominate his curriculum. As he declared,

> October first marks the beginning of the academic year when we cease having so much physical labor and devote ourselves to mental exertions. I look forward with pleasure to the prospect of having something to occupy my mind. Mental work is to me more of a diversion than physical labor, especially when I am interested in what I am doing.

After Alfred drew his books, he and his peers received their new room assignments. Half were among the first 150 midshipmen ever to live in Bancroft Hall; the other half, including Alfred, lived in temporary quarters such as Annex B. He described moving there in this letter dated September 29. It was the last he wrote during Plebe Summer and it read,

> My dear Mamma, Am now all settled in my new quarters where I received your letter this morning. We were excused from drills and recitations yesterday so that we could do our moving. This was a regular circus. Bloebaum [Chester Bloebaum, his roommate] and I put our two mattresses together, piled our bed clothes, dress suits, service suits, and whites upon the middle and then carried the whole thing between us from one building to the other. The sight was too ridiculous for words . . . In the afternoon Charlotte came in to walk with me, and when I described this performance to her she laughed herself nearly sick.

IV

Alfred's writing habits changed when classes resumed. He wrote less often, his letters became shorter, and his penmanship suffered—probably due to his rigorous schedule. Even so, Alfred did write about two key events, which occurred during his first academic semester at the Academy: the Army-Navy football game and Christmas.

Navy football dominated local newspaper headlines as players prepared to face Army on November 26. The news wasn't good. Consider these front-page *Evening Capital* reports:

> The Naval Academy football squad is giving friends of the Navy great concern . . . The prospects are anything but hopeful at present." "The Navy is suffering from the same old trouble . . . the condition of the team is chaotic." And worst of all: "[Army] is a decided favorite . . . some of its most ardent admirers are offering odds that the Navy will not be able to score.

Despite this gloomy forecast, the Brigade looked forward to the contest. As Alfred wrote to his mother,

All of us are becoming more interested in the game so close at hand . . .
I am looking forward to having a good time at Philadelphia with the
entire family, so I hope Papa gets all the tickets he wants.

Alfred's father wanted five tickets for his immediate family. Securing that
many, however, would be difficult for two reasons. First, Franklin Field had limited seating. While nearly 70,000 fans attended the game in 2004, the stadium sat
only 25,000, including about 1,000 in special boxes, in 1904. Fans bought most of
the boxes at a live auction in Philadelphia, and the regular tickets were distributed
equally among the University of Pennsylvania and the two academies.

Franklin Field's size wasn't the only reason tickets were scarce in 1904;
there was also an unprecedented demand for them. The *Evening Capital*
explained why. It stated that many were eager to watch Navy's new coaches
in action. The team had just made significant changes to its coaching department, including hiring Naval Academy Professor Paul J. Dashiell as
head coach.

He was the perfect person for the
job. Born in Annapolis in 1867, Dr.
Dashiell was a stellar athlete. He competed in football, baseball, tennis,
wrestling, and gymnastics over his
ten-year college career. (A lack of eli-
gibility rules at the time allowed him
to do so as an undergraduate student,
graduate student, and instructor.)

In 1892, Dr. Dashiell began
teaching at the Naval Academy,
where he became known as "Skinny
Paul." His physique didn't inspire
this nickname; rather, it referred to
his position as a professor of chemistry, the subject that the midshipmen
called "skinny."

"Skinny Paul" made meaningful
contributions to football while at the
Academy, even prior to taking
charge of its team. He joined the
coaching staff in 1892, officiated at
major national intercollegiate
games, helped to organize the sport's
National Rules Committee in the
mid-1890s, and chaired the committee until 1911.

*Lt. Paul J. Dashiell. Courtesy of Special Collec-
tions & Archives Division, Nimitz Library,
U.S. Naval Academy.*

Dr. Dashiell was demanding, according to the 1905 *Lucky Bag*. He insisted that players had "to reach a higher physical standard" if they "were to be in the same class with Army," and took steps to improve their fitness. He added boxing and wrestling to their training regime and required them to use a "charging machine"—a task one midshipman described as "not fun."[8]

Navy hired new assistant coaches to aid Dr. Dashiell in 1904. Unlike years past, most of them were amateurs, not professionals, and only four were non-Academy graduates. This number included Dr. Dashiell, and three ex-Yale football stars.

The paper also attributed the high ticket demand to Navy's players. It said that despite a "subsequent slump," their early upset over Princeton had convinced fans of their potential. And, as a result, more wanted to watch them battle Army than ever before.

Alfred's father did what many failed to do: he secured multiple tickets and his entire family attended the game. Unfortunately, Navy lost it. Army won its fourth consecutive victory over the midshipmen, and its fifth since the contest began in 1890.

Alfred returned to Annapolis after Saturday's match with most of the Brigade, and the team followed on Sunday. He was probably among the large crowd who welcomed them at the train depot, where "they were heartily cheered . . . and given to understand their game fight was appreciated," to quote the paper.

Alfred's letter writing habits changed after the Army-Navy game. In fact, he almost stopped. He wrote only five in December, which makes sense given all that there was to do then. Academics, athletics, drills, hops—and for some such as Alfred, hobnobbing with local elites—left little time for corresponding—let alone Christmas shopping. This prompted Alfred to ask his mother to do this for him. As he wrote,

> I think that any Christmas presents which I want to give you can get for me if it will not be too much trouble for you. We do not get a chance here to do any Christmas shopping whatsoever. And even if I were to buy some things here I should have to pay express on them.

Alfred asked his mother to buy his gifts for another reason: local merchandise didn't impress him. He complained that, "Besides this, the stuff I could get here is of an inferior quality as most of the Annapolis people do their shopping in Baltimore."

Alfred was right. Many locals shopped in Baltimore and, as two newspaper articles from December 1904 reveal, local merchants viewed Baltimore stores as competition. The first article encouraged Annapolitans to shop in town. It praised stores such as Frank Munroe's for having "goods as cheap as those to be found in Baltimore," and ordered readers to "do your Christmas shopping at home." The second celebrated the reopening of the Severn River Bridge—an event that "turned the tide against the loss which would have been suffered . . . by the local merchants by a deflection of trade to Baltimore."

This article ran on December 24: the day the Academy closed at noon for a three-day holiday. Midshipmen could go into town and enjoyed extended liberty during this time; however, unlike today's Brigade, they had to sleep on the Yard.

The Christmas Eve ball was the highlight of the midshipmen's holiday. It was held in the school's new Armory, and the newspaper hailed it as "one of the most important and formal hops of the season." Alfred probably attended the ball with his parents, who were visiting from New Jersey. They stayed at Carvel Hall hotel and returned home on Christmas Day via train. Alfred described their difficult trip on December 27 in a letter that began, "My dear Mamma,

> . . . It is too bad your train was so much delayed as the journey is tiresome without delays and becomes positively vile when the trains are slow. However, the little surprise of seeing the tree already trimmed must have been considerable of a relief as it let you out of the job so nicely.

Several lines later, Alfred shared this amusing story. He was sleeping soundly on Christmas morning until upperclassmen began attacking his peers with water. As he recalled,

> Strange to say, Bloebaum and I were the only "Plebes" who did not get any water thrown on us . . . It was lots of fun for us to watch the other fellows shivering. Their bed clothes were drenched as were also their pajamas. Annex B was cold that morning too as even we two dry chaps felt unusually cold upon getting up at four A.M.

Alfred composed his last letter of 1904 on December 29. It describes an incident in which midshipmen were caught trying to smuggle "contraband drinkables" onto the Yard over the holiday. More importantly, it reveals much about Alfred's values, his respect for Academy regulations, and how seriously he took his responsibilities as a midshipman. "My dear papa," he began,

> A jug is a dangerous playtoy almost anywhere, but at the U.S.N.A. it becomes positively fatal to sport one about. Those unlucky fellows who are now aboard our 'houseboat' [the prison ship *Santee*] were not by any means the only chaps who had intoxicating drinks on Christmas. When I left you on Saturday high and came in here I met at least a dozen midshipmen who were listing to starboard and to port like a ship with a hole in the bottom. This cannot be helped as there are black sheep in every fold. You need not give me a single thought in this respect as I am perfectly well able to control myself. My companions are all of my own selection and they imitate me, not I them.

He then concluded his letter with this passage: "I hardly think that anyone will be dismissed or that any were even recommended for dismissal. All, however, have been given one hundred demerits, sent to the ship for the rest of the year, and deprived of September leave. This in itself is a heavy punishment although the Supt. [Superintendent] issued an order on the subject, in which he called it 'this comparatively light punishment.' The Supt. deals fairly with all of us and although I belong to a small minority who think the Supt. right I shall maintain my stand against all comers."

V

Winter of 1904 was mild until the New Year. At that point, the Weather Bureau began bringing nothing but bad news to Annapolis. Each day it delivered a dismal forecast, and each day locals braced for more of the same: freezing temperatures, violent winds, and the possibility of yet another snowstorm. Alfred described these miserable conditions in his letters. He also noted how he, and his peers, coped with them.

Dances offered some relief, including a New Year's Eve Hop and Graduation Ball. Alfred mentioned the first affair in this paragraph:

> Last night there was a big hop in the armory at which they watched the old year out and the new in. At twelve o'clock there was a bell rung and a bugler blew 'taps.' Immediately afterward the bugler blew reveille to awaken the New Year. A large number of 'plebes' staid to see this part of the show but Bloebaum and I went to bed at the usual hour.

Alfred's family came to the second dance. They enjoyed what was "perhaps the most brilliant and beautiful [ball] ever held" at the Academy—especially his sister Florence.[9] She had bought a new dress for it even though, as Alfred joked, "her closet was probably full of dresses."

The ball was held in honor of members of the Class of 1905, who graduated midway through their senior year to satisfy the fleet's need for junior officers. When describing their early departure Alfred wrote, "In three weeks [they] will be officers. Six of them have been physically disqualified and have been notified that their resignations will be accepted. . . . I feel sorry for these poor chaps; it seems like a pretty hard streak of luck to get through four years of hard work and then be disqualified on account of weak heart or eyes."

Parties offered further relief, and Alfred attended as many as possible. He was—to be frank—a social climber, who tried to hobnob with distinguished officers and their families. Consider this letter, which he wrote to his mother:

> The Superintendent and Mrs. Brownson gave a reception on Monday, January 2, to all of the midshipmen, and to any officers and ladies who cared to attend. Bloebaum and I went as big as life. Admiral Dewey would have been jealous of me if he could have seen the way in which I strutted up to Mrs. Supt. and shook hands at the same time handing her a game of jolly as to how very much pleased I was to

be able to come, in answer to the jolly she gave me about how kind it was of me to come.

The next person I braced was Miss Badger, otherwise known as Miss Commandant. I jollied her into giving each of us two chaps a plate full of some sort of salad, cake, etc. I then walked over to Mrs. Halsey for ten minutes while I ate my grub. The next lady I struck was Miss Supt. [Superintendent Brownson's daughter]. She dealt me out a glass of coffee sherbet which I ate while she talked at me a streak which took away my breath . . .

The room was crowded and I managed to work my way from the parlor into the dining room. My stomach gauge registered a full cargo, so I got busy dodging things to eat. Whenever I saw a lady with a plate, glass, or cup, making toward me I broke out in some other direction and butted into some new circle. At last I honed up alongside of Miss Halsey who very kindly asked me to sit beside her and help her eat some olives. She is daughter of Captain Halsey, Head of the Department of Seamanship, so I just made good right then and there.

After a little while I saw Miss Terry, whose dad is Head of the Department of Physics and Chemistry. I managed to slip away from Miss Halsey while she happened to be looking some other way, and came up alongside Miss Terry. She is a Wellsley grad so we two talked shop for a quarter of an hour . . . No one there knew that I did not attend a reception at the White House every week. I wish the Supt. and Suptess would receive every week; it's a circus.

Alfred also socialized with well-to-do civilians that winter. Sometimes he visited them alone. Other times, he brought a friend: Asahi Kitagaki (USNA 1909), who he called Kitty when he was "in a hurry."

Asahi was one of sixteen Japanese students who attended the Academy in the 19th and early 20th centuries. They came as a result of Emperor Mitsuhito's effort to modernize his country in 1868. That year, Japan's government asked permission to enroll select students (from Japan's nobility or samurai caste) in foreign schools, including the Academy. Congress granted its request, "provided that no expense shall thereby accrue to the United States," and the first Japanese midshipman arrived in 1869.[10] Asahi entered in 1905 but did not graduate. He died in 1929 in Japan.

Alfred mentioned him for the first time in this passage, dated January 26:

I am quite friendly with the Jap candidate here in town. He comes here three times a week together with two other Japs who teach the First Class "Judo" or Juicy Jitsu or whatever else they call it . . . [They] are pretty good at throwing our biggest and most powerful men around on the mats. They seem to have a wonderful gift in using their legs just as if they were arms . . . [They] are quick as lightening; so very quick, in fact, that we cannot see how holds are made until after it is all over and the victim is rubbing his joints. We all have the Jiu Jitsu fever now and keep choking and otherwise mameing [*sic*] each other all the time.

Later, Alfred noted that Asahi was "still a little behind the times with his English, but [was] getting up to date better every day."

In addition to social events, sports helped midshipmen to cope with winter's cold. Alfred, who had been a star gymnast in high school, joined the gym team in February. His timing was perfect. He joined just in time to prepare for, and perform in, a special exhibition. As he wrote, "On March 18th there is to be a grand tournament in every branch of athletics here. Among the amusements there is to be a gymnastic exhibition to be given by the gym team. I am one of the stuntsmen and shall do my best to give the spectators their money's worth. Admission is free, so you can imagine what my ability must be in order that they do not feel cheated."

The team trained rigorously for the event, which was a success. In fact, one week after it occurred, Alfred declared,

Our gym exhibition is still more or less talked about by everyone as it was quite a surprise to the whole place to have the team come out and do something worth looking at. Until this year the gym team has never amounted to much.

It's a good thing that Alfred joined the gym team. Otherwise, he might not have been able to maintain his svelte, 143-pound frame in winter of 1905. Alfred had a sweet tooth; his family knew it; and, therefore, they sent him many boxes filled with desserts that season. Consider these lines from his letters:

My box [of sweets] reached me two days ago and I received it without trouble. It is nearly empty and almost time for another.

My box of cake and candy was delivered to me on Wednesday without the least question . . . When Florence has her masquerade and there should happen to be anything left after the fun you can pack it up into a box and send it this way. Bloeb. and I will be pretty sure to clean up all you can send us.

Last Friday's mail brought me a box of the finest fudge I have ever eaten . . . [It] lasted about three hours.

If Barbara makes any cakes which are too large for the mail try the express . . . The young lady whom Bloebaum had here sent him a large box of candied dates and fudge by express and he received it without the least trouble.

Alfred's family sent him more than comfort food to help him through the winter. They also sent magazines, toothpaste, drawing materials, underwear, calling cards, and most frequently, stamps for his letters.

The highlight of Alfred's winter occurred on March 4, when the Brigade marched in President Theodore Roosevelt's inauguration in Washington, D.C. He recorded the event in several letters including this one, dated February 12:

> Our program for March 4th has already been pretty well fixed. We are to leave here about 10 A.M. arriving at Washington at noon. Then we march until 4 or 5 o'clock until the parade is over. The entire brigade of midshipmen is to be entertained at luncheon by Mrs. Mc Laine. I do not however know whether we shall be turned loose or not. As we must return to Annapolis upon the same day we shall get but little time to ourselves even if we are turned loose . . .

Alfred hoped that he would be "turned loose" for a reason: he wanted to visit a family friend, Mr. Linnett, who would be in town that day. He described his plan to see him in this letter, dated February 28:

> About seeing Mr Linnett in Washington I can make only this arrangement. Between four and four thirty I shall fall out of ranks at a place near the Shoreham. I shall proceed at once to that hotel and ask for Mr. Linnett. If he is not there I shall wait a half hour or so and then skip. If Mr. Linnett goes there and I do not show up by four forty he had better give me up. You might tell Albert the same. I am not absolutely sure of permission to fall out on that day but I guess there will be no trouble on that score.

Alfred mentioned the inauguration for the last time, on March 5 in this letter to his mother:

> The inauguration has come and gone but I am just the same as ever in spite of the strenuous march we had. Our brigade most certainly was at its best as you may know by what the papers have to say about us. I do wish you could have been down at the capital to see the parade. I do not believe there has been one as good since the Grand Army parade of 1865. We chaps worked hard and tried our level best and I am of the opinion that we met with success. You should have heard the cheers we received during the entire march. Navy! Navy! Navy! Sounded from every stand and every street crowd we passed. It was enough to give us all a heap of conceit but everyone is normal.
>
> Unfortunately I did not get permission to fall out and, as a result, missed seeing Mr. Linnett, Albert, Mary, and everyone else. Only those who had visiting parents or brothers or sisters were given liberty. Those who had brothers or sisters there were given one hour off while

Inauguration parade, 1905. Courtesy of Special Collections & Archives Division, Nimitz Library, U.S. Naval Academy.

those who had parents were allowed to remain all night and return this afternoon. On Friday afternoon I received a letter from Mary in which she asked me to take supper at her house. I telephoned to her that I could not do this and Mrs. Haron spoke up and said she wanted me to stay over night. She said she was going to ask Captain Brownson to let me do this as a personal favor to her. Evidently the Captain refused. I should like to catch him alone in the dark.

We were served a very fine luncheon after the parade by Mrs. McLean. All the pretty debutantes were there to serve us. Her house is one block beyond the Shoreham. There I was within hollering distance of Mr. Linnett and could not get loose. That was tough. Mrs. Mc's luncheon was the finest thing of the kind I have ever seen. There was music during the whole thing (one hour) and in spite of the fact that there were five hundred of us to serve everything went smoothly. Beside the girls and young ladies there were a lot of waiters who did the principal part of the waiting. It was certainly slick. Mrs. Mc was the best of all. She came to our table and said 'children do have some more croquettes.' Just think of us *children* marching eight miles, with our overcoats and rifles.

Why Midshipmen Toss Their Hats at Graduation

Alfred didn't do what most midshipmen do today: he didn't toss his hat at graduation. This story explains why, and explores the origin of this century-old Naval Academy tradition.

Hearing from readers is one of the best parts about writing my column. While some write or call to tell me about Annapolis's past, others ask questions about it. Take Gracie Booth, a budding young historian from Annapolis, for instance. She was just seven years old when she asked, "Why do midshipmen toss their hats at the Naval Academy's graduation?" At first, I assumed the answer was simple: they threw them in the air to celebrate.

I was wrong. There's a fascinating story behind this tradition, as James Cheevers, Assistant Director and Senior Curator of the Naval Academy Museum, explained.[1] The hat toss tradition began in 1912, when a crucial change in U.S. Navy policy occurred. Until then, Naval Academy graduates weren't commissioned as officers on graduation day; they only received a diploma or certificate. At that point, they had to serve two years in the fleet before being commissioned as ensigns in the Navy, or second lieutenants in the Marine Corps. During their two years at sea, they were called naval cadets, or "passed midshipmen," after 1902.

This system worked well until the early 1900s, when new, bigger battleships, and cruisers began to define the Navy's fleet. These ships required more junior officers to man them, and several steps were taken to meet this need. First, the Academy graduated members of the Classes of 1903–06 in the middle of their First Class, or senior years. It also split the Class of 1907 into three parts according to class rank; the first third graduated in September 1906, the second in February 1907, and the third in June of that year.[2]

At the same time, Congress considered legislation to allow the school to commission its graduates as officers on graduation day. Unfortunately, it took over a decade to pass the necessary act. This delay frustrated midshipmen such as Alfred Schanze, who wrote these lines to his father on February 5, 1905:

> Speaking of bills reminds me of the bill now before Congress ... If this bill, as it now stands, goes through I shall be an ensign in 1908 at the age of 22 . . . If you have any influence in Washington in any form whatsoever, use it to shove that bill through head first.[3]

Alfred mentioned the bill again in April 1906 when he wrote,

> There has been some talk here this week about the Vreeland bill [Edward Vreeland was a U.S. Representative from New York from 1899-1913],

which provides that midshipmen be commissioned as ensigns upon graduation . . . That bill means a great lot to us in money right from the start.[4]

Six years after Alfred wrote this passage, Congress passed the necessary bill on May 12, 1912. One month later, members of the Class of 1912 became the first to be commissioned immediately as officers. Their *Lucky Bag*, or yearbook, reveals just how significant this was to them. Its second page contains a copy of the bill titled "An Act authorizing that commission of ensign be given midshipmen upon graduating from the Naval Academy," and references to it appear throughout the book.

Newspaper accounts also prove that the bill marked a turning point for the school and Navy. For instance, the *Evening Capital* reported on June 6, 1912 that, "The graduation ceremonies of tomorrow will be epochal in nature as it will be the first time that graduates have been commissioned immediately upon graduation . . . 150 odd young men who represent the members of the graduating class are . . . keyed up to the highest pitch of enthusiasm, for tomorrow . . . they will get their diplomas, as well as commissions as full fledged officers of the American Navy."

Members of the U.S. Naval Academy Class of 1926 toss their hats at graduation inside the Armory, later called Dahlgren Hall. Courtesy of Special Collections & Archives Division, Nimitz Library, U.S. Naval Academy.

That the graduates were commissioned immediately had at least two results. First, it influenced the graduation ceremony. The event occurred on Friday, June 7, in the school's Armory, where "fond papas and mamas and a host of other relatives and friends . . . gazed in admiration at the new junior officers."

Several officials gave speeches, President William Howard Taft distributed the diplomas, and then something unexpected happened. Because the graduates were ensigns and second lieutenants—and not midshipmen—they didn't need their old uniforms, including their hats. This prompted them to hurl them spontaneously in the air, which launched the hat toss tradition that continues today.

That the men were commissioned also influenced what happened after the ceremony. It inspired an unprecedented wave of weddings among the new officers and their sweethearts. Previously, a midshipman's slim pay had made it nearly impossible for him to marry soon after graduation. In 1912, midshipmen earned $600 per year while at the Academy, and $1,400 per year after graduating. However, as Alfred's second letter implied, Congress's bill changed that. They made $1,700 per year once they left the school as ensigns or second lieutenants.

About ten weddings took place shortly after graduation day, 1912. When describing this unusually high number the *Evening Capital* said, "This is the outcome of the changed status of the graduates, who become ensigns at once with the pay and privilege of officers."

Three of the weddings occurred on June 8. Ensign Harold Grow was the first to marry. He and his bride, Edith Brady of 11 Revell Street in Annapolis, wed at 2 P.M., at St. Mary's Roman Catholic Church. An hour later, Ensign Roscoe Martin married Dorothy Knox of Howard County. Finally, Ensign Thales Boyd married Lillian Martin of 198 Prince George Street at 6 P.M. at St. Anne's Church. According to the newspaper, the ensigns who attended this particular wedding "wore the uniform of their rank," including their new hat.

French Soldiers—Buried at St. John's?

While Gracie asked a question about Naval Academy history, Dan Paulsen, a waiter at Café Normandie in Annapolis, inquired about the history of St. John's College.

Dan made his inquiry after students on a scavenger hunt ordered something that wasn't on Café Normandie's menu: help. They wondered if he knew where to find the monument that France gave to Annapolis during the Revolutionary War.

This was either a trick question, or Dan misunderstood it, because no such monument exists. What does exist, however, is one honoring the French troops who died in the area while fighting for America's independence during that war. It was built in 1906 on St. John's campus, near today's Hodson Boathouse.

The monument's story begins with Henri Marion, a Naval Academy professor, who traveled to Cherbourg, France, in 1905 for a momentous occasion. General Horace Porter had just discovered John Paul Jones's remains in Paris, and a U.S. ship squadron had gone to Cherbourg to return it to the Academy.

During his stay, Marion was touched by Cherbourg's hospitality—specifically, how well its residents had cared for the graves of American sailors located in their city's cemetery. The sailors had perished in 1864, at a nearby sea battle between the USS sloop of war *Kearsarge* and the Confederate cruiser *Alabama*.

Professor Marion thought that America should offer a similar gesture of respect. Therefore, upon returning home, he proposed an idea. He suggested building a monument in Annapolis to honor the French who died there while supporting America during the Revolution. He also thought that work on it should start in 1906, when the French Squadron would be in Annapolis for the commemoration exercises in honor of John Paul Jones.

Many agreed with Marion, including the General Society of the Sons of the Revolution. The society made the monument possible and, in spring of 1906, its cornerstone was laid on St. John's campus overlooking College Creek.

This site was chosen for a reason: It's where the French troops who died in Annapolis during the war were probably buried. Oral history suggests that it is. As the *Evening Capital* reported in 1911, "The precise location of their [the French soldiers'] graves has been hopelessly lost to posterity . . . But . . . Old—very old—Annapolitans can recall their great-grandfathers speaking of a few simple tombstones that marked the graves of some of the French dead buried here."[1]

We don't know how many Frenchmen were buried at St. John's during the war, their exact causes of death, or even their names. We do

The French Monument at St. John's College. Courtesy of St. John's College Archives SJC-P-1707.

know, however, that they were among the 4,000 French troops who stopped here in September 1781 while marching from Newport, Rhode Island to Yorktown, Virginia.

The march was long. It was difficult. And, it was "excessively hot," according to Jean Francois Louis, Comte de Clermont-Crevecoeur, who recorded the feat in his journal. There was no spring along the away and the troops "suffered extreme discomfort," he wrote.[2]

The Comte de Grasse was commander of the French fleet at the time of the march. His great-granddaughter, Amelia Fowler, placed the first bit of mortar under the monument's cornerstone and Mme. Jusserand, wife of the French ambassador, laid a wreath upon it.

The monument was finished and dedicated five years later. And, although the dedication ceremony was supposed to happen on April 19, 1911 (as the date on its plaque states) it occurred one day early, so that President William Howard Taft could attend.

Taft's visit was important for two reasons. For one, it was his first trip to Annapolis as president. "For the first time since he took his seat in the presidential chair, William Howard Taft, with all of his two hundred and sixty pounds of smile and good nature is in Annapolis this afternoon" the *Evening Capital* declared.

And second, he wasn't just coming to the Naval Academy. The newspaper said that, "[this is] the first time in many, many years—possibly since George Washington was President, says the oldest inhabitant—a President of the United States has come to Annapolis—not the Naval Academy, mind you, but the city itself."[3]

President Taft arrived on Tuesday, April 18, at 3 P.M. He traveled from Washington, D.C. in a new parlor car that the Washington, Baltimore & Annapolis Railroad had recently purchased for special events. According to the newspaper, "many of the high muck-a-muck of the General Society Sons of the Revolution," had already come from Washington, where they were celebrating their triennial convention. They spent the morning sightseeing in Annapolis and had lunch at Carvel Hall before joining the president.

The dedication ceremony started at St. John's in the late afternoon. Hundreds of spectators gathered for the event, including the city's police force, and the St. John's College Corps of Cadets, wearing "their natty full-dress uniforms."

College President Dr. Thomas Fell opened the occasion with a brief address. He described how the famous French military leader, the Marquis de Lafayette, had "visited this College in years gone by; how he was entertained in our college halls, and how the maidens greeted him, strewing flowers at his feet as he passed along the streets, waving banners . . . "

Next, President Taft spoke about the good relationship that France and America had enjoyed since the Revolution. Finally, Jean Jules Jusserand, the French Ambassador to Washington, said a few words, and the society's

Chaplain offered a prayer. Afterwards, Miss Fowler and one of Lafayette's descendants removed a canvas that had covered the monument.

What the canvas had concealed is still visible today. Designed by Baltimore sculptor J. Maxwell Miller, the monument features a bronze tablet affixed to a tall, pink granite shaft. The tablet shows a female bearing a laurel garland, standing near a shield. Behind her are French troops marching to their ships, and in front of her are two graves marked with the words "ci $+$ git un soldat de La France" and "ci $+$ 3 git un marin de La France."

Before submitting my column, I went to Café Normandie to ask Dan if he knew what these words meant. This time, he had the answer. After consulting with a fellow employee, he said they translated roughly to "Here rests a soldier of France" and "Here rests a sailor of France."

Annapolis's Other Military School

The French monument was built at St. John's when it was a military school. This story explores this surprising part of the college's past.

That St. John's offered—let alone required—military training seems ironic given its charter. Issued by Maryland's General Assembly in 1784, the document exempted students "from all military duties, except in the case of actual invasion of the state, and when general military law is declared."[1]

St. John's introduced military training to its curriculum in 1826, when its Board of Visitors and Governors appointed Thomas Sudler as Professor of Civil Engineering and Military Tactics. The board's timing made sense, according to Tench Francis Tilghman. Tilghman, a former St. John's tutor, wrote that,

> Annapolis had become very military minded recently; the papers of these years are full of notices of the various city companies: the United Volunteers, the United Guards, and the Sharp Shooters. The board got the fever badly . . .[2]

At first, the board made military training optional for students. It became mandatory three months later. Students were called "cadets," and were assigned to one of two companies. They assembled at 6 o'clock each morning at the school's Parade Ground, wearing uniforms designed by the board. They wore blue jackets with white buttons and collars, which rose to "the tips of the ears;" white or gray pantaloons depending on the season; as well as a black cravat, black hat, and ankle-high "Jefferson shoes." The college appropriated $75 for music for the military department in its early days, and it borrowed arms from the state.[3]

Military training at St. John's wavered between being optional and mandatory for many years. In 1831, college president Hector Humphreys, reversed the board's decision and made it an elective; this must have pleased the students since they "had always disliked" the training, and many had tried "their best to evade it." He also changed the title of Professor of Civil Engineering and Military Tactics to "Professor of Mathematics and Civil Engineering."[4] President Cleland Nelson, in turn, made the training compulsory again in the late 1850s. At that point, each cadet had to buy his uniform, which cost $17.50.[5]

St. John's closed in 1861 due to the Civil War. When it reopened in 1866, students could choose whether or not to receive military instruction; it was "regarded as sort of a physical culture course," used mostly for ceremonial events.[6]

Tilghman offered this amusing anecdote of what was called the college's "Corps of Cadets" at the time. When quoting the Class of 1873 historian, he wrote, "The most heroic deed performed by this gallant little band was their march to Governor Bowie's inauguration . . . They were brought back from the Inaugural Exercises if not upon their shield at least by the kind assistance of

Battalion of St. John's College Cadets in full dress, 1923. Courtesy of St. John's College Archives SJC-P-1848.

their more sober companions. Their Alma Mater following the example of the severe Grecian Mother was displeased."[7]

Military training intensified at the college in 1884, under President William Hopkins's administration. He made it mandatory, and it stayed so for forty years. He also strengthened the Military Department; he persuaded the U.S. War Department to station an officer on campus as Commandant of Cadets and Professor of Military Science and Law. As the college's *Catalogue* for that year noted,

> Under Section 1225 of the Revised Statutes of the United States, relating to Military Instruction in Colleges and Universities, this College has secured the services of an Officer of the U.S. Army [at no cost to the college] . . . and, by the same authority, is supplied with arms and accoutrements for the use and instruction of students as Military Cadets.[8]

Lieutenant Charles William Foster was the first to hold this position. He arrived in 1884 and received the title "Charles W. Foster, U.S.A., Professor of Military Science and Tactics and Lecturer on International and Constitutional Law."

The college's 1884 *Catalogue* was the first to list a Department of Military Science and Tactics at St. John's. It also noted what life was like for its cadets. They drilled four times per week in army tactics, infantry, and artillery. Each cadet had to participate in the drills, unless he was physically unable.

The Staff of the St. John's College Military Department, 1905. Courtesy of St. John's College Archives, 1905 Rat Tat.

Cadets wore uniforms, but only during drills and parades. They consisted of dark blue suits, with matching caps made of "good material and workmanship." They were made in Annapolis under the "supervision of the [school's] President and Military Instructor."[9]

By 1886, the college's Military Department had grown in size and stature to the point that it was listed separately from the regular faculty. And, at that point, cadets received two kinds of military training: practical and theoretical. They took military theory courses such as Infantry and Artillery Tactics, U.S. Army Regulations, and Military Law. They also attended lectures on Strategy, and Grand and Minor Tactics.

For practical training, cadets drilled for one hour, four days per week. They participated in artillery tactics, bayonet exercises, group formations, skirmishing, military ceremonies, and target practice. The college received ammunition for these activities from the U.S. Army Ordnance Department. It was kept in McDowell Hall's basement, which proved to be disastrous on February 20, 1909: the day the building burned, and 30,000 rounds of ammunition exploded during the fire.[10]

Cadets bought their own uniforms in 1886. They cost between $15 and $20, "according to the size of the cadet." The letters "S.J.C." embroidered in "old English characters" decorated their dark blue caps, which matched their blue uniforms.[11] In later years, the uniform was gray and was a "modification of that worn at the U.S. Military Academy, [at] West Point, N.Y."[12]

By the late 19th century, the Military Department had become a crucial part of St. John's. In fact, "the cadet corps . . . was easily the main feature of life" there, according to

> ## ST. JOHN'S WEEK
> ### BEGINS SUNDAY.
>
> #### The One Hundred And Twenty-Sixth Annual Commencement At Old Institution.
>
> St. John's "June Week," put forward some three or four weeks this year, will be held in May, instead of the last week in June.
>
> The exercises attendant upon the 126th annual commencement will begin on Sunday. On account of war conditions, many of the St. John's students having answered the call to colors, or joined the various training camps, the exercises are considerably shortened, and many of the usual features, will be conspicuous by their absence.
>
> The following is the complete progarm:
>
> Sunday, May 26—11.00 A. M.—Baccalaureate Sermon in St. Anne's Church, by Right Rev. Thomas J. Garland, D. D., Suffragan Bishop of Pennsylvania.
>
> Monday, May 27—8.00 p. m.—Junior Oratorical Contest and Dramatic Club.
>
> Tuesday, May 28—11.30 a. m.—Presentation of Class Shield by Senior Class.
>
> 4.30 p. m.—Battalion Parade and Review.
>
> 8.00 p. m.—Farewell Ball to Class of 1918.
>
> Wednesday, May 29—10.30 a. m.—Graduation Exericses.

The St. John's cadets' activities often made the Evening Capital's *front pages. Consider this update, which appeared on March 24, 1918.*

Enoch Garey during his senior year at St. John's College. Courtesy of St. John's College Archives, 1903 Rat Tat.

Tilghman.[13] It's importance increased further in the early 20th century. Cadets began to wear their uniforms at all times—not just for drills and parades. And, since they were required, the college advised parents to "omit the purchase of articles of civilian dress" for their sons.[14] They drilled for at least one hour, four times per week—although "quite frequently, more time [was] expended." Everyone had to participate in the drills, and even those who applied "to be excused because of physical disability" had to obtain a "physician's certificate."[15]

But the cadets' military obligations did not stop there. They participated in ceremonies, practice marches on nearby country roads, and target practice year round. They received gallery instruction in the school's armory in the winter and trained at encampments in the summer. This tradition began in 1903 in Kent County, Maryland. There, at Tolchester Beach, the cadets took lessons in fieldwork, target practice, military hygiene, and castrametation (the art or act of making or laying out a camp).[16]

Edmund Berkeley Iglehart was crucial to the Military Department's strength in the early 1900s. Born in Annapolis in 1874, he entered St. John's Preparatory School at age thirteen, and graduated from the college at age twenty. He excelled at baseball and football while a student, and later, coached the football team as an alumnus.

Edmund served in the Navy Pay Corps during the Spanish-American War. He accepted a commission as a Second Lieutenant in the Army after the conflict. He was detailed to his alma mater and in 1907 was appointed as its Commandant of Cadets and Professor of Military Science, Tactics, and Law. He held that position until poor health forced him to resign in 1909.

Thanks in part to Lt. Iglehart, St. John's Military Department was recognized for its rigor. The U.S. War Department ranked it among the nation's top six military colleges in 1905. Yet despite this achievement, not everyone approved of the department. It was "threatening to engulf the whole college," to quote Tilghman, and relations between it and the college's faculty were souring.[17]

The faculty complained that the department put excessive demands on their time; for instance, it required them to act as "officers of the day" during hall duty to ensure order among the cadets. Cadets also complained about the department's demands. And, in 1908, college President Dr. Thomas Fell warned the college board that it made "life for the students extremely onerous."[18]

Despite these complaints, however, the board supported the department until a tragic incident occurred. In May 1914, an upper-classman tried to force his way into a freshman's room in order to haze him. In response, the freshman shot him through his door, and he died the next day.

The investigation that followed stripped the Military Department of much of its power. The investigating committee concluded that St. John's "military atmosphere was conducive to the hazing tradition." It also noted that it promoted the wrong kind of discipline and made students feel as if they were accountable only to the department.

The board took the committee's conclusions seriously and appointed another committee to make recommendations for improving the college. It made three, including one regarding the Military Department. It said that the power to enforce discipline at St. John's belonged to its faculty, not the department. The board agreed and its decision marked the beginning of the end of military training at the college.[19]

St. John's Military Department enjoyed a brief, final growth spurt when the United States entered World War I. The campus received an Army ROTC (Reserve Officers Training Corps) unit in 1917. A branch of the Students Army Training Corps followed, which enrolled approximately 320 young men. All in all, 705 St. John's students or alumni served as officers or

---

During St. John's military years, each sophomore class developed a set of rules for the incoming class. The rules were "designed to cause the maximum amount of discomfort" for the freshmen, sometimes called "rats." Here is a sampling of rules:

1. Part the hair in the middle.
2. Keep off the grass of the front Campus.
3. Stay off the Sacred Walk.
4. Cut all corners at right angles on the sidewalk.
5. Speak when spoken to.
6. Do not speak to an upperclassman, unless seeking advice.
7. Be inspected by an upperclassman before going downtown.
8. Freshmen are not allowed to eat while in uniform, downtown.
9. Freshmen are not allowed to speak to girls, unless they have been properly introduced to them.
10. All freshmen have to carry matches at all times.
11. Call all upperclassmen by their last names. No nick-names at all.
12. Cannot put their hands in their pockets.
13. Come when you are called. Drop everything you are holding. Come at once.
14. Keep trousers creased at all times.
15. Not allowed to wear overcoat collars turned up.[24]

COLONEL AMOS W. W. WOODCOCK
President of the College

Col. Amos W. W. Woodcock, 1935. Maj. Garey had much in common with Amos Woodcock. This native of Salisbury, Maryland, also graduated from St. John's in 1903. He served in the army after graduating as well; in World War I, for instance, he led units on the Mexican border and France as an infantry captain. After the war, Woodcock returned to civilian life. He served two years as assistant to the Maryland Attorney General, was appointed U.S. Attorney for Maryland in 1922, and was appointed by President Herbert Hoover as Director of the U.S. Bureau of Prohibition in 1930. Woodcock left the Bureau in 1933 and became Special Assistant to the U.S. Attorney General. The next year, he became the president of St. John's College. Unfortunately, Woodcock's administration was brief. The board asked for his resignation in 1937, mainly because he vetoed a faculty decision and granted a degree to a student who had failed to meet the degree's requirements. This act had caused the Middle States Association of Colleges and Secondary Schools to revote the college's accreditation. Courtesy of St. John's College Archives, 1935 St. John's Yearbook.

enlisted men in the armed forces during World War I; only West Point provided more.[20]

St. John's Military Department dissolved quickly after the war. In 1923 Major Enoch Barton Garey succeeded Dr. Fell, who had been president since 1886. Maj. Garey was a native of Williston, Maryland. Upon graduating from St. John's in 1903, he graduated from the U.S. Military Academy in 1908, served in the U.S. Army, taught at Johns Hopkins University from 1920–23, and attended Washington College.

St. John's had improved dramatically during Dr. Fell's administration. Old buildings were renovated, new ones were built, it earned national acclaim as a military school, and its registration doubled. After the war, however, its enrollment and reputation waned.

It was up to Major Garey to restore the school's prestige. He succeeded. During his administration, the college acquired historic properties in Annapolis including the Brice, Hammond-Harwood, and Pinkney Houses; its library was improved; and an art library was founded.

Maj. Garey also enlarged the school's faculty and abolished its Military Department, mandatory military training, and Cadet Corps, to allow students to focus on academics. A voluntary ROTC unit replaced the Corps, whose participants drilled two hours per week, and took limited military coursework. First-year cadets studied rifle marksmanship, scouting and patrolling, and military courtesy. Second-year cadets took lessons in infantry weapons, musketry, military hygiene, sanitation, map reading, and sketching. Third-year students studied military law, and handled machine guns, 37 mm guns, and trench mortar. Finally, seniors focused on tactics, military history, and pistol marksmanship.[21]

Maj. Garey also brought the nation's first Naval Reserve Officers' training unit to St. John's in 1924. As that year's *Catalogue* noted, "This is the only college at which such a unit is maintained. In the future there will be many other colleges having such a course, but St. John's has the honor of being the first." Participation in the unit was voluntary; its members took an oath to serve in case of national emergency, were appointed as midshipmen, and were appointed as ensigns in the Naval Reserve upon graduating.[22]

St. John's ROTC unit disappeared in 1926 due to a lack of interest. By 1929, its Naval Reserve program, and Department of Naval Science had vanished as well. Tilghman offered one explanation for why military training at St. John's did not last. He wrote that,

> In spite of the excellent records of many of its graduates, it [the military department], was always a misfit at St. John's, because it meant that the college was trying to be two things at once: a liberal arts college—which was what its founders had intended it to be—and a military school. It demands all of an institution's efforts to be successful at one of these attempts; no college can be simultaneously successful in both.[23]

How Spanish Influenza Attacked St. John's and the Academy

As St. John's alumni fought abroad during World War I, their alma mater was fighting a battle of its own in Annapolis. This is the story of how it, like the rest of the city, survived Spanish Influenza.

As Germans battled Americans abroad in 1918, an equally lethal enemy was attacking Annapolis: Spanish Influenza. "The flu hit Annapolis at an exceptionally unfortunate time," said author and historian Jane McWilliams. "The town was already tense; people were worried about the war and those who were fighting overseas."[1]

The Naval Academy was influenza's first local target, and even the healthy young midshipmen were defenseless. Midshipman Orin Haskell, a member of the Class of 1920, described the flu's early impact there on September 22, in this letter to his girlfriend:

> Dearest Audrey,
>   . . . Rather a sad thing happened to us today as the brother of my roommate, who is a lieutenant in the Navy, died last night of Spanish influenza, which has had such a run in the Navy and especially the northern states. It was mighty hard as he was a splendid officer and has been flag officer of the Pacific fleet for the past year . . . they say that the Germans introduced the disease into this country. This is one thing more to hate them for . . .[2]

Midshipman Haskell mentioned the flu several other times, including on October 6. As he wrote that day,

> Perhaps you have heard that the influenza has us here. We have 1,000 cases and four deaths so far. The fellow in the next bed to me in the hospital passed on. He was a fellow from Georgia and as he was a Scotchman was a mighty fine chap. I was mighty surprised to get your letter saying that all the Portland schools are closed and that you are at home. I only hope that the flu doesn't get you. If you get the influenza, get in bed and keep covered as if your life depended on it as it is very easy to catch pneumonia and if you get that it is 'good night.' The main thing is not to get cold . . . Be careful and do not get the flu . . .[3]

The next day he recorded,

> Since I came back from the hospital Saturday I have been to no recitations as they are keeping me on the sick list although I am feeling fine aside from a slight cold. Four mids have died so far and some others are

very sick. The flu is having a big run and is hitting them much harder in some places than it has us here. Even the postmaster has the flu because the mail hasn't come yet . . .[4]

The Academy quarantined the Brigade of Midshipmen in late September, which "probably saved the town," Ms. McWilliams said. But the flu had already begun its in-town assault. Each day the *Evening Capital* reported the latest casualties: "Death claims colored preacher;" "Young mother claimed by death;" "Flu claims prisoner in jail;" "Death of faithful colored man;" "Double funeral of influenza victims;" and so forth. The headlines were sobering, and left many wondering, "Who'd be next?"

Citizens tried to stop the flu from spreading by canceling sports contests, dances, and other public

Midshipman Orin Haskell (USNA 1920). Courtesy of Special Collections & Archives Division, Nimitz Library, U.S. Naval Academy.

events. City Health Officer Dr. William Welch went further and closed public schools on October 3, when 288 cases were reported in the Annapolis Grammar School alone. Next, he shut down the movie theaters and poolrooms. Finally, even the churches closed on October 13. Yet the crisis escalated until it climaxed in mid-October—the deadliest month in the nation's history.

In just thirty-one days, the flu killed approximately 195,000 Americans, including 151 Annapolitans.[5] Yet this total is questionable, according to Ms. McWilliams. After careful research, she concluded that approximately 108 Annapolitans died of flu-related complications that month.[6] Twenty-eight of the 1,100 midshipmen who became ill died. So did numerous Naval Academy employees.

Several St. John's students also perished, even though the school imposed quarantine and converted Randall Hall's top floor into a hospital to isolate patients.

Many who treated the sick also became victims. Twenty-five-year-old Gladys Wigley graduated from the Annapolis Emergency Hospital's nurse training program in 1916. She left her home in Millersville to serve in Annapolis in late September and died within a week. In contrast, "the local African-American population fared very well," according to historian Janice Hayes-Williams.

She estimates that African-Americans accounted for about 150 of Anne Arundel County's 1,000 flu-related deaths in October 1918, half of which occurred at Camp (later called Fort) Meade. They also accounted for between twenty and thirty such deaths in Annapolis, Camp Parole, and Eastport that month.

Dr. Ambrose Garcia of Clay Street probably treated many of the African-Americans who became ill in town. It's likely that many also treated themselves. As Ms. Williams said, "Without the benefit of viable health care, and a small number of available doctors, members of the African American community have always used healing remedies passed down by their ancestors such as poultices, salves, teas, and prayer, before, during, and after slavery."[7]

Dorothy Purvis Thomas recalled the peak of the local flu crisis during a 1990 interview for Mame Warren's book, *Then Again . . . Annapolis, 1900–1965*. "People in Annapolis were dying like flies from the flu epidemic in 1918," she said. "Almost all the doctors were gone. The undertakers couldn't keep up with it."[8]

*Series of newspaper headlines about the flu (*Evening Capital *October 2 and 7, 1918).*

St. John's converted part of Randall Hall, above, into a hospital during the flu crisis in 1918. Courtesy of St. John's College Archives SJC-P-486.

In fact, three of the doctors at the Annapolis Emergency Hospital had accepted commissions in the Army and were gone. Margaret Wohlgemuth, R.N., the hospital's superintendent and director of its nurse training program, was also serving overseas.

The city's undertakers were also overwhelmed. James S. Taylor & Son prepared ninety bodies in October alone—fifteen times greater than their monthly average. B. L. Hopping also prepared forty bodies, which was eight times his average.

After a month of intense suffering, the flu finally began to wane in Annapolis. Dr. Welch lifted the quarantine on October 24 "after due thought and consideration," and "conference and advice of the state Health Department," to quote the *Evening Capital*.

Movie theaters were the first public centers to reopen. In advertising the Republic theater, its proprietor, Philip Miller, declared that it had been fumigated and inspected by Dr. Welch. City churches reopened that Sunday, as did the Naval Academy. Midshipman Haskell recorded this event on October 27 when he wrote that, "The quarantine was lifted today with a bang. Liberty, football game with Newport Training School—we won 47-7—and a big hop last night . . ."[9]

St. Mary's Parochial School reopened on October 29, and the public schools followed a week later. They had scrubbed and sprayed the floors with formaldehyde, and burned formaldehyde candles with the windows closed to prepare for it.

"A Pretty Piece of Land": How ROTC
Saved St. John's from the Academy

Shortly after Annapolis battled the flu, the city's colleges engaged in a battle of their own. In 1945, the U.S. Navy needed more officers and the Naval Academy needed more space. It looked across King George Street, at the tree-lined grounds of a small liberal arts school struggling to survive, and pictured the site as a midshipman's dormitory and mess hall. Backing the Academy were military supporters, civic groups, the Chamber of Commerce, the daily newspaper, and seemingly, most of Annapolis. This is the story of how St. John's fended off their attack and achieved one of the shining moments in its history.

Conditions were ripe for a thunderstorm on July 26, 1945, as nearly 100 women marched to the Maryland State House. Led by Mrs. Morden (Nancy) Rigg, they were coming to protest the Naval Academy's plan to annex St. John's College—a plan that pitted the Academy, and its many ardent supporters, against a small, financially struggling college.

Rumors that the Academy planned to annex St. John's began in 1940, and resurfaced during the war. In 1945, the Academy announced its proposed expansion, and began an aggressive campaign to annex the 32-acre St. John's campus—a campaign that would take a fight in Congress to settle.

Underlying the Academy's effort was a need for space. World War II had brought sweeping changes to the school, especially an increase in its student body. While about 3,200 midshipmen attended in 1945, postwar estimates predicted that this figure could soar to 7,500. At that point, the Academy could not handle such an influx; most of its facilities were built when the enrollment numbered 800, and its dormitory was designed to house just 2,500.

This housing shortage, among other factors, prompted the Academy to pursue a three-phase, $70 million expansion. First, it sought to annex and erect academic buildings on 3 acres belonging to the city of Annapolis. It also planned to acquire land in West Annapolis owned by the Naval Academy Athletic Association. The third phase called for purchasing St. John's for a suggested price of $750,000, razing its buildings, and replacing them with a dormitory, among other buildings. While the plan's first two parts met little opposition, the third created a storm of controversy.

The Naval Assault

From the mayor to the media most locals, 80 percent according to the *Evening Capital*, favored the proposed takeover.[1] Citizens feared losing the Academy—and the $17.5 million that the Navy injected into the economy each year.

Their fear was justified since in 1945, congressmen from the West Coast, Midwest, and South sought to relocate the Academy—or at least part of it—to their areas of the country, where space was abundant.

1945 also marked the Academy's 100th year of operating in Annapolis. Surely, Annapolitans were influenced by the school's weeklong centennial celebration, which was covered by the national press, *Time* magazine, and the *Evening Capital.*

This local newspaper was among the Academy's staunchest supporters. Throughout the conflict it ran pro-Navy editorials such as "Back the Academy," "Annapolis Must Act," and "Academy Expansion Assured." The paper's president and publisher, Talbot Speer, also belonged to the Citizens' Committee for the Retention of the United States Naval Academy in Annapolis.

Sponsored by the Chamber of Commerce (another pro-Navy group), the committee consisted of community leaders including Speer; William McCready, then-Mayor of Annapolis; Cary Meredith, president of Farmers National Bank; Chris Nelson, president of the Annapolis Yacht Yard; Willis Armbruster, manager of Carvel Hall (the premiere hotel in Annapolis at the time); and Annapolis insurance broker Joseph Lazenby, who was its chair. Under his leadership, the committee produced a petition with over 4,000 signatures in support of the annexation.

Maryland's General Assembly also passed a resolution urging the school's expansion, the Annapolis City Council voted to support the takeover, and civic groups such as the Rotary, Civitan, Kiwanis, and Lions Clubs were all willing to forsake St. John's for a bigger, better Academy. So were members of the Academy's Employees' Association.

But St. John's also had its champions, especially its alumni. "Save St. John's" was the theme of the Alumni Association's annual meeting in June 1945, at which Stringfellow Barr, then-president of St. John's, addressed a crowd of 150. During the four-and-a-half hour rally Barr labeled the Navy's plan a "coup to try to grab a pretty piece of land" and urged alumni to voice their opposition.[2]

They responded with gusto. Many wrote impassioned letters to

Stringfellow Barr, above, was president of St. John's College when the Academy tried to seize it. Courtesy of St. John's College Archives BAR-P-0015.

the editor of the *Evening Capital*. Others, such as Herbert Fooks, class of 1906, took a more creative approach. He wrote a poetic defense of his alma mater, which the newspaper published on July 25. Titled, "O, Hallowed Ground of Old St. Johns," it began,

> O, hallowed ground of Old St. Johns!
> Let no one dare profane thee,
> Nor greed, nor gold, nor want of soul
> Seek ever to enchain thee . . .

Several St. John's alumni, including returning veteran Andrew Witwer (1944), even testified before Congress. He said, "None of us went off to war in order that we might return and find the place where we had begun to learn about a free society was being moved out from under us . . . It is for such institutions that men go to war. It is through the lack of such institutions that men make war."[3]

In addition to the support of its alumni, St. John's was backed by historic preservationists, the Severn River Association, and 100 prominent citizens who signed "An Open Letter" to the *Evening Capital* calling for the college's preservation. Many of the women who protested at the State House in July signed the letter. So did well-respected local men including Colonel D. Murray Cheston, medical Dr. J. Oliver Purvis, Maryland State Archivist Dr. Morris Radoff, and Frank A. Munroe. Yet they, like the others who favored the college, were clearly in the minority.

The College Fights Back

As World War II continued to rage abroad, a "small but highly explosive war" was erupting in Annapolis in spring of 1945.[4] What had once been a rumor: that the Naval Academy planned to annex St. John's College for as little as $750,000—had just been confirmed as fact.

In response, an outraged St. John's Board of Visitors and Governors wrote and sent a policy statement to then-Secretary of the Navy James Forrestal. Their message was clear: the college would only consider the sale if it received enough funds to relocate and if the national interest required its relocation.

"[St. John's will] cheerfully accede to genuine national necessity, if such necessity as distinguished from convenience, is formally declared by the Navy," said Richard Cleveland on behalf of the college at the time.[5]

Unfortunately, the Navy mistook the board's policy as an offer. In fact, Secretary Forrestal informed its Chairman, Dr. Thomas Parran, that negotiations for the purchase would start immediately. Fortunately for the college, things weren't that simple. The Academy couldn't annex its campus unless the U.S. House and Senate Naval Affairs Committees approved the plan.

Congressional hearings on the matter began in May 1945. Less than a month later, the House Committee dealt a harsh blow to St. John's: it approved the acquisition, but deferred from taking final action until a subcommittee explored other sites for the Academy's expansion in Annapolis.

Several weeks later the subcommittee delivered its verdict. It concluded that St. John's was the only suitable site and should be forced to move. Other options such as relocating the Academy to 850 acres across the Severn River were deemed impractical. This scenario, for instance, would require the school to revamp its class schedules, build new facilities, and transport midshipmen back and forth either by boat or over a new bridge.

Others agreed with the subcommittee including architects, the Academy's Superintendent Vice Admiral Aubrey Fitch, and Vice Admiral Ben Moreell, Chief of the Bureau of Yards and Docks.

Vice Admiral Aubrey W. Fitch, U.S. Naval Academy Superintendent during the climax of the proposed takeover. Courtesy of Special Collections & Archives Division, Nimitz Library, U.S. Naval Academy.

At the same time, new sites were proposed for St. John's. Annapolis-area real estate men advised Congress that Holly Beach Farm and Hillsmere would make ideal spots. Local resident Dorothy Strickland declared that a 100-acre farm near the South River "would be perfect." As she wrote in her letter to the editor of the *Evening Capital*, "[W]e realize the necessity of an enlarged Naval Academy and welcome its enlargement. Many colleges have moved from the city into the country . . . It would be advisable for St. John's to do the same. Beautiful farmland may be purchased within five miles of Annapolis . . . The lovely old brick college buildings could be torn down and erected on the same plans . . ."[6]

She was not alone. Many other locals offered their suggestions, according to this sarcastic recap from the *1945–46 St. John's Yearbook*:

> The Annapolis Roads Club offered us their site and bathhouses and suggested we save McDowell Hall by moving it out there to the beach stone by stone. Innumerable 10-room 'great estates' were offered to us at only three or four times their normal value, and many chambers of commerce, embarrassed by their lack of local culture, invited us to bring our ideals to fruitification in their sylvan neighborhoods where, they assured us, the folk were particularly warm and responsive to new ideas . . .[7]

After hearing the subcommittee's report, and testimony from both St. John's and Academy supporters, the House Committee declared that it would wait until Congress reconvened in October before making a final decision. The Senate Committee concurred. Yet both committees shocked the public in late July when, in a surprise move, they approved the acquisition.

Even then, however, St. John's board remained unconvinced that the annexation was a "national necessity." It protested, and, as Emily Murphy documented in *A Complete and Generous Education,* meetings followed among board members, Navy officials, and Committee Chairmen Senator David Walsh and Representative Carl Vinson. During these meetings, it became clear that the committees had only approved negotiations between the Navy and the college, and not the college's actual annexation.[8] When St. John's refused even to negotiate, further hearings were postponed until October.

Showdown in Congress

In the interim, a plan was gaining support that would reduce the Academy's need to expand and impact Congress's final choice. Officials predicted that the postwar navy would require about 500,000 enlisted men, and 50,000 officers. And, since it was impossible for the Academy to produce that number, Secretary Forrestal and Vice Admiral Louis Denfeld created a board to explore other options for officer training.

McDowell Hall. Courtesy of Historic Annapolis Foundation.

Chaired by Rear Admiral James Holloway Jr., the "Holloway Board," proposed three solutions for producing more naval officers. The first called for converting the Academy into a two-year postgraduate school for those who had completed three years of college; it was rejected. So was the second solution, which suggested creating an entirely new Academy, most likely on the West Coast. The third proposal had two parts: it recommended retaining the Academy's current site and four-year structure, and expanding NROTC (the Naval Reserve Officers Training Corps) at civilian colleges and universities to produce more officers.

Officials embraced this idea, which became known as the "Holloway Plan." The plan became law by an act of Congress in August 1946.[9] However, Secretary Forrestal approved it in October 1945, as hearings about the Navy's plan to annex St. John's persisted in Washington.

Congress was expected to make a final decision about the annex on October 24, yet failed to do so until spring. Finally, on May 22, 1946, by a vote of eleven to seven, the House Committee declared that, "the national emergency neither justifies nor warrants the proposed acquisition of St. John's campus."[10]

At that point, Secretary Forrestal notified St. John's that the Navy would no longer try to annex its campus. And, in response, Dr. Parran asked the Senate to "drive the third nail in the coffin of the project," which it did on June 12.[11] Several months later, St. John's celebrated its 250th anniversary—freed from the fear of losing its home, and the horrific vision of a midshipmen's dormitory in place of McDowell Hall.

St. John's Artist Designs a Special Stamp

Franklin Townsend Morgan came to St. John's shortly after the Academy tried to annex it. This is his story, and that of the special stamp he designed: the Annapolis Tercentenary 3-cent Stamp, issued on May 23, 1949.

The stamp's story begins in 1948. Annapolis was astir that year, as citizens prepared for Tercentenary Week: a seven-day celebration that would honor the city's 300-year anniversary in May 1949. The first group of Europeans had arrived in Anne Arundel County, Maryland, in 1649. They founded a settlement called Providence. And, while it was concentrated on the north side of the Severn River, it included some areas across the river on land that is now Annapolis.[1]

The Annapolis Tercentenary Commission planned the celebration. Chaired by Elmer Jackson, Jr., the Commission thought the government should issue a stamp to honor Annapolis's anniversary. So did the local Chamber of Commerce.

The groups shared their idea with Annapolis's Postmaster, William Strohm, in 1948. He embraced it, as did two Maryland Congressmen: Senator Herbert O'Conor and Representative Landsdale Sasscer.

O'Conor and Sasscer prepared bills regarding the stamp for the House and Senate in 1948. The Senate passed O'Conor's bill that spring. However, the House failed to consider Sasscer's bill before session ended. This was unfortunate. Congress wouldn't be able to reconsider the bill until it reconvened in January 1949—just four months before the celebration was scheduled to occur. And much had to happen before then. Passing the bill would only be the first step. Next, President Harry S. Truman would have to sign it, an artist would have to design the stamp, and officials would have to approve it. After that, plates would have to be engraved, and the stamps would have to be printed, and distributed. Incredibly, all of this happened by May 23. Here's how:

O'Conor reintroduced his bill when Congress reconvened. The Senate passed it unanimously on February 8 and that night, he shared the good news with the Commission. He sent its members a telegram that read, "Senate today passed my bill directing issuance Annapolis commemorative stamp after I explained its urgency."[2]

Next, Sasscer set to work. He reintroduced his bill in the House, and on March 1 the *Evening Capital* reported that he had "urged early and favorable action on his bill authorizing the issuance of a commemorative stamp on the 300th anniversary of Annapolis . . . "

The Commission was confident that Sasscer's bill would pass. Therefore, while he worked in Washington, it forged ahead with plans for the stamp. Together with Postmaster Strohm, it appointed a group to oversee its design. The group was called the Committee on Design for the Annapolis Tercentenary Stamp, and Colonel Earl Thompson, a Senior Professor of Electrical Engineering at the Naval Academy, was its chair. Its other members were Walter Norris, a historian and Senior Professor at the Academy; Thomas Gillmer, an authority on early ships and Assistant Professor at the Academy; Dr. Morris Radoff, Archivist of the State of Maryland; Jennie Richardson, an artist at the Calvert Studio on Church Circle; and Captain Frank Munroe, Jr., USN.

The Annapolis Tercentenary Stamp issued May 23, 1949. From the author's collection. First day of issue sales for the stamp were 910,623. All in all, 107,340,000 of them were eventually issued. The stamp measured .84-by-1.44 inches. The U.S. Naval Academy Museum possesses the original watercolor on paper (21-by-34 inches), which Morgan created for its design. He gifted it to the museum in 1951.

Capt. Munroe was born in Annapolis in 1904. He graduated

from the Naval Academy in 1925, and was President of the Annapolis Stamp Club in 1949. The club held a contest to choose a design for the Tercentenary stamp's cachet. Barbara Droll, a St. Mary's High School student, won the contest, and the Commission, and several other companies created additional cachets.

Franklin Townsend Morgan completed the committee's roster. Born in 1883 in Brooklyn, New York, Morgan studied at the Pratt Institute and the Art Students' League in that state. He started printmaking in 1912, and his portfolio included prints of the American West, New England, the Atlantic Seaboard, Florida, and the West Indies.

By the 1930s, Morgan had earned a sound reputation as an artist. He received awards including the first prize medal of the Philadelphia Sketch Club, two honorable mentions from the Print Club of Philadelphia, and an honorable mention from that city's Arts Alliance. He also received the J. Frederick Talcott prize at the Society of American Etchers in New York in 1935.

From that year until 1941, Morgan worked with the WPA (Works Progress Administration) Artists in the Florida Keys. The Depression had devastated Key West. This prompted the city and Monroe County to seek help from Florida Governor David Sholtz in 1934. They asked him to appoint Julius Stone, Florida's administrator for FERA (the Federal Emergency Relief Administration), to assess the problem.

Mr. Stone reached a swift conclusion; he said that the only way to save Key West would be to make it an attractive tourist destination. Therefore, Public Works of Art Project artists came from across the country to beautify it and to promote tourism in 1934. They painted murals, designed monuments, staged theater shows, formed an art gallery, and drew and painted postcards and pictures that were sent nationwide to attract vacationers.

Their efforts, in combination with other improvements, worked. Key West attracted roughly 40,000 tourists that winter, FERA's programs phased out that summer, and the WPA took over many of its ongoing projects. It was at that time that Morgan arrived. President Franklin D. Roosevelt appointed him as the second director of the Key West artist's group working under the WPA. He collaborated with the other artists on several projects, and also taught printmaking.

Morgan stayed in Key West after the WPA program ended. He became the second Art Director of the Key West Art Society, the precursor to the Key West Art and Historical Society. He also helped to found the Key West Art Center, which sold and exhibited his and other artists' creations.

By the late 1940s, Morgan had received national acclaim for his work. He moved to Annapolis at that point, and became Artist-in-Residence at St. John's College in 1948: the year that "two of the so-called Fine Arts [music and art]" came to the school.[3]

Morgan was the most important member of the stamp design committee. He created its image based on input from the other members and Postmaster Strohm. At first, the group considered these options: an early ship carrying Puritans, the

Liberty Tree with settlers and Native Americans, an early map of Annapolis, the city's historic State House, the Maryland State Flag and Seal, and a skyline of Annapolis showing its prominent steeples, cupolas, and towers.

The committee agreed on a final design in early March. It featured a map of the Annapolis harbor and Severn River in 1649 and was painted a brilliant aquamarine. Morgan consulted several historic maps of the Virginia, Maryland, Severn, and Chesapeake areas to develop his map. The stamp also showed a ship carrying Puritan settlers to Greenbury Point, and symbols such as a compass rose, a northeast wind blowing the ship, the Maryland State Seal, trees, hills, a rockfish, and a blue crab.[4]

At about the time the committee agreed on a design, Sasscer sent its members a telegram. On March 3, he notified them that the House Committee had reported favorably on his stamp bill.

The House passed the bill unanimously on March 7. Four days later, the committee's members visited the U.S. Post Office Department in Washington, D.C. They shared their design with two officials: the Superintendent of the Division of Stamps, and the Chief Engraver of the Bureau of Printing and Engraving, and it was approved.

Morgan had saved the committee crucial time. He was familiar with the department's requirements, and the engraving process. Therefore, it was able to approve and accept his image with but few changes. Several of the changes involved the stamp's wording. For instance, the abbreviation "Md." was added after the word "Annapolis" to avoid confusion with Annapolis, Missouri.

President Truman signed a joint Congressional resolution regarding the stamp on March 16. Postmaster General Jesse Donaldson officially announced the stamp's design public shortly thereafter. And, at that point, stamp enthusiasts began ordering first-day covers. Those who wanted one could send up to ten self-addressed envelopes to Postmaster Strohm, along with remittance to cover the cost of the stamps to be affixed. By early May, the Annapolis Post Office had received over 200,000 such orders from across the globe. By mid-May, this figure had soared to over 450,000.

The stamp was finally issued on May 23. The day was called "Maryland State Day," and launched Tercentenary Week in Annapolis. The city's Post Office opened at 7 A.M. However, a swarm of stamp collectors had lined its walkway long before then. So had a number of regional stamp dealers, who had set up stands to sell their goods.

A presentation ceremony occurred near the Post Office, on the South East Portico of the State House, at 10 A.M. The Naval Academy band entertained the crowd that had gathered for the event, which included the city's former postmaster, eighty-two-year-old Joseph Armstrong; Joseph Lawler, the Third Assistant Postmaster General; Maryland Governor William Preston Lane, Jr.; Tercentenary Commission and Stamp Design Committee members, and about 300 other citizens.

The band finished at 11 A.M., at which point Postmaster Strohm welcomed the crowd. Mr. Lawler then gave a brief speech and presented an album of the stamps to Morgan, Col. Thomson, Capt. Munroe, and others.

After the ceremony, the Commission held a luncheon at Carvel Hall hotel for 200 distinguished guests. Each guest received a copy of an original sketch by Morgan, and a Tercentary stamp, courtesy of the hotel. Among those present were John Kieffer, the President of St. John's College; William U. McCready, Mayor of Annapolis; Thomas D'Alessandro, Mayor of Baltimore; Jesse A. Wallace on behalf of the Naval Academy's Superintendent, Rear Admiral James Holloway, Jr.; and the Postmasters of Annapolis, Baltimore, and Washington. Governor Lane, who also attended, praised Annapolis as "probably the best preserved of the colonial cities of America."[5]

Two days after the stamp was issued, "Organizations Day" occurred in town. This day was also part of Tercentenary Week, and it featured a festive parade. Civic, fraternal, and military groups marched or rode in floats from Amos Garrett Boulevard to West Street, to Church Circle, down Main Street, around Market Space, up Randall Street, up King George Street, along College Avenue, around Church Circle, back to West Street, and finally, back to the assembling point.

Franklin Townsend Morgan at his Annapolis studio. Courtesy of St. John's College Archives SJC-P-0973.

Three judges watched the parade including Judge Benjamin Michaelson of the Anne Arundel County Circuit Court. They conversed and chose their favorite entries. Appropriately, they gave the Grand Prize for Best Entry to the Employees of the Annapolis Post Office.[6]

Ogle Hall's Many Owners

Other special events occurred on "Organizations Day" in Annapolis. For instance, the League of American Pen Women held an open house at Ogle Hall, at 247 King George Street. This story celebrates this historic building, and its many owners.

Annapolis, Maryland: February 5, 1776

With her home in chaos and workmen throughout, Mrs. Benjamin (Henrietta) Ogle retreated upstairs to write to her mother-in-law in London. She had so much to share about life in Annapolis—the only question was, where to begin?

Of course she had to convey the sense of imminent danger. Rumors that a Man of War was coming to destroy Annapolis had many on edge. Yet this potential threat did breathe life into what she called a "vastly dull" town. From a lack of "balls and bouts" to very "little dining and supping out" local entertainment was scant at best. Goods were also terribly "scarce and high priced," she complained.[1]

Despite these inconveniences, the Ogles had stayed in town for the winter—perhaps to oversee their home's construction. Ah yes, she mustn't forget to mention this seemingly endless effort! Nevertheless, the work was almost done, and Mrs. Ogle worried that the ship would destroy her house if it came. As she wrote,

"Miserably afraid of a Man of War coming here and destroying our Town. It would be horrid provoking to have our House beat down now we have almost finished it."[2]

Fortunately her fear did not come to pass. And today, over two centuries later, her residence at the corner of King George and Tabernacle Streets (now College Avenue) stands intact as Alumni House, or Ogle Hall—a term that wasn't officially used until 1923.

Contrary to what its name suggests, the Ogles were not the building's first owners. Dr. William Stephenson, an Annapolis surgeon, built the house in 1739, yet died before its completion in 1742. Five years later, his widow leased it to Samuel Ogle, the first of three Maryland Governors to live there.

Ogle Hall viewed from King George Street. Photograph by George Smyth, 2005.

Samuel was nearly three decades older than his wife, Anne, who outlived him by many years. When he died, Anne's brother Benjamin Tasker bought the house for 70 tons of Baltimore pig iron. He in turn sold it to Anne in 1760.

Ogle Hall changed hands again in 1773, when Anne sold the property to her son, Benjamin Ogle, who governed Maryland from 1798–1801. George Washington was among Benjamin's esteemed guests and dined with him at his house on October 1, 1773.

Meanwhile, new Georgian mansions rivaling Ogle Hall's grandeur were emerging nearby. The William Paca House (1765), Chase-Lloyd House (1769), and Hammond-Harwood House (1774) had all raised the bar for elegant living standards in town. Not to be outshined by their neighbors, Benjamin and Henrietta made several minor home improvements.

In 1774, they erected an outdoor, 10-foot high, brick "party wall" to separate their land from the adjacent Lloyd property. They also added a grand staircase, second story master chamber, and semi-octagonal ballroom wing with an ornate cornice inside the building. This construction had clear drawbacks as Henrietta confided to her mother-in-law in 1776,

"Have not yet seen the Miss Anderson's—our House hear being in Confusion and litter with Workmen and most of our furniture sent to Bell Air has prevented me from inviting them over . . . "[3]

Although Benjamin Ogle died in 1809, Henrietta remained there until her death in 1815. Next, James Steele purchased the property; his son, Henry, married Francis Scott Key's daughter, Maria. The Steele family owned Ogle Hall until Sally Scott Murray Lloyd purchased it in 1839. Eight years later, she sold it to Thomas Pratt, the third Governor of Maryland to reside there, who owned the property until 1867. And it is there that Ogle Hall's rich Naval heritage begins.

Ogle Hall has enjoyed a continuous association with the U.S. Navy for nearly 150 years. Judge John Mason of the Maryland Court of Appeals forged this tie when he leased it from Mr. Pratt in 1865 and purchased it 1867.

Mason's two daughters, Bettie and Louisa, were probably overjoyed when they moved to Ogle Hall. What more could two young, single girls ask for than to live paces from the Naval Academy and its students?

Not surprisingly, both girls married Naval officers in 1873—the year of their father's death. Bettie, the youngest, married Theodoric Porter, son of Admiral David Dixon Porter. Sadly, she saw little of her husband who spent twenty of his forty-three year military career at sea. During his absence she lived with their children at Ogle Hall, which she received after her mother's death in 1899. Bettie lived there until her own passing in 1909, leaving behind two heirs: Marguerite Cusachs and Rosalie Van Ness.

Like her mother, Marguerite married a Navy man: Carlos Cusachs, who taught French and Spanish at the Naval Academy. Starting in 1914, she and Rosalie co-owned Ogle Hall, until Rosalie transferred her portion to Marguerite in 1923. Marguerite then lived there until 1944, when she sold it to the U.S. Naval

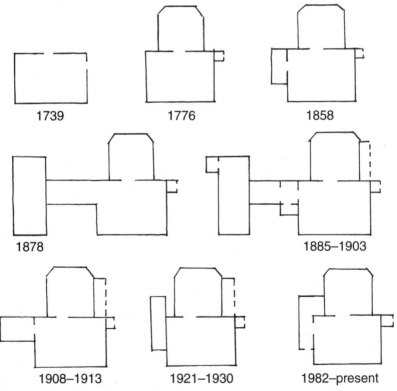

How Ogle Hall's form has evolved from 1739–2005. Illustrations by the author.

Academy Alumni Association. The property was dedicated as "Alumni House" during the Naval Academy Centennial celebration the following October.

Since then, the Association has restored Ogle Hall to reflect its original colonial grandeur. Even so, Benjamin and Henrietta Ogle might not recognize the building, as it has evolved steadily since the 1700s. Initially, the property contained a stable, its backyard had a courtyard with a brick kitchen, and it's possible that the front yard was once a garden.

Guests also entered Ogle Hall through a "jib door" in colonial-era Annapolis. The jib door, which can be used as a door or window, is located in the larger of Ogle Hall's two entertainment rooms that face King George Street.

Ogle Hall changed considerably in the 19th century. By 1858, a small addition had been made to its southeast side. At about that time, the building was also painted white. By 1878 a wing had been added to the property's smaller unit, and within a decade, its northwest side received a porch, which was removed in the 1940s.

Ogle Hall witnessed extensive changes in the 20th century as well, including the addition of a balcony. The building was restored in the 1930s, and again after a fire struck in July 1971, which damaged the stair hall and northeast corner. It received its red wood fence eight years later.

Today, Ogle Hall's décor enhances its appearance and historic significance. Antiques such as the Hepplewhite sideboard, which belonged to the first Secretary of the Navy, grace its entrance foyer. Paintings of Naval ships and portraits of figures including Commander Franklin Buchanan also offer lessons in American Naval history.[4]

How Maryland Considered Taxing
Bachelors to Fund Education

Ogle Hall is just across the street from St. John's College campus, including McDowell Hall. This story explores how Maryland considered taxing bachelors to fund this building's completion (among other things) in the 18th and 19th centuries.

Bachelorhood has always had benefits. Yet it's also had drawbacks—including in colonial Maryland, where the legislature considered taxing bachelors to help fund a college for the province. Maryland started taxing its bachelors in 1756, when the General Assembly passed a "Supply Act for His Majesty's Service." The act appropriated 40,000 pounds to fund new troops, arms, ammunition, a fort on Maryland's western frontier, and other items for the

"Defence and Security of this Province." While the Loan Office provided part of this sum, new bills of credit were issued to raise about 34,000 pounds.[1]

To repay or "sink" these bills by 1763, legislators proposed a wave of new or increased taxes. Among the taxables were pitch, tar, Negroes, and writs; as well as land, liquor, horses, billiard tables, and bachelors. Taxing bachelors was a last minute idea; the Lower House proposed it only after the original act's provision, to levy a 5-shilling tax on newly issued marriage licenses, was defeated by a vote of twenty-eight to nineteen.[2]

Bachelors age twenty-five or older, whose estates were worth at least 100 pounds, had to pay the tax. And, what each paid depended on the assessed value of his estate; he paid 5 shillings if it was worth between 100 and 300 pounds, and 20 shillings if it was worth over 300 pounds.[3]

Lawmakers gave two reasons why "the Rank of Men called Batchelors" should be taxed. First, unlike married men, they could "contribute a larger Tax towards the Support of the Community" since they were not "burthened with the Charge and Expence that usually attends a Matrimonial Condition." They were also less beneficial to Maryland's overall health and development. As the act declared, "Forasmuch as Divine Institutions ought to be strictly observed in every well-regulated Government, and as that in Regard to the entering into the holy Estate of Matrimony may tend to the more orderly Propagation of Mankind, it ought, not only in a religious, but political View, to be promoted and the continuing in a State of Celibacy discountenanced, especially in every Infant Country."[4]

The act became law in May and offered instructions for levying the tax. Ideally, this is what would happen: First, a rector from each parish would make a list of his parishioners who were eligible to pay it. Next, he would give the list to his parish's Register in July. At that point, anyone who thought that his age or estate had been misjudged could dispute the matter.[5]

Once these disputes were resolved, the Register would forward two copies of the list. He would send one to his county's sheriff, who in turn, would submit a copy to the Loan Office; he would send the other to his county's Collector of Excise, who would collect the taxes by August 10. The Collector could seize the "goods and chattels" of anyone who refused to pay and had to deliver the taxes to the Loan Office by September 29, keeping "5 Pounds per Cent" of the proceeds as his salary.[6]

Unfortunately, levying the new tax was easier said than done. Rectors failed to make and deliver their lists, bachelors failed to pay the tax, collectors failed to collect it, and so forth. In response, the Assembly appointed a series of committees to investigate this problem, Loan Office accounts, and other matters in the 1750s–'60s.

The committees' findings were shocking. In 1758, for instance, one found that many had violated the law including James Dickson, Frederick County's Collector. He had "returned no . . . Money on Account of the Batchellor's Tax for the Year 1757 or rendered any List of Batchellors for that

Year."[7] Dickson wasn't alone. Over the next few years, officials from Charles, Calvert, Cecil, Kent, Talbot, Anne Arundel, and Baltimore Counties, among others, all failed to fulfill their duties.

Yet this did not stop legislators from levying another tax on bachelors, one to help establish an institution for higher learning in Annapolis. In 1761, the Assembly appointed a committee to report what funds would be necessary "for Erecting and Establishing a College within this Province."[8] Its members reached two conclusions. First, it would cost about 2,500 pounds to finish the school's grounds, including the building that was begun in 1744 as Governor Thomas Bladen's official residence. Its "outhouses, gardens, and yards" also had

In 1763, Maryland's General Assembly voted to tax bachelors to fund the "annual Expence" of a proposed college. It voted to use money from the Loan Office to finish the college's grounds including the building that began in 1744 as Governor Thomas Bladen's official residence. Nothing was done to carry out the proposal, however, and work did on the building didn't resume until 1786, two years after St. John's College was chartered. The building was later named McDowell Hall, after John McDowell, the college's first principal. Illustration by the author.

to be built or finished, and furnishings were needed for its kitchen, dining room, and rooms belonging to its masters, students, and servants. To raise this sum, legislators proposed selling "all the Lands, Goods, and Chattels, belonging to the Free-School in the several Counties within this Province."[9] The committee also concluded that the "annual Expences" for the college, including the president's salary, and that of its masters, and servants, would total 1510 pounds. To cover this cost, legislators proposed taxing items such as "batchelors, wheel-carriages, Negroes, and Irish Papist Servants."[10]

The Assembly adjourned before legislators could take final action on the bill; they made two choices when it finally resurfaced in 1763. They voted to use money from the Loan Office to finish the college's grounds, and to fund the "annual Expence of Supporting" it through a graduated tax on bachelors among other means.[11]

This was the last time the General Assembly voted to tax Maryland's bachelors, although it considered doing so in the 19th century. In December 1806, it considered "An act to tax bachelors and bank stock for the education of poor children in the several counties in this state." The bill was read for "the first time and ordered to lie on the table."[12] However, legislators didn't consider it again until 1808. At that point, the House rejected this suggested amendment to it: "That all bachelors or unmarried male persons, over the age of thirty years, shall be fined twenty dollars annually, to be paid and applied agreeably to the provisions of this act."[13]

The Assembly also considered taxing bachelors to relieve the state's debt in 1842. On February 14, a delegate from Harford motioned that "The committee on Ways and Means be instructed to inquire into the propriety of reporting a bill laying a tax on bachelors, to aid in paying the debts of the state." House members then offered several amusing amendments to the introductory bill. One suggested using the tax revenue "to support indigent old maids," rather than to relieve the state's debt. Another proposed making it apply only to "old" bachelors. Legislators eventually defeated the bill—it would be interesting to know how many who voted against it were bachelors.[14]

Bygone Naval Academy Dating Traditions

Walter "Lou" Gerich was happy being a bachelor—until he saw Mignon "Non" Jenkins. This is the story of how they met, courted, and married during a bygone era of dating at the Naval Academy.

Lou will never forget the first time he saw Non. It was January 1942, and the stunning blond in an orchid sweater caught his eye as soon as he entered the hop at Carvel Hall hotel. The handsome midshipman told his friend "that's the girl I'm going to marry," mustered his courage, and crossed the dance floor to meet her.

He introduced himself, and the rest is history. The couple married two days Lou graduated from the Academy in 1944. Yet spending time together before then was difficult. "I had to walk two paces behind her or else I'd get put on report," he said. Non also had to hide him in her father's car to sneak him off the Yard, since midshipmen couldn't ride in private automobiles at the time. And once, Lou even skated across the frozen Severn River to see his favorite "drag."

Non didn't mind being called a drag because the word had a different meaning then, In 1942, Kendall Banning defined the term as "a young woman guest of a midshipman," in his book *Annapolis Today*.[1] Chapter 12 of the book, "What Every Drag Should Know," offers an amusing glimpse into dating protocol at the Academy at the time.

Winning a midshipman's heart was hard work for a girl in the 1940s. According to Banning, it took a lot in order to become his OAO ("One-And-Only," and not just "One-Among-Others"). To simplify matters, he compiled this list of "Don'ts for Drags" with help from the Brigade of Midshipmen:

1. Don't keep a midshipman waiting. Liberty hours are too precious to waste;
2. Don't chew gum in public. The midshipmen don't like it—and besides, the regulations forbid them to chew it themselves;
3. Don't suggest anything that cuts into your host's bankroll. He's putting up the best show he can on the little money Uncle Sam lets him have;
4. Don't try to induce your host to violate any regulation. Remember that it is he and not you who pays the penalty;
5. Don't smoke in the Yard, on the street or on the dance floor. Special compartments are set aside for cigarette addicts;
6. Don't bring liquor into the Yard and don't offer your host any at any time. Serving drinks to midshipmen is a felony in Annapolis, and no reputable restaurant will serve it to anyone at a table at which a midshipman is seated;
7. Don't indulge in loud actions or in daring clothing. Drags have been ruled off the dance floor for both offenses—and your host is accountable for your conduct;
8. Don't wear "bunny wraps"—meaning any kind of white fur. The hairs come off and mess up the blue uniforms;
9. Don't suggest that your host take you to places. If he is allowed to take you to them, he will ask you himself—if he wants to;
10. Don't hold hands in public. Unless they are your own; and

11. Never, never commit the unpardonable sin of "late dating" with a St. Johnny . . . after your midshipman host has been required to report back to Bancroft Hall. If a blacklist of drags is ever started, double-daters will head it.[2]

To complement this list of "Don'ts," Banning offered helpful tips for female guests such as packing light when visiting the Yard. He advised them to leave all riding, canoeing, and swimming costumes at home "no matter now well they set off their charms."

Banning also advised young women about their temperament. He said that a drag should be "merry and uncomplaining, adapt herself to conditions and to the rules and regulations as she finds them," and "find them good!"

However, a drag had to more than optimistic and flexible. Looks were also important, even though Banning advised midshipmen to "regard beautiful girls with a lot of suspicion" since they were often spoiled. Intelligence mattered as well. But, according to Banning, it was only a plus if a drag kept her "mental attainments and esthetic tastes under restraint," and gave "her attention to the pleasures immediately at hand."

A drag's career and income also counted—to a degree. Most of the midshipmen who Banning surveyed said that what a girl did during the week made

From left to right: Mr. and Mrs. Walter (Mignon) Gerich, and Jim Cremins in San Francisco, at Fisherman's Wharf, at Joe DiMaggio's Yacht Club, 1945. Courtesy of Mr. and Mrs. Walter (Mignon) Gerich.

Midshipman hop, 1938. Courtesy of Special Collections & Archives Division, Nimitz Library, U.S. Naval Academy.

little to no difference. However, a working girl, "coed," or debutante, had a "slight edge over the high school lass."[3]

A Brigade publication called *The Log*, classified drags into nine types in 1938. Three of the types were Clinging Vines, Athletic Girls, and Natural Girls. Clinging Vines were "blonde, dainty and couldn't open doors or light cigarettes." They could be counted on to "henpeck" their husbands for the rest of their lives. *The Log* advised midshipmen to treat such girls "rough in the true style of the caveman" if they wished to woo them successfully.

The Log gave a slightly more favorable account Athletic Girls. It praised them as being "tall, tanned and muscular, healthy, clear-eyed and candid." However, it criticized them for "leaning over bars . . . being too mannish . . . and beating men in sports." It also warned any midshipman who pursued an Athletic Girl that he would probably have to "stay at home with baby while she's out playing golf" if they married.[4]

Midshipmen found Natural Girls to be the most appealing according to Banning. They were "naïve, truthful, modest, sincere, and straightforward;" they were also "of medium height," and most had "brown hair, innocent-looking features, and bright teeth."

Non was—and still is—a Natural Girl, according to Lou.[5] The couple celebrated their fiftieth wedding anniversary in 1994. And, that year, Lou wrote
this entry about their time together, for his Class's fiftieth year reunion book:

"Life goes on pretty much as before. Still associated with the same European trading group, now twenty-two years . . . We split our time between here,
Canada and Europe, but home is still Old Annapolis Road [Baltimore Annapolis Boulevard] . . . On June 9, Mignon and I will celebrate our 50th wedding
anniversary. Will probably go somewhere and hide, and start all over again. It's
been that good."[6]

The Naval Academy's Other Golf Course

The Gerichs built their home on "Old Annapolis Road" in 1962. It's a minute's
walk from where Mignon was raised, and a minute's drive from the U.S. Naval
Academy Golf Course. This chapter celebrates the history of that course and of
the one it replaced.

The Naval Academy's new golf course was astir in June 1916, as players prepared for one of its first tournaments. The contest would start July 3 and have
three parts: a co-ed club championship, and separate match play events for men
and women.[1] Some bought new balls for the occasion, others cleaned their brass-
ies and mashies, and everyone practiced their drives or tee shots. These shots
would be crucial—since the course required players to hit across Route 450.

This is just one of many surprising facts about the Academy's golf course
that opened in 1916. That it was built then makes sense, given trends in golf at
the time. The sport's popularity was soaring nationwide, and the PGA (Professional Golfers' Association of America) had just formed.

On January 17, 1916, amateur and professional golfers gathered in New
York City. They met at the Taplow Club, where they discussed forming a na-
tional group to raise awareness about the sport. By spring, the group had a for-
mal constitution and, on April 10, eighty-two charter members established the
PGA. Seven months later, the Association's first championship occurred at
New York's Siwanoy Country Club.[2]

Golf was also becoming popular among Annapolis-area military officials.
Consider what happened in 1913 for instance. The Admirals' Golf Cup Association formed that year, thanks to Colonel Robert Means Thompson
(USNA 1868). In 1912, Col. Thompson had presented a cup to be played for
at a tournament at Maryland's Chevy Chase Country Club. Only members of

that club who had graduated from the Academy before September 1, 1870, were eligible to play.

The tournament was a success. A second one occurred in 1913, and players chose to make it an annual tradition at a luncheon following the event. As the *Army and Navy Journal* reported, "It was proposed by Capt. John C. Wilson and unanimously accepted that an association be formed to bring together annually the 'Old Timers' at the Chevy Chase Club." They called it the Admiral's Golf Cup Association and chose Col. Thompson as its Vice President.[3]

Shortly thereafter, Army and Navy officials proposed building an Army and Navy Golf Club in Washington, D.C. Washington already had many fine golf clubs; however, officials insisted that " . . . there should be an Army and Navy Club, which would be managed to suit the conveniences of officers stationed at the Capitol."[4]

Officials cited golf's health benefits to justify their proposal. As the *Army and Navy Journal* noted, "Golf is now being recognized in the Service as one of the best methods of keeping in good physical condition and at no place is there as much need of a golf club as at Washington." Army officials argued that a club would be "almost an absolute necessity" if the "annual test ride" (a system that was used to keep officers in "physical condition") was abandoned. Their Navy

Apartment Houses at the Naval Academy with golf holes, 1939. Courtesy of Special Collections & Archives Division, Nimitz Library, U.S. Naval Academy.

counterparts stressed the "need of a service golf course to keep them in condition for their required walk."[5]

Perhaps golf's health benefits influenced the Academy's choice to build a golf club. It stood on the Severn River's south bank and was a humble course, according to Cary Meredith. This native Annapolitan and avid golfer recalled that, "The original links had just nine holes with sand greens."[6]

The first hole finished at the bottom of the hill where Perry Circle Apartments now stand. Number 2 required a blind 60-yard straight uphill shot. Golfers rang a bell once they finished this hole to let those behind them know it was safe to hit, since they couldn't see the green from the tee. From there, the course progressed counterclockwise towards West Annapolis, and the Wardour community, where it bordered the old Washington, Baltimore & Annapolis Railroad tracks.

Next, Number 7, a par 5, ran parallel to the Academy's Post Graduate School, housed in Halligan Hall. This long hole began near today's water tower, continued over the current swimming pool, and finished at a blind green.

Numbers 8 and 9 were the course's signature—and most hazardous—holes. They played across Route 450 and back, and were Numbers 1 and 2 until the early 1920s. On Number 8, players hit their tee shots across the road, and their second shots to a green by the Academy's old seawall near the hospital. The ninth hole required players to drive short of the road and hit their approach shots to a green by the clubhouse. By about 1927 however, increased traffic forced the Academy to move these holes north of the road. The new Number 8 dipped to the base of the Severn River Bridge, and Number 9 looped back to the clubhouse.

F. Marion Lazenby's "regular golf foursome." Pictured from left to right are Elmer Martin Jackson, Jr., Dr. Claude Handy, Dr. Robert Welch, and Mr. Lazenby. Courtesy of Capt. Richard D. Lazenby, USN (Ret.).

Shortly after the holes moved, the club's membership began to change. Only military personnel could belong to it at first. However, the Academy invited an initial group of seven civilians to join in the 1930s. The group included F. Marion Lazenby, Dr. Claude Handy, Elmer Jackson, Jr., and Dr. Robert Welch: a regular foursome that came to the course in rain or shine. They played golf several times per week in good weather and played cards inside the clubhouse if conditions were foul. Gin rummy was the game of choice if four men were present. Yet if another joined in—as the club's golf professional often did—they played a game called "Ship, Captain, and Crew."[7]

Captain Dan Hunt, USN (Ret.), who captained the Academy's golf team in 1942, recalled the clubhouse at the time. "It was a modest wood clubhouse, and a kind gentleman by the name of Brown worked there," he said.[8] He and Mr. Lazenby's son, Captain Richard Lazenby, USN (Ret.), remember the Academy's first golf club well. They also remember when it moved to Greenbury Point, across the Severn River, in the 1940s.

Golf initially came to Greenbury Point in 1928: the year that the Point's longtime occupant, the Remsen Brothers Dairy Farm, folded. The *Evening Capital* had praised the farm in this passage dated 1908:

> Pure milk means good health and longevity of life, and that hundreds of the citizens of Annapolis get it from the Greenberry Point Dairy is shown by their healthy appearance and robust constitutions. No man in this section of Maryland has paid closer attention to procuring pure milk than has Mr. Charles E. Remsen, proprietor of this splendid dairy, which is pleasantly located three miles from Annapolis. It is from here that the United States Naval Academy receives its supply. The milk of ninety cows is required for the daily consumption of the midshipmen, and Uncle Sam is well aware that when his "babies" are being supplied from this dairy they are receiving pure and wholesome milk. The cows of Greenberry Point Farm Dairy are inspected by government officials and no unhealthy milkers are allowed to remain in the herd. The stables are splendid structures, fitted with every modern convenience for the handling, care and health of the finest blooded stock . . . Mr. Remsen is justly proud of his place, and well he should be, for nothing can compare with it in this section.[9]

Two Washington lawyers took advantage of the dairy's closure: Fred Rhodes and Judge William Richardson. One was a zealous golfer, the other had a keen eye for real estate, and both had an ambitious plan for the foreclosed property. They bought 150 acres of it to create "The Greenbury Point Yacht and Country Club." They thought that the Point would be ideal for such a posh facility; its surrounding waters, including deep Mill Creek, would attract yachters, and even Mr. Rhodes (the non-golfer) recognized the land's potential as a golf course. They also planned to build waterfront homes and a public recreation area onsite.

As the entrepreneurs refined their vision, a board of trustees ensured the project's financial backing. Five well-to-do men comprised the board including Harvey Cox, special assistant to the U.S. Attorney General; William King, President of the W. H. West Company of Washington; Douglas Murnham, President of the D. M. Burnham Company; A. Houghton, an insurance broker and leading local golfer; and George See of the District National Bank of Washington.

Rhodes and Richardson presented their plan to the local Chamber of Commerce, at Carvel Hall, on January 19, 1928. So did another group of developers: those who were rebuilding Annapolis Roads. The *Evening Capital* claimed that this golf course, once called Belmont, would "offer those interested in the game the best golf within six minutes' ride of the city." Yet Greenbury Point would be equally attractive with its 18-hole course, tennis courts, saltwater bathing pool, boathouse, pier, recreation center, and clubhouse, which would have a locker room, ballroom, dining room, and grand foyer. Both presentations impressed the Chamber, and it promised to "lend all possible cooperation" to them.[10]

Progress was well under way at Greenbury Point by late January 1928. Most of the land had been cleared to make way for its new golf course designed by Harry Collis. Collis was a renowned golf course architect, contractor, and golf professional based in Chicago. He practiced during the "Golden Age" of golf course design, which spanned from about 1910–37, and was a master of his craft. For instance, he is credited with renovating nine holes and adding 600 yards to Medinah Country Club's famous Number 3 Course. *Golf Digest* chose Medinah, originally designed by Tom Bendelow, as a charter member of "America's 100 Greatest Golf Courses" in 1966.

Richardson was responsible for bringing Collis and his talents to Annapolis. He was a member of Manor Country Club, where Collis was creating the club's "Woods Nine" in 1928. His work there impressed Richardson and others who, in response, awarded him the contract for Greenbury Point. Collis finished his work at Manor, and then came to Annapolis with laborers such as "Pete" Linton and "Babe" Enthswiler.[11]

The course that they built at the Point was different from the site's current course. It stood on the right side of the road leading to the Point's Naval Radio Station. The front nine was flat and led directly to the old towers; in contrast, the back nine was hilly and stood where the front nine is today.

Mr. Rhodes's son, Fred Rhodes, tended the course during its early, or what he called "primitive days." Workers hand-mowed the greens, a team of horses mowed the rough with a sickle-bar mower, and a gang mower kept the fairways in good condition. He recalled that, "We were always behind in cutting the rough and so the poor golfer often found himself with a shot out of an area which must have looked like a hay field."[12]

Mr. Rhodes made it clear that the "real story" of maintaining the course must include the men who worked there, who lived in the Mulberry Hill community. They were from the Little and Stansbury families and were faithful stewards of the course. Ed Little was "the best and most careful green mower," Jim Little was the caddy who used to carry bags that were "as big as he was," and Perry Stansbury, whose father was "the patriarch of the Mulberry Hill folk,"

Hole Numbers 8 and 9 at the U.S. Naval Academy Golf Course with the course's clubhouse and Chesapeake Bay Bridge in the background. Photograph by Roger Doyel, 2005.

had immense strength. When recalling Perry's strength Mr. Rhodes wrote, "Perry was perhaps the strongest man I've ever known . . . Once in March we were planting some fruit trees . . . Because of the muddy ground we could not get the truck very close to the holes. Perry solved the problem by taking each of these fairly good-sized trees (with trunks of two to three inches) on his shoulder and wading to each hold through mud that came halfway up his knee-high boots—he made the trip six different times."[13]

Mr. Rhodes did more than work at the golf course. He also enjoyed its amenities including its clubhouse, which was built from one of the old Remsen milking barns. Members could eat "delicious meals" in its dining room, dance in the ballroom, or rent the entire facility for $50 per night.[14]

The club offered other forms of leisure. It had a beach, with sand that had been "dug by shovel," and "hauled by truck" from behind the Academy's Rifle Range. Just beyond the beach, there was also a miniature golf course—a game that was "just then becoming the rage."[15]

The Depression forced the Greenbury Point Club to fold shortly after it opened. "People were not joining country clubs and they were not spending much money to do anything including playing golf," according to Mr. Rhodes. It went bankrupt in the 1930s, the course fell into disrepair, and the site was abandoned.[16]

Meanwhile, the Academy's golf club continued to thrive across the Severn River. Golf's popularity was also increasing at the school. It became part of the midshipmen's physical education program in 1928. James Roche was its instructor; he was paid on a per-lesson basis and earned about $350 annually.

Shortly after Roche arrived, the headline "Middie Seniors Must Take Golf Lessons: Practice in Sail Loft" hit the *Evening Capital* (and *Washington Post*). The story claimed that the Academy had "become the first college of importance in the country . . . to make golf a compulsory part of the curriculum." It also quoted school officials as saying "compulsory golf was necessary to the Midshipman's life because it would be an asset . . . after the student's graduation, when he would associate with groups who followed the pastime. The navy develops men not wallflowers . . . For purely social reasons, aside from the physical benefits of the game, Naval officers should know their golf."[17]

The Associated Press had dispatched this story. And, while most of it proved to be false, this part of it was true: during the winter, midshipmen did practice the sport on an "indoor golf course" in the school's sail loft.[18]

The Naval Academy had acquired an informal golf team by 1934, and it earned varsity status in 1935. Its members practiced outdoors at the Navy course, indoors using driving nets in Bancroft Hall, and played most their matches at Sherwood Forest. Bob Williams, a Baltimore-based golf professional who had assisted Roche since 1931, became the team's first coach in 1936.

Two years later, the Navy decided to expand its Radio Station at Greenbury Point. It purchased the old Greenbury Point Club for that reason, and to rejuvenate its golf course. It built an administrative building, power plant, and new radio towers on top of the course's front nine holes and opened the other nine for play in October 1940. William Flynn, a nationally renowned golf course architect, designed the course's final nine in 1942. They cost about $80,000 and opened for play on May 1, 1944.

Much has changed about the course since then, especially its layout. What were initially its first two holes are now Numbers 8 and 9. The front nine's remaining seven holes were located on the north side of Greenbury Point Road where the back nine stands today (except Numbers 13 and 14).

In 1944, the back nine started where the first tee is now, and Numbers 12 and 13 ran past the building behind the current Number 2 green. Number 13, a long par 5 dogleg right, played towards today's gas station. The course changed form in about 1954, when the Naval Radio Station expanded again, and a building was erected behind the current Number 2 green. At that point, the nines were reversed, two new holes were carved from the woods to replace Numbers 12 and 13, and the current Numbers 13 and 14 were added.

Here are just a few other ways that the course has changed. First, caddies no longer work there. Two types of caddies assisted members in the club's early days: Class A Caddies and Class B Novices. The Caddies enjoyed higher wages. They earned $1.25 for carrying one bag for eighteen holes, 75 cents for nine holes, and 50 cents for each hour that they spent chasing players' shots. In contrast, the Novices received $1.00, 60 cents, and 35 cents for the same jobs.

Second, the Academy's golf coach no longer lives onsite. Coach Williams lived there until 1954, in a small concrete house once occupied by the Greenbury

Point Club's greenskeeper. This arrangement was crucial since Williams was more than a coach; he was also the club's professional and groundskeeper. Officials gave two reasons for why it was important for Williams to live there: He had to be on the job early in the morning to supervise watering the greens and had to stay late at night, until after the midshipmen left the course.

Williams (and other men) enjoyed greater privileges at the club than women did—another fact that has changed. Women couldn't play on Saturday afternoons, or Sunday and holiday mornings in the late 1940s. Their status improved slightly in the early 1950s when they were only restricted from teeing off between 12 and 3 P.M. on Saturdays, and before 11 A.M. on Sundays and holidays. The only time women had starting priority was on "Ladies Day" from 9 to 10 A.M.

Despite these restrictions, women paid the same membership initiation fee, monthly dues, and practice and playing and fees as men. Of course, these fees were much less than the club's current rates. Civilians paid about $15,000 to join it in 2005 (military personnel paid less); yet it cost just $10 to do so in 1948. Practicing was also less expensive then. A bucket of balls cost 10 cents, and midshipmen paid half that price. In 2005, however, players paid between $3.50 and $11 per bucket depending on its size.

Greens fees have also soared. While playing eighteen holes cost civilian guests $39 on weekdays and $50 on weekends and holidays (excluding cart fees) in 2005, it cost just $1.50 to play during the week and $2.50 on weekends and holidays in 1946.

Since then, the club's membership has increased dramatically. In 1947, the club had just 206 members comprised of 177 officers, 10 civilians, 2 wives, 3 widows, 10 "specials," and 4 enlisted personnel who paid on a monthly basis. In contrast, about 630 people belonged to the club in 2005 including 200 civilians.

Halligan Hall: Home to Marines and Midshipmen

The Academy's old golf course stood across the road from Halligan Hall. This chapter features this building's history—including why its first occupants, the U.S. Marines, were forced to leave.

The Naval Academy: September 24, 1917

Bill Magruder, nicknamed Doc, never minded a good stretch of the legs. Long walks had been a part—one of the best parts, in fact—of growing up in rural Arkansas. Yet this morning was different. Classes resumed today, it was raining, and the thought of trudging a mile to class was unpleasant. At times like this, Bill wished that he lived with most of the Brigade, at the heart of the Academy, in what his peers called "Bancroft Hotel."[1]

Midshipman Magruder and 200 other members of the Class of 1921 did not live in Bancroft Hall as plebes. Known as "Barracks Plebes," they occupied the old marine barracks, later called Halligan Hall, at the far end of campus.

Like many of the Yard's buildings, Halligan Hall can trace its roots to 1895. That year, the Academy's Board of Visitors condemned the school's facilities. The Board's Committee on Grounds, Buildings, and Sanitary Conditions submitted a chiding report that stated, "It is not going too far to say that many of the present buildings are entirely unworthy for present use and all together inadequate . . ."[2]

The marine barracks was among the "unworthy" buildings. Its condition prompted Congress to allocate funds to raze it, in order to make room for part of Ernest Flagg's "New Naval Academy." This decision outraged the Marine Corps's Commandant, Colonel Commandant Charles Heywood, who wrote the following to Secretary of the Navy John D. Long in 1898:

> In the naval appropriations act approved May 4, 1898, provision was made for the erection of new buildings at the Naval Academy . . . and the removal of old buildings from the desired sites. The plans which were adopted provided for the erection of the new armory on the site of the marine barracks and officers' quarters, thus necessitating the demolishing of these buildings. I was unaware that any such action was contemplated, as no notification was sent to me until after the bill had become a law and the work of tearing down the barracks and quarters was about to be commenced when I received a notice from the Superintendent of the Naval Academy requesting the removal of all marine property and stores from the barracks as they were going to be immediately torn down to make room for the new Armory.[3]

Securing funds to raze the old barracks had been easy; however financing its replacement was difficult—although this task had seemed simple at first. In March 1899, Congress approved $50,000 to build new barracks, $14,000 for two new Junior Officers' quarters, and $9,000 for a Commanding Officer's house on the Yard—with an additional 25 percent increase if they were to be fireproof. Unfortunately, these figures failed to consider an important fact: labor and supply costs had risen since estimates had been made for the buildings in 1898.[4]

This increase caused all of the construction bids to come in well over budget. And, when they did, General Heywood asked lawmakers to increase their appropriations. In 1900, he asked them to approve $95,000 for the barracks, $20,000 for the Junior Officers' Quarters, and $14,000 for the Commanding Officer's house. Unfortunately, they denied his request.[5] Another year passed before they approved enough money to allow construction to begin.

By then, several of Flagg's buildings were already taking shape. The Armory, Boat House, and Bancroft Hall were all under way. Yet the new barracks would look nothing like these buildings—because they had a different architect: Henry Ives Cobb.

Born in 1859 in Brookline, Massachusetts, Cobb attended the Massachusetts Institute of Technology and Harvard University. He also studied at the Écoles des Beaux Arts in Paris, but he was uncomfortable using the Beaux Arts style of architecture so crucial to Flagg's design.

Cobb launched his architectural career in 1881, when he established his practice in Chicago. While there, he won national acclaim for designing a fortress-like mansion called the Potter Castle, the Yerkes Observatory, and buildings at the University of Chicago among others. In 1895, he moved to the East Coast, where his reputation earned him contracts including the Academy's barracks.[6]

While Cobb designed the barracks, the Charles McCaul Company of Philadelphia built it. First Lieutenant Logan Feland, a Marine officer and Civil Engineer stationed at Annapolis, also oversaw the building process.

Unfortunately for Lt. Feland, this process was just as tedious as securing funds had been. Postponements plagued the project once a site was chosen along the County Road. Three factors caused the delays. First, steel manufacturers failed to deliver the steel on time. Good labor was also scarce. Even when the necessary materials arrived, a national construction boom made securing skilled workmen difficult. Finally, winter of 1901 brought miserable weather to Annapolis. This forced the builders to cease all exterior work on the barracks for about sixty days.[7]

The Marine Barracks at Halligan Hall, early 1900s. Courtesy of Special Collections & Archives Division, Nimitz Library, U.S. Naval Academy.

Building the quarters was just as tedious. Cobb had to redraw his plans for them three times in order to stay within his budget, and excessive rain made grading the grounds around them impossible for several months. These and other obstacles forced the builders to finish the quarters, like the barracks, well behind schedule. The marines moved from temporary tents to the barracks on February 21, 1903, and the quarters were ready in November 1904.

Despite their tardy completion, the new buildings were well received. General Heywood had been exactly right in 1902 when he predicted that, "The new marine barracks at Annapolis, when finished, will be a model of its kind, substantially constructed, roomy, light, well ventilated, well heated, and imposing in appearance in keeping with the general improvements going on at the Naval Academy . . . In my opinion, it would not have been possible with the money provided by Congress to construct a more convenient and complete barracks than at Annapolis . . ."[8]

Those who lived there agreed. After being quartered on the USS *Santee*, the USS *Monongahela*, and in tents, the barracks was a welcome change. Its open arcade overlooked the Yard, and it had modern features including a brick bake oven, large refrigerator, electric lighting, and a sewer system. It received further improvements after the marines arrived; its floors were stained and

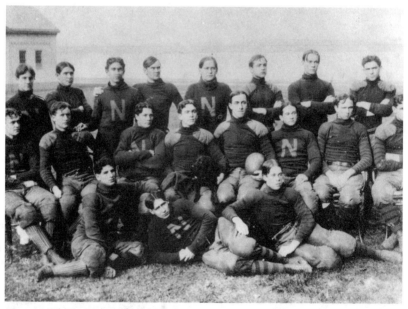

Rear Admiral John Halligan graduated from the Naval Academy in 1898. He captained the school's 1897 football team and is shown above, in the 1898 Lucky Bag, *fifth from the left in the second row. Courtesy of Special Collections & Archives Division, Nimitz Library, U.S. Naval Academy.*

oiled, a piano and "pianola" arrived in September 1903, and a modern water system was installed in 1904.

Inspectors praised the new building. So did the *Evening Capital*, which said, "There is always an air of busy life about the Naval Academy marine barracks. Everything about the place is speck and span."[9]

The barracks provided the marines with more than comfortable quarters; it also offered social opportunities. It hosted social events, such as a series of dances that ended on October 23, 1903. Nearly 300 guests attended this dance in the building's ballroom, which the "hop committee" had decorated with lights, plants, blue and gold bunting, and brass cannons mounted on carriages.

Unfortunately, the marines didn't enjoy their new home for long. World War I brought significant changes to the Academy, including a surge in its student body. Congress authorized the school to increase the strength of the regiment from 1,094 to 1,746 in February 1916. Seven months later, the school opened its academic year with 1,240 midshipmen (over 300 more than in 1915), and over 700 plebes arrived the next year. Their Class was twice as large as the entire regiment had been only eighteen months prior.[10] The newspaper announced their arrival in June:

> The largest class on record will enter the United States Naval Academy this summer, the number being estimated at between 750 and 775. This increase is due to the granting of one extra appointment to each Senator and Representative in Congress . . .[11]

This population increase caused a housing crisis on the Yard—especially since Bancroft Hall could only hold 1,200 students at the time. Plans to enlarge Bancroft were being drawn; however, a short-term housing solution was needed: somewhere sturdy, somewhere sizeable—somewhere like the barracks.

Superintendent Captain Edward W. Eberle recognized this opportunity, seized the structure in May 1917, and officials transformed it to assume its new role. For instance, they partitioned its interior with screens to create a suitable study atmosphere for the midshipmen.

The marines were forced from the barracks at an ironic moment: just prior to Marine Corps Week, which was celebrated nationally from June 10–16. During the week, the Secretary of the Navy stressed the importance of the Corps, and officials tried to recruit 4,000 men to join its ranks.[12] To entice recruits, the government promised to furnish them with necessities including "board and lodging." Where they planned to lodge them in Annapolis is a good question.[13]

Members of the Class of 1921 became the first midshipmen to occupy the barracks when they arrived in 1917. They were called "Barracks Plebes," operated almost as a "separate body of midshipmen," and enjoyed many benefits. They had their own officers, drum and bugle corps, striper organization, "fine mess hall," and views of the Academy's new golf course, located across the

County Road.[14] A Brigade publication called *The Log* even claimed that living there "was pretty much fruit."

But barracks life also had drawbacks, and *The Log* noted them as well. First, the building was a mile from the heart of campus. Second, unlike Bancroft Hall, the barracks lacked "comfortable little individual cells" for sleeping, and "individual showers per apartment." Finally, its walls were "all windows," many of which had to be kept open "even in the coldest weather."[15]

"Barracks Plebes" were also more apt to cause trouble than their peers. They were issued a "Barracks Routine Pamphlet," which outlined the building's policies. It said that their routine should conform as closely as possible to that of Bancroft Hall, and the Yard, and that they were still subject to normal Navy and Academy regulations. However, they often disregarded these regulations. As the 1921 *Lucky Bag* noted,

> Those were the days when a Plebe rated Plebe; the days of Conduct Grades, and liberty for Plebes once every two weeks, if they were very good or very lucky, that is, with the exception of the Barracks Plebes. And while they can't be envied for their lack of plebe training, still they are not to be blamed, because their isolation was due to the lack of space in our Bancroft Hotel, for a class the size of ours had never before been heard of . . .[16]

Midshipmen occupied the barracks until 1919. Yet much to the marines' dismay, neither it, nor the quarters, was returned to them that year. The quarters were turned over permanently to the Navy, and the barracks became home to the Naval Postgraduate School, which reopened there on June 12, 1919. The building was renamed Halligan Hall in 1937 to honor Rear Admiral John Halligan, Jr. Admiral Halligan (USNA 1898) had been among the Postgraduate School's organizers, and promoters, and was its first director.[17]

Over a century has passed since the barracks were built at the Academy. About fifty years have also passed since the Postgraduate School left Halligan Hall in Annapolis for Monterey, California, where appropriately, a building with the same name stands today.

Part 4: Preservation

Henry Sturdy's Colonial Guide Service

Edwin (Ed) Weber wasn't your typical Annapolis history tour guide. He was only twenty years old, greeted tourists at an umbrella stand, and drove their cars to show them the town. This is the story of how he and other local youths held this unique job in the 1930s–'40s.

Born in Newport, Rhode Island, Mr. Weber moved to Annapolis in 1920. He came when his father, a U.S. Navy petty officer, joined the Naval Academy's band as a clarinetist. His family lived in Cedar Park when that area, near today's Navy-Marine Corps Memorial Stadium, was still what he called "wide open, rural country."

That Mr. Weber's father was enlisted—and not an officer—influenced how others treated him. "It was almost 100 percent taboo for enlisted kids to play with officers' sons—strict segregation. It was difficult, but you got used to it," he said.

Mr. Weber walked or biked to many places as a child, including Germantown Elementary School. His trip there took him across the WB&A (Washington, Baltimore & Annapolis) Railroad tracks, where he also went on Navy football days. As he recalled,

"Back then, when the Navy team played its away games, the whole Brigade went too. They went on steam locomotives that came in on a track line that terminated on West Street. And when their whistles blew, kids would jump out of bed and line up along the tracks to see them. It was a big event for us—really something."

Mr. Weber and his peers often rode the WB&A and joked that it stood for Wobble, Bump, & Agony. "The WB&A was quite a ride," he explained. "This electric railway made about twenty-seven stops between Baltimore and Annapolis—but took just twenty-eight minutes! It started like a bat out of hell then slammed on the breaks for the next station. When it got up to 60 miles per hour it swerved from side to side . . . and it didn't have air conditioning."

Mr. Weber graduated from Annapolis High School in 1936, then left for flight school and college in the Midwest. He always came home for summer break, and when he returned in 1939, his friend, Bob Reynolds, shared this exciting news: he was recruiting guides to work for Professor Henry Sturdy's Colonial Guide Service. The guides would have an opportunity to learn about local history and give tours of historic sites in downtown Annapolis, at the Naval Academy, and north of the Severn River Bridge.

Professor Henry Francis Sturdy. Courtesy of Special Collections & Archives Division, Nimitz Library, U.S. Naval Academy.

Mr. Reynolds had joined the guide service in 1937, while working as a movie extra. He was a background extra in two films that were shot partially in Annapolis: *Navy Blue and Gold,* starring James Stewart, Florence Rice, and Lionel Barrymore; and *Annapolis Salute,* with Marsha Hunt, James Ellison, and Van Heflin.

Mr. Weber also appeared in *Annapolis Salute.* "We got $5 a day for being extras and all we had to do was wear a midshipman's uniform. We met in the Armory to shoot a June Ball scene; there were hundreds of nice looking college girls there—a real mob scene," he said.

One day, two of Professor Sturdy's guides recruited Mr. Reynolds near the State House. As he recalled, "They approached me, sent me to Professor Sturdy, and he quizzed me. I knew a lot about local history having attended Cochran and Bryan's [U.S. Naval Academy] prep school . . . and so, he said I'd make a good guide."

Soon, Mr. Reynolds was wearing the service's uniform: a white shirt, orange and black striped necktie, and an orange armband with the word "guide" on it, and setting up umbrella stands on Church Circle to attract customers. "They'd stop for a tour and we drove their cars—since they couldn't maneuver them through the narrow streets. There were about twelve of us, all males," he said.

Mr. Reynolds recalled the warning the Professor gave to his guides at the time. "He warned us not to be like the guides at Gettysburg," he said. "And I knew what he meant. I'd spent a lot of time there and remembered those guides.

They used to jump on the automobile running boards in their uniforms, which scared the tourists!"

Mr. Reynolds transferred from Johns Hopkins University to St. John's College in 1938. The scope of his work for the service increased at that point. He was in charge of recruiting new guides, training them, and even used to "cut class to take tours or special excursions" he said.

One of his recruits, Bill Carter, wasn't familiar with local history. "Bill said he didn't know a damn thing about the Naval Academy. But he made do. He used to sneak up close to me so that his group could hear what I was saying to mine!" Mr. Reynolds said.

He also recruited Mr. Weber, who jumped at the chance. After all, he needed a summer job, was familiar with local history, and knew of Professor Sturdy's fine reputation. Before joining the Naval Academy's faculty in 1917, he had distinguished himself as a teacher at Wilmer & Chew's Naval Academy Preparatory School, and at his alma mater, St. John's College.

Professor Sturdy was more than a history teacher; he was also a student. He was "a good student of colonial Annapolis history," said Orlando (Lanny) Ridout IV, another of his guides. Based on his research, Professor Sturdy co-wrote *Seeing Annapolis and the Naval Academy*, the pocket-sized book on which his tours were based. As Mr. Weber recalled, "We studied the book, he lectured us on it, and then we had to pass an exam before he turned us loose on the public."

Mr. Ridout joined the service in 1938. He was still attending Annapolis High School when two St. John's students, Osborne Duvall and Albert Hodges, recruited him. Like Mr. Reynolds, he recalled setting up stands on Church Circle. "They [the stands] were on the pavement. And we would sit there and wait for a tourist's car to come along and pick us up and take us on a guided tour, driving around Annapolis . . ." he said.[1]

By the time Mr. Weber became a guide, the service had also expanded to include a stand on Maryland Avenue. "We sat on a plot of grass in front of the Hammond-Harwood House [on Maryland Avenue] in beach chairs under a beach umbrella with Maryland's colors. Cars would stop for information about the tours. We used the customers' automobiles to give them tours from memory—one guide per group," he said.

Working for the service had several benefits. First, it enabled the guides to learn more about local history. For some, including Mr. Ridout, history and historic preservation remained an integral part of their lives.

Being a guide also paid well. Tours took about four hours and cost $1 per hour; the guides kept 90 cents per dollar, and the rest went to the Annapolis Chamber of Commerce, which sponsored the tours. "The whole thing was a good deal—especially the wages," Mr. Weber said. "We made 90 cents, plus tips, and clerks at the A&P made just 25 or 50 cents."

Guides even ate for free—if they timed their tours correctly. As Mr. Weber explained, "We tried to extend our morning tours to the lunch hour. That way,

SQUARE DANCE
AT THE
SEVERN BRIDGE Inn
TO THE MUSIC OF NELSON'S AMBASSADORS
TONIGHT 7 TO 12

Seafood of all kinds.   Beer and Mixed Drinks.

Dine And Dance Over The Severn
SEVERN BRIDGE INN
SPECIAL FLOOR SHOW TONIGHT   11:30 AND 1

Dine And Dance Over The Severn
SEVERN BRIDGE INN
HALLOWEEN PARTY
Thursday, October 31st
Prizes given for best and funniest costume
For Your Halloween Night—No Cover Charge

Severn Bridge Inn advertisements from the Evening Capital *(May 5, 1939; October 12, 1940; and October 30, 1940).*

customers would always ask us if we knew any good restaurants. We'd make a suggestion and nine times out of ten they'd buy our meal."

Many guides, including Mr. Weber, suggested the Severn Bridge Inn at the base of the Severn River Bridge. "We tried to stop there. It had a nice restaurant and bar—although its complexion changed in the evening, when everyone came to drink," he said.

The guides also timed their afternoon tours. They tried to end them by 4 P.M. to take advantage of Everett Smith's new bar, the Port Lounge Grill, at 2

Maryland Avenue. "The bar opened at four and we always liked to be the first ones there," Mr. Weber said.

Mr. Weber will never forget the first tour he gave as a guide. It was for a young married couple and, as he recalled, "We were touring the Naval Academy and the next thing I knew, I was walking hand in hand with the lady in the group—and they were newlyweds! I don't know how it happened," he said.

He also recalled touring a University of Pittsburgh history professor. "This was quite an anxious moment. I knew that I had to be very careful about what I said," he said.

Mr. Weber gave his final tour in 1940, one year before Professor Sturdy's service dissolved due to World War II. And, while much about his guidebook is outdated, its "Foreword" still holds true. As Professor Sturdy wrote,

> "It is hoped that the pilgrimage [or tour] through Colonial Annapolis will develop an ever-growing appreciation of the quiet charm and substantiality of the colonial period. Those of us who are resident Annapolitans, but whose constant sojourn in the midst of this colonial setting tends to dull our appreciation, should also make the pilgrimage. . .[2]

Over sixty years have passed since Mr. Reynolds and Mr. Weber gave their final tours for Professor Sturdy in 1940 and 1941. However, they still remember these facts about them: locals rarely took the tours, and most of the tourists who did "wanted to talk about their hometowns rather than listen to the guides."

They also remember that Annapolis was a special place to grow up. "It was fabulous growing up there," Mr. Reynolds said. Mr. Weber agreed. "It was just a great town," he said. "It was charming—not overrun by tourists. We had St. John's and the Naval Academy, and there were cobblestones everywhere . . ."[3]

Rats: Unlikely Preservationists

Professor Sturdy's tour included a stop at the venerable Hammond-Harwood House, which was built in 1744. This vignette reveals how rats have helped to preserve and educate people about the house's history.

Rats: They're ugly, disease-carrying rodents with long tails, and sharp teeth. Yet in Annapolis, they're helping historians to learn more about the Hammond-Harwood House. Here's how.

Rats build nests, and those that used to live in this house were no exception. They built and maintained a sizeable one from the 18th to the mid-20th century, using an array of materials. "The rats weren't picky," said Heater Foster, former Curator of the Hammond-Harwood House. "They were industrious little creatures."

The nest remained a secret until 1994, when architectural conservators discovered it in the house's attic. "The attic had been examined before, but this was the first time its nooks and crannies had been investigated," Ms. Foster said.

The nest is approximately 1 foot long, 1 foot wide, and several inches deep. "It's the house's best surviving artifact," she said. "It's a time capsule of things that were in the home, that were used by people and no longer survive in any shape, context, or form." The nest is also the only link historians have to the 18th-century house, aside from the building itself, since there are no surviving inventories of its residents' belongings, visitors' first hand accounts, or other documentation.

So far, the nest has yielded three main types of artifacts: human hair, paper fragments, and textiles, which are the most common. Rope, architectural fragments, stays for a woman's corset, and leather shoes were also discovered in, or near the nest.

In April 2004, Ms. Foster took the textile artifacts to Williamsburg, Virginia, so that Linda Baumgarten, who she called the "the guru of 18th-

The Hammond-Harwood House on Maryland Avenue, c. 1926–30. Courtesy of the Hammond-Harwood House Association. Photograph by E. H. Pickering.

and 19th-century clothing," could study them. Using a microscope to look at their fibers, Ms. Baumgarten determined that most of the fabrics were silk, cotton, or linen. Wool was also discovered; and although it was more commonly used for men's clothes, the nest contained a large piece from the mid-to-late 19th century that was probably the underlining of a woman's petticoat.

The rats' nest. Courtesy of the Hammond-Harwood House Association.

All together, thirteen distinct fabrics have been identified in the nest. And, while the majority have faded, a few, such as a red and ochre print, remain brilliant. One fabric, dating to about 1830, also appears iridescent. Very few of the fabrics contain patterns. However, there are exceptions. One piece, from the mid-19th century, features a beautiful trellis motif, and another, from the Victorian period, has a beige, yellow, blue, and green floral pattern.

The most important textile discovery to date is a hand-sized piece of cotton dimity. This white, washable, ribbed material was among the most popular fabrics in the late 18th and early 19th centuries. Thomas Jefferson and other affluent citizens decorated their homes with dimity bedcovers, curtains, and case covers. Case covers "were a way of protecting upholstery, which would have been removed for special guests," Ms. Foster said. That dimity was found at the house shows that "whoever was living here at the time was taking style seriously. It helped us learn more about its [the house's] original appearance," she said.

In addition to textiles, the nest has yielded an abundance of paper fragments including newspaper scraps. Researching their typefaces could reveal the general period during which they were printed, and it's possible that some are from the *Maryland Gazette*.

The most interesting paper artifacts identified to date are two large, fairly intact sales receipts. Both bear the marks of rats' teeth. Both are also addressed to Miss Hester Loockerman. Born in 1803, Hester Loockerman (Harwood) was the granddaughter of Jeremiah Townley Chase, who rented the house before purchasing it in 1811 from Ninian Pinkney, Sr. Mr. Chase put the house in trust for his daughter, Frances Townley Chase, who in turn, lived there with her family, including her daughter Hester. Hester moved to Alabama after marrying William Harwood in 1834; however, the couple later returned to Annapolis, where they lived with Hester's mother in her home.

Claude & Hammond of Annapolis issued the first receipt in about 1825. It records Miss Loockerman's purchase of eight books from "Claude & Hammond . . .": "*Abbot's Young Christ*—[illegible], —*of a Good Man, Britain's*

The attic where conservators discovered the rats' nest in 1994. Photograph by David Hartcorn, 2005.

Apology, Pilgrims Progress, Summer on the Locke, —Richmond, —Hymns, and Improvement of Society." Her bill totaled $5.25 and the most expensive book, *Summer on the Locke,* cost 94 cents. Unfortunately, the teeth marks obscure the bill's other details such as the date of sale.

The second receipt records Miss Loockerman's purchase of a guitar from what appears to be the name Josiah Hughes in the 1820s for $15. This receipt is extremely important according to Ms. Foster. It "corroborates that she was practicing music . . . Like many affluent young girls, her education was all encompassing including music, the arts, and sewing."

In addition to the receipts, the nest also contained pieces of a ledger from June, October, and November in an unidentified year, and January of 1833. It lists debts paid or received during that time, from locals such as a Mr. Hart, Mrs. Simmons, Mr. David Ridgely, and a "Richard Harwood of Thos." among others.

As of 2005, only a fraction of the rat's nest had been sorted and studied. Yet Hammond-Harwood House officials hope that will change; they are seeking an intern to undertake this task in the near future. Of course there are a few requisites. According to Ms. Foster, candidates "can't get grossed out, can't be too allergic, and should either be undergraduate or graduate students, or be interested in history."[1]

Woodworkers Help to Preserve Local History

Five years after conservators found the rats' nest at the Hammond-Harwood House, Carter Lively made another remarkable discovery there—this time, in his office on the second floor.

Winds were howling outside the Hammond-Harwood House as Hurricane Floyd approached Annapolis in September 1999. Inside, however, things were quiet as Carter Lively worked in his office—until a strange sound began in the fireplace. "Drip, drip, drip. Drip, drip, drip," it echoed. Rising from his desk, Mr. Lively walked to the sound's source. He removed a chair that was blocking the hearth and made this surprising discovery: a box stuffed full of paper scrolls—that he had never seen—since he became Executive Director of the house in March.

One of the scrolls looked much older than the rest. And indeed, unraveling it revealed that it was; it contained six plans for the house's garden drawn by Alden Hopkins in the 1940s.

Alden Hopkins was among America's leading landscape architects. To name several of his achievements, he helped to define the Colonial Revival garden style in the early 20th century; he was Colonial Williamsburg's official Landscape Architect for many years; and he designed gardens for Woodlawn, Stratford Hall, and UVA (the University of Virginia) among other sites.

Mr. Hopkins was practicing in Williamsburg and working simultaneously at UVA when he designed the Hammond-Harwood House garden. He submitted his plans for it in 1949: the year it was finished, and the year the Federated Garden Clubs of Maryland presented the house with its brick wall along Cumberland Court.

The garden has changed since then, although not by much. "What it is now is what has evolved," Mr. Lively said. "Its plantings have matured, and an herb garden has been added, as have several compressors."

One of the garden's most dramatic changes was the condition of its white wooden gate, which opened to Cumberland Court. "The gate is [was] a work of art," Mr. Lively said. "It was designed by Hopkins down to the hardware. All of the ironwork was made on Duke of Gloucester Street—in Williamsburg, not Annapolis."

Unfortunately, over fifty years of everyday use, weather damage, and negligent drivers (several cars hit the gate) took a toll on the gate's appearance and stability. Fortunately, however, one of the plans Mr. Lively found was Hopkins's original design for the gate. This prompted him to explore options for building a replacement for it in 2003.[1]

The front entrance to the Hammond-Harwood House. Author's note: The entrance does not have a bannister or staircase to the left. These features were added to this illustration, which was created for a children's book in 2003. Illustration by the author.

At that point, he contacted the AWG (Annapolis Woodworkers' Guild): a nonprofit organization founded in 1989 to "advance fellowship among persons interested in the art of woodworking; preserve the tradition, culture, and history of woodworking; promote the knowledge and understanding of all aspects of woodworking; and enjoy and appreciate the woodworking skills of others."

Since 1989, the AWG has undertaken many historic preservation-related projects. Its members have helped to restore the Maryland State House cupola; built park benches for the William Paca House and Gardens on behalf of Historic Annapolis Foundation; and created a bench, stand-up desk, trestle table, and other items for Historic London Town. The group also provided much of the "everyday grunt work" at London Town, as the site built a replica of its original settlement. Over 200 members belong to the group, and while most are older retired males, membership is open to anyone, eighteen years or older, who believes in the AWG's purpose and is willing to participate in its work.

Mr. Lively contacted the AWG with the hope that it would build a much-needed replacement, or replica, of the gate as a "special project." According to AWG President Michael Arndt, the group accepts "special projects" from nonprofit or community groups through the following process. First, its Board of Directors must approve the project; next, a volunteer team leader is identified to spearhead it; he or she then forms a team of volunteers to accomplish the task; and finally, although the site pays for the materials, the AWG "provides the expertise and people [at no cost]" Mr. Arndt said.

The AWG Board approved Mr. Lively's request, and work on the gate began in October 2003. Eight AWG members, mostly novice woodworkers, built its replica using Hopkins's plan. Mr. Arndt was the project's chairman, and his teammates included his son Brad Arndt, Fred Goldstein, Gary Metzler, Harlan Ray, Doug Richardson, Richard Valentich, and Vicki Kunde.

The team spent a total of 222 hours on the project. Yet it wasn't easy. "The gate was designed by an architect with entirely too much time on his hands," Mr. Arndt said, while pointing out its intricacies. Working at their woodshop in Severn, Maryland, the team followed Hopkins's design to the tee. Each piece of the new gate, including its field panels, is identical to its original counterpart. They also used hardware, including hinges, and hand-forged nails, which were custom made at a blacksmith shop in Williamsburg. They even had a company custom-mix the gate's original dark red color: Pittsburgh Paint No. 27164.

The team did, however, make two concessions to the original. The new gate's mortise and tenant joints are sealed with a modern adhesive instead of lead. And, while the first gate was "most likely made of mahogany," to quote Mr. Arndt, the new one is built of Spanish cedar obtained from a Mennonite lumber mill in Hagerstown, Maryland.

The gate that Alden Hopkins designed for the Hammond-Harwood House. Illustration by the author.

Mr. Arndt and his teammates finished the gate in August 2004. It took a total of three days to disassemble the old one and to mount its replica. Shortly thereafter, they completed a second project at the garden. They repainted its other gate that opens to King George Street and was also designed by Hopkins.[2]

Anne St. Clair Wright: Annapolis's "First Lady of Preservation"

The AWG has also done historic-related work for the Hammond-Harwood House's neighbor: the William Paca House and Gardens. This story celebrates the woman who helped to save this landmark from destruction.

I've only had writer's block once. It occurred in April 2004 and lasted two weeks. The problem wasn't a lack of inspiration; nor was it spring fever, since the weather was miserable. Rather I was overwhelmed by this task: how to honor St. Clair Wright, a woman remembered as "the savior of Annapolis, unquestionably the savior," in 1,000 words or less.

I struggled to weave these (and other) facts about her into a coherent whole: that she was a founder of HA (Historic Annapolis, Inc.) and served four terms as its president; that she helped to save the William Paca House and Gardens and secure the city's National Historic District Landmark status; that she received awards including the highest conferred by the National Trust for Historic Preservation, as well as honorary degrees from the University of Maryland and Towson State College; that she was an accomplished author; and that she devoted over forty years to historic preservation, without ever being paid.

Finally, after a long impasse, I decided to change my approach. I chose not to describe how Mrs. Wright did more for Annapolis "than any other single person in the city's history by saving it from being Anywhere USA," as Roger Moyer said in 2002.[1]

Instead, I focused on these lesser-known facts about the woman remembered as the "First Lady of Preservation:" She was not a native Annapolitan, she lacked formal training in historic preservation, and she was a gifted artist.

Anne St. Clair Smith was born in 1910, in Newport News, Virginia, to Rear Admiral Arthur St. Clair Smith, and Anne Lena Salley. Because of her father's career, she spent much of her youth abroad in China, Japan, France, Panama, and the Philippines. During this time, she became fascinated with art and architecture, two interests that later complemented her work in historic preservation.

St. Clair, as most called her, initially came to Annapolis for the first time in 1912, when her father was stationed at the Naval Academy. He was an instructor there, and the family lived on the Yard until their home on Southgate Avenue was finished. And, although they moved in 1914, the city remained the family's permanent residence.

Mrs. Wright married U.S. Navy Captain Joseph M. P. Wright in 1932. As in her youth, she traveled extensively due to her husband's career; the couple lived in California, Virginia, and Hawaii before moving to Annapolis in 1942. They lived there off and on, before settling permanently in town in 1952: the year Mrs. Wright was Secretary at HA's inaugural meeting, which occurred in McDowell Hall at St. John's College.

Anne St. Clair Wright, 1983. Courtesy of M. E. Warren and Historic Annapolis Foundation. Copyright © 1983 by M. E. Warren.

Although Mrs. Wright helped to launch the city's historic preservation movement, she lacked formal training in the field. Rather, she employed her "intellect and catalogue memory" to become a self-taught expert. She developed "an intense interest in history and read widely and voraciously" at about the time HA was founded. She also consulted experts in law, architecture, archaeology, economic development, and horticulture and was herself a knowledgeable gardener and horticultural historian.[2]

Mrs. Wright's commitment to learning bore fruit. She "never appeared to be an amateur," said Dr. Mark Leone, Professor of Anthropology at the University of Maryland, who made Mrs. Wright's acquaintance in 1981. "The quality of her education [in historic preservation] was irrelevant; the quality of her mind was significant," he said.[3] And, as the *Baltimore Sun* noted in 1982, "You do not want to argue with St. Clair Wright unless you have done your homework, because she knows all the Annapolis answers."[4]

Nancy Avallone, who served on HA's Board of Trustees, recalled Mrs. Wright's vision for historic preservation in Annapolis. "She saw what a little jewel this town was and how important it was to save the city," she said.[5]

Maryland Governor Millard Tawes presents a Distinguished Maryland Citizens Citation to Anne St. Clair Wright, with U.S. Secretary of the Interior Stuart Udall in the background, July 1965. Courtesy of M. E. Warren and Historic Annapolis Foundation. Copyright © 1965 by M. E. Warren.

Anne St. Clair Wright (center), Pringle Symonds (far right), and U.S. Protocol officials in the William Paca Gardens, 1975. Courtesy of M. E. Warren and Historic Annapolis Foundation. Copyright © 1975 by M. E. Warren.

Mrs. Wright knew that everyone didn't share her vision. In a 1981 interview she lamented that, "Local people viewed Annapolis only as an old obsolete city. They did not feel that it had any value of any kind from an economic point of view, a cultural point of view. To them, it was nothing."[6]

While Mrs. Wright lacked formal training in historic preservation, she was formally trained as an artist. She studied at Mary Baldwin College in Virginia, and received her Bachelor of Arts degree from the Maryland Institute of Fine Arts in Baltimore in 1932.

She worked as a professional artist upon graduating. In 1936, for instance, she painted large, decorative murals for the Willard Hotel in Washington, D.C. They hung in the Navy Relief Ball Room on Thanksgiving Day and were "the talk of the town," to quote the *Washington Herald*. The paper praised her as "a first class" artist and remarked that she had "been painting since she was a pig-tailed Annapolitan."[7]

Mrs. Ronnie Carr, a friend of Mrs. Wright's since 1947, recalled that she was also a gifted ceramicist. "She had a kiln and little studio on Southgate . . . she made a beautiful figurine of the Peggy Stewart and a plate showing the Liberty Tree," she said.[8]

Later, Mrs. Wright used her artistic talent in pursuit of historic preservation. "She was always sketching," to quote Dr. Henry Wright, her youngest of
three sons. "Any argument about preservation or restoration was likely to be accompanied by plans and drawings from Mother," he said.[9] She designed pam-
phlets and brochures for HA, as well as its Historic Building Markers, which
are present throughout the city's Historic District.

Ann Fligsten, former president and current Trustee Emeritus of HA, remembers Mrs. Wright as "a brilliant, creative artist in the way she approached
life and did things." She also remembers that she "liked to mentor young people."[10] Linnell Bowen, the current Executive Director of Maryland Hall for the
Creative Arts was among those she mentored.

Mrs. Bowen began volunteering for HA in 1976, and later, served as its
Director of Education, and Director of Fundraising among other capacities.
When describing her former mentor she said, "St. Clair Wright was an artistic visionary. She saw beauty in our shabby, neglected capital city. Her pas-
sion for preservation and her ability to never let you say no saved Annapolis
for all of us."[11]

It is appropriate that, fifty years after Mrs. Wright helped to found HA,
both she and Mrs. Bowen were recognized in the book *Women of Achievement in
Maryland History*.

Saving the Historic Market House

Captain and Mrs. Wright moved to Annapolis just after officials tried to raze
the city's market house. This story features how this historic building escaped
from destruction—for the first time.

Robert Campbell was only twenty when his father died in 1940. He took
charge of his family's business that year and received this shocking letter in 1941:

October 21, 1941
Mr. Robert H. Campbell
City Market
Annapolis, Maryland

Dear Mr. Campbell:
    You are hereby notified to quit and deliver up to the Mayor,
Counselor and Aldermen of the City of Annapolis on December 1,
1941, the premises, market space or stall now held by you as its tenant

from month to month in the City Market located on Market Space, Annapolis, Maryland.

Dated this 21st day of October, 1941.

> Albert J. Goodman, Special Attorney
> for the Mayor, Counselor and
> Aldermen of the City of Annapolis[1]

Robert wasn't the only one who got this letter. So did every other market house tenant—for a reason. The city was going to raze and replace the building with a USO (United Service Organizations) center for white servicemen.[2]

Discussions about the center had started that summer at a city council meeting. On July 21, Richard Elliott, Secretary of the Parks and Recreation Committee, announced that the "Federal government had tentatively allocated $40,000 to Annapolis to construct a temporary recreation center as part of the national defense program."[3]

Mayor William McCready reacted quickly to the news. He appointed a committee that met with federal officials to discuss their offer on July 23.[4] That day, the committee learned that while the city wouldn't have to pay for the center, it would have to provide a site for it.

The committee searched for one immediately. It explored several options before concluding in October that the market area was the only possible place for a "permanent recreation center."[5] (Since July, officials had agreed that the center could be permanent, instead of temporary, if the city could pay $30,000 to cover the difference in cost.)

The council considered the committee's choice on October 20. Everyone thought it was a good idea, except for Alderman Arthur Ellington. He "wanted to know what would be used for [a] Fish Market" if the market were razed? Alderman Jesse Fisher addressed his concern. He said that of the two tenants who sold fish in the market, one also ran a local seafood store, and the other would be able to relocate "in the vicinity."[6] He added that, "The only thing we are going to lose are the few tenants [in] the market, and

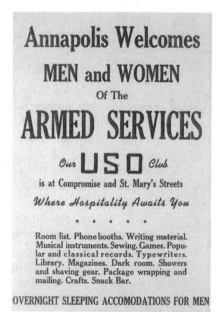

Annapolis Welcomes

MEN and WOMEN

Of The

ARMED SERVICES

Our **USO** *Club*

is at Compromise and St. Mary's Streets

Where Hospitality Awaits You

★ ★ ★ ★ ★

Room list. Phone booths. Writing material. Musical instruments. Sewing. Games. Popular and classical records. Typewriters. Library. Magazines. Dark room. Showers and shaving gear. Package wrapping and mailing. Crafts. Snack Bar.

OVERNIGHT SLEEPING ACCOMODATIONS FOR MEN

Sign welcoming servicemen to the city's USO Club. Courtesy of the city of Annapolis Department of Recreation and Parks.

we are not going to lose them. They can go outside the market like the open markets on the West coast and in other cities."[7]

Fisher's remarks satisfied Ellington, who then made a motion. He urged the council to accept the government's offer, inform the government of its choice, and "request that a representative be sent here for a conference so we can all move speedily for construction."[8]

Ellington's motion passed unanimously. So did another by Fisher who moved "that the site of the Market House be turned over to the proper authorities for a recreation center."[9]

Choosing a site for the USO center had been easy for officials. However, enforcing their choice would be difficult—and they knew it. With that in mind, they hired "Special Attorney" Albert J. Goodman who, on October 21, wrote the letter ordering the market's tenants to vacate.

Several tenants (and nearby merchants) took legal action upon receiving it. Roland Brown, Pasquale Tarantino, George Lawton, Marion Sanders, Edwin Bangert, and George Graefe hired Eugene Childs as their attorney and prepared to file suit against the city.

Meanwhile, the city forged ahead with its plans. It worked with federal officials and architect Earl Harder to design the center. His design called for a two-story, 56-foot wide, 120-foot long brick building, with recreation equipment and areas including tennis courts.

The council also held a special session on November 6. Its members took two steps regarding the center that night. They accepted the conditions that would accompany the government's grant for the building. These were the conditions, as reported by the *Evening Capital* on November 7:

- The site must be leased to the United States for five years at $1 a year, with the right to renew for five years at the same price;
- The site will be the city market, the city to clear the ground;
- A masonry type of construction will be used with the city's plans to be followed;
- The total cost includes architect's fees;
- The city must provide $35,000 to meet cost of permanent construction;
- Plans and specifications to be completed not later than November 15;
- The government is to award the contract and supervise construction;
- The city's share of the building cost must be deposited to the credit of the United States with a finance officer; and that
- Any remaining Federal funds, not required by the building, will be used for a colored recreation building in the city.[10]

They also asked Guy Hendry, the city's USO representative, a question that many were wondering: Would the center be open to civilians as well as servicemen? Mr. Hendry said that, "as far as he knew [it] would be open to citizens

The USO Club eventually became the city of Annapolis's Annapolis Recreation Center. Its exterior is shown above in 1969, and its interior, below, in the 1950s. Courtesy of the city of Annapolis Department of Recreation and Parks.

generally," but that facility's control would be in the "hands of a local commit-tee."[11] He also "expressed appreciation of the council's action" and promised that he and his team "would feel a keen sense of responsibility to do their best taking into consideration the entire community."[12]

The council made a final choice regarding the center on November 24. It authorized Mayor McCready and Counselor Edward Chaney to execute a lease for the market house property to the U.S. government for the building.[13]

The tenants took their stand four days later. Roland Brown had already testified at the November 10 city council meeting. Speaking on behalf of the tenants, he had asked "what provision would be made for them when [the] market is demolished?" To his question, the council replied, ". . . only an open air market may be expected."[14]

On November 28, however, he and the others took concrete action; Mr. Childs filed a bill of complaint for them at the county Circuit Court to stop the city "from turning over the site of the market house or dispossessing the tenants therefrom until a Court hearing on the merits of the allegations of the bill could be had and the matter properly adjudicated."[15]

The bill contained many allegations, including:

- That "the Mayor, Counselor and Aldermen of the City of Anna-polis . . . did arbitrarily pass a resolution to turn the site of the market house over to the proper authorities for a recreation center, which resolution is not only deceiving, but is unlawful, oppressive and in utter disregard of the trust reposed in [them] . . ."
- "That no provisions have been made, or space appropriated for a new market in compliance with the charter, and the proposed taking away of the present market is in violation of charter provisions, all of which has been done against the will and without the consent of your orators and the people . . ." and
- "That a public market is essential to the health and welfare of the people . . . It is the hub for barter and trade, and serves not only its own people, but the people of surrounding counties in the state . . . [and that its destruction] . . . would be to the great and irreparable damage, loss, and injury to your orators, as well as to the municipal-ity for which no adequate compensation in damage could be had."

The city neither admitted nor denied the bill's allegations. It also claimed that its acts had been "proper and lawful."[16]

The case went to court on December 8, with Judge Eugene Boylan, Jr. pre-siding. The plaintiffs argued that the city had no authority to take over "prop-erty dedicated to public uses" for any purpose. As Mr. Childs said,

"We most earnestly contend not that they cannot lease or sell the market house, but they can do it only if they have the proper authority which resides with the [Maryland State] legislature." He also called the city's action "unreasonable and unnecessary," since there were "plenty of places in Annapolis where they could destroy unsightly sore spots" to build the center.[17]

Counselor Chaney offered three counter arguments on the city's behalf. He said the city's Charter granted it the "power to erect and regulate markets;" referenced City Code, which stated that, "markets cannot be used for any other purpose except with written permission from the council;" and quoted law cases "in which the right of the governing body had been upheld in like instances."[18]

Judge Boylan ordered the case to be reargued on December 29. He found in favor of the tenants two days later, and said that the city did "not have the power to dispose of the market house as contemplated" for this reason:

It lacked the legislative authority. He said the city was a "creature of the state," which could exercise "only those powers conferred either expressly or by fair and reasonable implication" by the State Legislature. And, he noted that, "the Legislature [had] not directly or impliedly empowered the city of Annapolis to dispose of any municipal property, except the burial lots."[19]

Judge Bolyan's ruling forced the city to find a new site for the USO center. It purchased land along Compromise and St. Mary's Streets in winter of 1942 and built the facility there later that year.

Although the tenants saved the historic market house in 1941, they still had to vacate it temporarily in 1942. The city's Health Officer and Chairman of the Market House Committee inspected the building that January. Their report, which they submitted to city council, condemned the market

The Annapolis Recreation Center. Photograph by David Hartcorn, 2005.

as "unsanitary," and recommended that it should "be closed temporarily and put in a satisfactory condition."

This prompted the council to pass a motion. It authorized the Market House Committee to do two things: to notify the market tenants "as soon as possible" to vacate their spaces, and to close the market temporarily in order to sanitize it.[20]

Saving the Historic Market House—Again

1941 wasn't the only time that the market escaped destruction. This story features how locals saved the historic building from becoming a parking lot 18 years later.

Annapolis had a "parking problem" in 1959—one that these quotes, taken from a study started a year later, reveal:

> The bugbear of Annapolis and many another town is its parking problem. Scrutinized by government, professional and civic organizations and private citizens' groups over the last several years, the subject does not want for an informed body of public opinion . . .[1]

> Local sentiment and survey conclusions indicate a severe parking problem. In the downtown area, there is little room for additional parking lots . . . space for future construction of parking lots is virtually non-existent.[2]

> Traffic and Parking—These two problems have created a dilemma . . . no two persons seem to agree on a solution. Many merchants themselves park in front of their stores in 'feed-the-meter-style,' thereby reducing curb space for customer parking . . .[3]

> The city, to date, has been responsible for the construction of 5 off-street parking lots in the downtown core area with a total of 363 spaces but this ambitions program has far from satisfied total parking demand.[4]

To solve this "parking problem," city officials considered converting several downtown Annapolis sites into parking lots. And, in summer of 1959, they contemplated destroying the market house for that purpose. The *Evening Capital* announced this possibility on July 29 in this article:

City Market Shift Eyed at Meeting: Site Would be Turned Into a Parking Lot

> The possibility of moving the city market to the Dock St. parking lot, and creating a parking area on the present site of the market, was dis-

cussed last night at a meeting of the Mayor's Committee on Off-Street Parking Lots and Traffic Movement, held in the office of Mayor Arthur G. Ellington.[5]

The feasibility of moving the market came up during a general discussion of all phases of the off-street parking situation in the city. It was pointed out that the Dock St. lot isn't being used many times to the full extent of its potentialities, and that a lot in the center of Market Space, on the Market site, would be convenient to that entire business area. The matter didn't go beyond the discussion stage.[6]

Although the idea didn't go "beyond the discussion stage," its very mention caused a local panic. HA (Historic Annapolis, Inc.), was among the first to respond. It circulated a petition, which urged officials to save the market. As the paper noted on August 7:

Petition Hits Idea of Razing City Market

More than 100 customers have joined merchants in the Old Market House at the city dock in petitioning the Mayor and Council to remodel and renovate rather than demolish the market house, F. W. Basil, retail meat merchant in the market, said today.

The petition, initiated by Historic Annapolis has been circulating in the area and will continue to do so until Monday Basil said. He added that it will then be presented to the City Council. Shoppers are brought into the Market Space area by the specialty shops there, the petition points out. It urges the city to refurbish the market to become an "attractive asset to the waterfront area."

Five hundred people signed the petition in eleven days, according to this August 12 newspaper report:

Mayor Arthur G. Ellington told the Council that he had been informed by Mrs. J.M.P. Wright [then-Vice President of HA], that a petition that was placed in the city market Aug. 1 already had 500 signers asking the city to restore or improve the market. Mrs. Wright pointed out that the large number of signers shows real interest in keeping the present market house . . .[7]

While many signed the petition in protest, others, including Don Riley, took a different approach. He wrote this letter to the editor, which the *Evening Capital* published on August 25:

Sir: At times in the alleged 'March of Progress' some are in the ranks who are badly out of step and I think the misguided element which, I understand, seeks to demolish the Market House and fill in the slip, are seeking to do Annapolis a disservice.

The city eventually built additional parking garages to accommodate the growing number of vehicles in Annapolis. It also established a ticketed parking lot near the Harbour House restaurant, shown above in 1972. Courtesy of The Capital. *Photograph by Ron Houghton.*

Mayor Roger Moyer, at right, emphasizes what Annapolis's new signs point out (where the parking is), while City Engineer William R. Jackson puts the last twist on a bolt holding the last sign to be placed. The Annapolis Businessmen's Association donated the signs to help locals and visitors find the municipal parking lots, April 1967. Courtesy of The Capital. *Photograph by Lee Troutner.*

Tradition, the 'Old Ancient City,' makes our hometown distinctive, a gem of a colorful and glamorous past when it truly won the sobriquet of the 'Athens of America.' It now has what Williamsburg, Va., hasn't and never will have and I don't mean the Rockefeller millions.

It is a city which has emerged from delightful and historic Colonial days with many of the splendid homes and other buildings intact. They have been replaced in many cases, converted back to regain their old charm, but not a la Williamsburg newly built from old blueprints.

The Market House has been a sign and symbol of Annapolis, the slip an institution, which we should not allow to slip out of our grasp.

To level the market . . . with the puny excuse that it will attract more shoppers to the county and possibly provide additional parking space, is unthinkable. Other places can undoubtedly be found for the road monsters. Improve the present market and restore its surroundings so that it will be a rendezvous for more shoppers. Don't seek to undermine Annapolis, make it more of a magnet for those who live there and the others who visit.

"Woodman, Spare That Tree!" is a well known . . . poem written by George Pope Morris. "Annapolis, Spare the Market and the Slip." Don't confuse any modern march that includes the demolition of tradition with true progress. It is nothing of the sort.[8]

Fortunately, Mr. Riley's efforts (and those of other citizens) worked. Public pressure prompted the council to dismiss the idea of razing the market—at least for a little while.

Saving the Market—One More Time

The city's efforts to raze the market in the mid-20th century were trivial compared to what happened in 1968. That year, city council voted to tear the market down: a choice that propelled historic preservationists into action. This is the story of how they—and other like-minded citizens—saved the historic building from destruction.

August 12, 1968, was a cool, still night in Annapolis: one last moment of calm before a storm of controversy that had been brewing for months finally hit. Temperatures had already dipped into the 50s when Mayor Roger "Pip" Moyer reached City Hall for a city council meeting. He arrived seven minutes late, at

8:07 P.M., after several hippies on Maryland Avenue stopped him to ask, "when police harassment" in the area would stop.[2]

This was not the night to be late for city council. For during the meeting, he and the aldermen would vote on a highly controversial resolution: a "Resolution Regarding City Market," sponsored by Alderman Charles Bernstein.[3]

At stake was the future of the city's 111-year old market house. If the resolution passed, the building would be "demolished and removed;" its tenants would be forced to vacate by December 31 to set the stage for demolition; and the area, many feared, would be redeveloped into a parking lot or high-rise commercial building.

The council wasn't the first to consider razing the market. In 1941, for instance, councilmen had voted to replace it with a USO center. Yet thanks to a county Circuit Court ruling, the center was built on Compromise Street instead.

Even then however, the market's future remained unclear as certain locals continued to press for its removal. The outspoken Elmer Martin Jackson, Jr. drove this effort in the 1960s. By 1968, he had campaigned "off and on" for twenty-five years to raze the market for economic, visual, structural—and as some suspected—personal reasons.[4]

Economically, Mr. Jackson claimed the market was a poor investment for Annapolis. Its tenants paid just 96 cents per square foot, which was much less than the going Annapolis rental rate in 1968. And, although this rate increased to $1.60 per square foot that September, it was still comparatively low.

Visually, the market was also in trouble. Since being built in 1857–58, its appearance had suffered several blows: part of its northeast end had been removed, stucco exterior walls had covered its original open-air sides, a monitor window structure had been built on the roof, and commercial signs had been allowed to clutter its windows.

By 1968, the market's infrastructure had also deteriorated. The "market as it is now [1968] is worthless," said William Jackson, the city's public works director.[5] No funds had been budgeted for its maintenance for some time, and professionals estimated that rehabilitating it would cost between $200,000 and $250,000.

These and other factors prompted citizens, including Elmer Jackson, to call for the market's destruction. And, as then-Editor of the *Evening Capital*, he had a powerful forum for expressing his view: the newspaper.

Starting in summer of 1968, the market house became the dominant theme of Mr. Jackson's daily front-page "Editor's Reports." In them, he emphasized the market's problems and denied that it was a historic asset to the city. He even dismissed a Department of Interior letter stating that Annapolis might "seriously" endanger its status as a National Historic Landmark if it lost its market as "just silly talk."[6]

One of Jackson's most scathing reports, "Keeping City Market House Foolish Idea," ran on July 29, 1968. It accused HA (Historic Annapolis, Inc.) and St. Clair Wright—whom he called its "militant leader"—of being inconsis-

> "I haven't been in that market in I don't know how long. I'm afraid to go in there. Somebody might say, 'There's an alderman,' and I'd get mobbed before they knew which alderman I was."
> —Alderman Noah Hillman (Ward One) December 21, 1968. Mr. Hillman was one of two aldermen who did not vote to tear the market down on August 12, 1968.[1]

tent. (Some suspected that Jackson's campaign to raze the market began as a personal conflict between himself and Mrs. Wright: a possibility that the *Washington Post* reported in December 1968.[7])

According to Mr. Jackson, HA and Mrs. Wright had opposed the Annapolis Hilton Hotel's erection because it looked modern and blocked the waterfront.[8] Yet he claimed that they wanted to restore the market using a "modern, contemporary" design. "To now wish to rebuild the market house, and make it modern in many respects, amounts to inconsistency," wrote Mr. Jackson, who added, "If the hotel blocks the waterfront so does the market house."[9]

Unlike Mr. Jackson's reports, the announcement for the August 12 city council meeting was discreet. It ran that day, was buried at the bottom left corner of page 2, and measured about 1 square inch.

The ad's discretion didn't keep market supporters, including Mrs. Wright and other preservationists, from attending the meeting. Representing HA, she read a Department of the Interior letter, which condemned the market's possible destruction: "We deplore the possibility of this action as one more step to reduce the old center of Annapolis to the mediocrity of the typical American downtown," it stated.[10] Carroll Brice, representing descendents of those who deeded market space to the city in 1784, was there too.

Eight of the council's nine members were also present: Mayor Roger Moyer, and Aldermen Noah Hillman (Ward 1), Charles Bernstein (Ward 2), Arthur Ellington (Ward 3), Roscoe Parker (Ward 4), Paul Clark, Jr. (Ward 6), John Chambers, Jr. (Ward 7), and Louis Hyatt (Ward 8). Only Howard Dignen (Ward 5) was absent.

After hearing public testimony, the council reached a swift, shocking conclusion: It passed the resolution by a vote of six to two. Even the two aldermen who opposed it weren't necessarily against the market's destruction. Mr. Clark thought it should be razed only after officials made plans to build a new market in the waterfront area. And Mr. Hillman, in response to the *Evening Capital*'s forceful anti-market editorials said, "In the end I may vote to tear that building down . . . But I hate to be pushed."[11]

The councilmen said four factors influenced their vote. First, rehabilitating the deteriorated market would cost between $200,000 and $250,000: money they said the city didn't have. Second, the market was not meeting locals' needs. In their opinion, the building was also not a historic asset. Finally, its removal was part of a larger plan to "open up" the city's waterfront; the council had already announced plans to raze other buildings in the area such as the Amoco Service Station, and properties along Compromise Street and Market Space.[12]

Many, however, suspected that something (or rather someone) else had influenced the council: Mr. Jackson. "Jackson admits he was the force behind the Council's decision to tear down the structure," reported the *Washington Post* in December 1968. "One Council member says publicly and a couple admit privately that . . . with citywide elections coming in May, those who want to retain their posts don't think they can afford to cross the town's newspaper editor," it said.[13]

Of course Mr. Jackson denied these reports. "I would not even think, let alone say that I control any vote of a member of the City Council," he wrote. Yet as former Mayor Moyer disclosed in 2004, "[Mr. Jackson] said he wouldn't support me any more if I supported the market house."[14]

While Mr. Jackson denied trying to influence the council, he did admit trying to sway public opinion about the market through his "Editor's Reports." One of the most forceful, headlined "City Fathers Display Vision for Dock Area," ran on August 13. In it, Mr. Jackson praised the council for having "courageously voted . . . to tear down the City Market" despite being "submitted to the greatest round of pressures that could be exercised against them."

His words must have outraged locals—especially those who feared Market Space would become a parking lot. "There is no parking downtown to accom-

The Annapolis market house in February 1968. Courtesy of The Capital. *Photograph by Lee Troutner.*

modate a huge throng," he wrote and added, "Opening up of Market Space will undoubtedly lead to the beautification of the entire area while providing some additional parking . . ."

Mr. Jackson wasn't the only one who pressed for the market's removal. So did then-President and Publisher of the *Evening Capital,* Talbot Speer. "The possibilities are unlimited for the area," he said. "When the market house goes, I predict most everyone will quickly recognize that the dock area has more beauty than we have yet seen."[15]

Many businessmen agreed. According to Mr. Jackson, over thirty local Chamber of Commerce members said they supported the council's stance during a chamber-hosted event in September 1968. Members of the Maryland-Delaware Press Association, which met in Annapolis that month, concurred. Most "agreed that the area would be enhanced through removal of the market house," he wrote. One visiting editor even declared, "The market house is awful looking. There is nothing to indicate that it is a city market . . . It would appear to me that the whole area suffers from its presence."[16]

At the same time, others fought to save the market. Crucial to this effort were preservation-minded citizens such as Mrs. Wright, George Hannon, Jr., L. Harvey Poe, Jr., Paul Pearson, and Pringle Symonds—citizens Roger Moyer recently praised as "visionaries."[17]

Shortly after the council cast its vote, they helped to form the "Save the Market Committee." This informal coalition believed in the market's historical and architectural value. And, together with HA, it campaigned to rescue it from destruction.

To counter Mr. Jackson's anti-market assault, the committee ran a paid political ad in the *Evening Capital* on September 27, 1968. Titled "An Open Letter to the Mayor and City Council," it called for a two-year delay in the market's proposed demolition. Over 300 people signed the letter including these familiar Annapolis names: F. Marion Lazenby; Morris Radoff; Phebe Jacobson; David Colburn; Stuart Christhilf; and members of the Carr, Trumpy, Sadler, Feldmeyer, and Florestano families.

Committee members and HA also produced petitions with over 3,000 signatures, distributed pro-market literature, made radio appearances, flooded city council meetings with supporters, and researched and financed a lawsuit they hoped would serve as a stay of execution for the historic market.

Mrs. Symonds, who moved to Annapolis in 1963, was an essential part of these activities. She recalled that, "The proposal [to raze the market] was outrageous. There was talk that its removal would increase parking, but that wasn't the real thrust of it. A larger development was presumed and everyone thought Mr. Jackson had a hidden interest."[18] Mr. Poe and Mayor Moyer, for instance, thought he favored constructing a 10-story building.

During the crisis, Mrs. Symonds collected signatures for two "Save the Market" petitions: one for downtown residents, and another for waterfront merchants. Getting residents to sign was "no problem," she said. Yet businesses such as Stevens Hardware were reluctant. Mr. Stevens "couldn't sign because he was told the *Evening Capital* wouldn't let him advertise if he did," she recalled.[19]

In addition to signing petitions, market supporters also flooded the paper with letters to the editor. Maryland State Archivist Dr. Morris Radoff penned one, as did young Stephen Carr who wrote

> Sir: I am 14 years old and I know my opinion on the demolition of the market won't make a bit of difference but I decided to express myself anyway. I have enjoyed the market area in many ways throughout my life and would find it a real crime to rip it down. . .[20]

While many took to their typewriters, others took legal action. This effort began on August 12, 1968, when Carroll Brice addressed city council—just before it voted to raze the building.

Representing descendents of those who deeded Market Space to the city in 1784, he spoke about the deed's possible "reverter clause," which would return Market Space to the heirs if it were used for anything but a market house.[21]

Yet Malcolm Smith, the City's Attorney, disagreed. "The deed contains no reverter clause," he said. "I've told the mayor that the city can legally demolish the market and use the property for any public use the same as any other property owned by the city."[22]

At first, Mr. Brice claimed that he had "no plans to go to court."[23] He changed his mind, however, once research funded by HA, and the committee, identified a more extensive list of descendents. And, on December 17, 1968, Baltimore attorney Lawrence Rodowsky filed suit on behalf of three of them: Dr. Douglas Carroll of Brooklandville, Maryland (who had never been to the market or heard of the controversy until he was contacted); Nancy Gordon Carroll Trimble, also of Brooklandville; and Julia Anne Walton Tyler of Ferry Farms, Annapolis.[24]

The suit was "a diversionary tactic, a monkey in the wrench," said Mr. Poe, who moved to Annapolis in 1954. "The reverter might not work, but at least we could hold things up," he said.[25]

In response to the suit, Mayor Moyer called an emergency council meeting on December 20, during which its members voted to "keep the market functioning until a final court decision was made." "There's no intention of putting anybody out of business—we don't want an empty market," said Moyer at the time.[26]

The market closed temporarily, was divided into smaller stalls, and then reopened. Tenants, however, would have to vacate on thirty days notice if the court found in favor of the city.

Meanwhile, three factors were improving the market's long-term chances for survival. First, groups such as the National Trust for Historic Preservation strengthened their support. The Trust's President, James Biddle, had already made his position clear in July, in a letter to HA. He wrote that, "The National Trust for Historic Preservation supports your organization in its efforts to preserve the Annapolis Market House. The pre–Civil War Market House is one of the major focal elements within the historic district of Annapolis and its destruction would be a serious loss to the character of the waterfront area."[27]

Second, a vital turning point occurred in December 1968. That month, Talbot Speer announced that Capital-Gazette Press, Inc. was about to be sold to Philip Merrill. It was, and shortly thereafter, Mr. Jackson—and his anti-market editorials—left the newspaper.

Finally, election time was approaching. Aldermen Ellington and Bernstein, both long-time advocates of razing the market, planned to retire. And, due to public pressure, Mr. Poe and Mrs. Wright's persuasive lobbying, and other factors, most candidates ran on a "pro-market platform," according to Mr. Poe.

Elections occurred in the spring and a new city council emerged. Mayor Moyer remained; Aldermen Bernstein and Ellington retired as planned; and three new faces joined the group: Alderman-at-large Stuart Whelan, Jr., Robert Spaeth who replaced Ellington, and Alfred Hopkins who defeated Paul Clark.

After the election, Mayor Moyer called a special council meeting on July 16. That night, Alderman Whelan made a motion to bring closure to what had been a tumultuous year for Annapolis.

Whelan, who chaired the Market House, Harbor and Docks Committee, based his motion on two of the committee's conclusions: that residents wanted to keep the historic market, and that it could make a valuable contribution to the city and state's plans to improve the downtown area.

Alderman J. Stuart Whelan, left; market house renovation architect James W. Burch, squatted; and George J. Hannon, Jr., a leading supporter of the renovation project, survey a hole knocked in one of the market's interior walls to allow for measurements. Courtesy of The Capital. *Photograph by Joe Gruver.*

Mayor Roger W. Moyer signs the contract for renovating the market house in April 1971. Present, from the left, standing are architect James W. Burch, Paul Pearson, a member of the Mayor's Committee on the Market House, and Stuart Christhilf, chairman of the committee. On the left, seated, David Brown, contractor for the job, looks on while Mayor Moyer signs the contract under the watchful eye of Alderman J. Stuart Whelan, chairman of the city's Market House, Harbor, and Docks Committee. Courtesy of The Capital. *Photograph by Stu Whelan.*

His motion had two parts. It called for the council to rescind its decision to destroy the market and directed his committee to suggest ways to make the market a "real asset" to the community.[28]

The council passed Whelan's motion and voted to renovate—rather than raze—the market. It reopened three years (and $160,000) later on August 2, 1972. When describing a special "sneak preview" of the facility, which occurred on August 1, the *Evening Capital* said, "Bitterness was either hidden or forgotten as city officials, Market merchants, historic preservationists, outside merchants and the buying public gathered under one roof to relish the products filling the brand new shelves, counters, and ice bins . . . The still-empty space leased by poultry tenant John N. Snyder was used . . . to display with pictures of the history of the Market House. . ."

"Hysteric, Historic Annapolis"

HA (Historic Annapolis, Inc.) was essential to saving the Annapolis market house in 1969. Yet people often confuse this organization, now called Historic Annapolis Foundation (HAF), with the city's HPC (Historic Preservation Commission). This chapter explains the difference between these groups and celebrates their accomplishments.

I don't usually eavesdrop. However, I couldn't help it one Sunday while having breakfast at City Dock Coffee in Annapolis. There, at the next table, three men began criticizing "Hysteric, Historic Annapolis;" specifically, how "it" was every Historic District homeowner's "nightmare."

I wondered what they meant by "it." Were they referring to HAF or the HPC? Upon asking, I learned that they thought these organizations were one and the same.

This is false. HAF and the HPC are separate entities. Incorporated in 1952 as Historic Annapolis, Inc., HAF is a private, nonprofit organization. Its mission is "to educate the public about the history of Annapolis and advocate for preserving the city's architectural integrity."

HAF achieves this mission in many ways. In its early years, it focused on saving historically and culturally significant buildings and creating educational programs to foster appreciation of the city's heritage. Since 1959, it has identified Annapolis's architectural assets through three surveys; instituted a historic building marker program; and developed "Annapolis: A Museum Without Walls": a walking audio tour narrated by Walter Cronkite, which interprets the city's Historic District.

HAF has also rescued the 18th-century William Paca House from demolition, and restored its

Mrs. Howard (Ruth) Keith, president of Historic Annapolis, Inc. pours punch for Mrs. Maynard C. Nicholl and Dr. Richard T. Weigle, president of St. John's College and former president of Historic Annapolis in June 1967. The three are discussing restoration of the William Paca House and Gardens following the organization's semi-annual membership meeting held on June 22. Courtesy of The Capital. Photograph by Lee Troutner.

HAF manages several museum sites, including the William Paca House and Gardens (upper left), Waterfront Warehouse, the Barracks, and, until recently, the Old Treasury Building. Illustrations by the author.

gardens; purchased three Annapolis buildings from the Revolutionary War era; developed "Archaeology in Annapolis": a partnership with the city and University of Maryland Department of Anthropology; and more.

In addition, HAF holds nearly sixty preservation easements on properties in Annapolis. It will open the Annapolis History Center at 99 Main Street in 2006 and currently manages these museum sites: the William Paca House and Gardens, Shiplap House, the Barracks, 77 Main Street, the Waterfront Warehouse, and until recently, the Old Treasury Building. It also sponsors events such as the popular annual Annapolis by Candlelight tour, and free lectures on a variety of historical topics.

HAF's mission is similar to the HPC's purpose: "to safeguard the city's heritage as reflected in its unique plan, in its three centuries of historic architecture, and its broadly visible waterfront." However the HPC does more than advocate for historic preservation; it enforces Annapolis's historic preservation law: its Historic District Ordinance.

The HPC formed in 1968 when city council passed the city's first enforceable Historic District Ordinance. Similar laws had passed before, including one in 1952. Unfortunately this ordinance was weak; it created an Annapolis Historic District, and a board to review plans for building changes within it, but the council could overrule the board's decisions.

The council passed a second Historic District Ordinance in 1967. It was also weak, found unconstitutional when challenged in court, and city officials "totally ignored" the board's recommendations, to quote former HAF president Pringle Symonds.

Annapolis finally received a strong Historic District Ordinance in 1968. The council passed it that year, and citizens approved it in 1969 by a citywide vote of two to one. The ordinance established a Historic District Commission, whose decisions were final. Renamed the HPC in 1996, appeals to its decisions must be taken to Anne Arundel County's Circuit Court.

Unlike HAF, the HPC is part of Annapolis's city government. It's one of three quasi-judicial boards with statutory authority, along with the Planning Commission and Board of Appeals. City Code requires the HPC to review all plans for work to the exterior of Historic District buildings before issuing a Certificate of Approval. The review is based on Chapter 21.62 of the code, which controls changes made to a building's entire exterior—including its

Mayor Roger W. Moyer swears in the members of the new Historic District Commission in July 1969. In front from the left, are Marcellus Hall, Pringle Symonds, and Carmine Blades; at back from the left, are Arthur G. Ellington and Michael V. McCutchan. Courtesy of The Capital. *Photograph by Lee Troutner.*

front, sides, rear, roof, and adjacent land and appurtenances. However, the code doesn't control exterior paint colors or building interiors.

The HPC has a staff and seven members. The staff consists of two full-time city Planning & Zoning Department employees: a Chief of Historic Preservation and Historic Preservation Assistant, and two part-time consultants (an architect and archaeologist). A plans reviewer in the city's Neighborhood & Environmental Programs Department also reviews applications for building code compliance.

These individuals help property owners prepare their applications to the HPC, review the applications, and advise the commission on zoning code and other matters. They also help prepare HPC-sponsored historic site surveys and publications and coordinate and distribute HPC paperwork and reports. They're compensated for their work.

In contrast, the HPC's members are unpaid volunteers—volunteers who spend countless hours at day and nighttime meetings, and in workshops, trying to make Annapolis a better place to live and work. The mayor appoints them, city council confirms them, and they serve three-year terms. Each member must live in the city of Annapolis, according to City Code. Each must also possess "a demonstrated special interest, specific knowledge, or professional or academic training in such fields as history, architecture, architectural history, planning, archaeology, anthropology, curation, conservation, landscape architecture, historic preservation, urban design, or related disci-

Newly elected Historic District Commission officers review plans for the restoration of the William Paca House in August 1969. From the left are Marcellus Hall, vice-chairman; Pringle Symonds, chairman; and Carmine Blades, secretary of the commission. Courtesy of The Capital. Photograph by Joe Gruver.

plines." Furthermore, at least two must have professional or academic training in one or more of these fields.

People might think that the HPC and HAF are one and the same for several reasons. First, HAF employees and officers served on the commission for many years. This was necessary since initially the city only provided minimum staffing for the HPC. It wasn't until the late 1980s that the city and HAF recognized that it was the city's responsibility to staff and support the HPC fully. HAF and Planning & Zoning advocated for professional staff for the HPC, and council approved a full-time preservation planner position, now called the Chief of Historic Preservation, in 1992.

HAF employees also attend HPC meetings, which are open to the public and occur at City Hall. "We [HAF] go to every HPC meeting and comment on proposed projects and so can anyone else who lives here," said HAF president Dr. Gregory Stiverson who added, "We do it as a matter of mission—preserving the architectural integrity of Annapolis is one of the principal reasons we exist—but we have no more authority than any other citizen or private entity."[1]

Making Sense of Annapolis's Historic Building Markers

As the last vignette noted, HAF instituted a Historic Building Marker Program in Annapolis. This story explores the program's origins, how the markers are awarded, and what they reveal about a property.

What object appears on over 150 buildings in the National Historic Landmark District of Annapolis? Here's a hint: It's 8-by-12 inches, weighs 2¾ pounds, and comes in one or more of eight colors.

If you guessed a "Historic Annapolis Foundation (HAF) Historic Building Marker," you're right. HAF launched its Historic Building Marker Program in 1965. Today, the program serves the same purpose as it did then: It informs people about the city's history and architectural styles; encourages the preservation, restoration, and maintenance of Historic District properties; and identifies buildings with architectural integrity that accurately convey local architectural history.

St. Clair Wright, a founding member of HAF and its four-term president, designed the marker. It features key aspects of Annapolis history and architecture including the city's bygone Liberty Tree. The Sons of Liberty held Pre-Revolutionary War meetings beneath this 400-year-old tulip poplar, which stood on St. John's College campus until Hurricane Floyd destroyed it in 1999.

The marker's four stars resemble those worn by Naval Academy midshipmen on their epaulets. Its elongated octagonal shape reflects the "wood window surrounds," created by carver Thomas Hall, found in 18th-century Annapolis buildings such as the William Paca and Hammond-Harwood Houses.

HAF issued its first markers in 1967. They cost $15 at the time—much less than their current price of $300. This amount covers costs associated with researching the property, and casting, painting, and maintaining the marker, which are HAF's responsibilities.

Not just anyone can buy a marker, however. HAF awards them based on specific criteria. Eligible buildings, both residential and commercial, must possess an overall integrity of design, materials, workmanship, location, and setting. They must also make architectural contributions to the streetscape.

Other criteria include a structure's siding and shutters. Buildings are ineligible if they have inoperable shutters, or artificial siding that covers original cladding material on highly visible facades. A building's overall condition, maintenance, and landscape also matter. On the other hand, its interior doesn't.

Once a property is deemed eligible for a marker, its owner must sign a "Historic Building Marker Agreement" in order to receive it. The agreement states that HAF retains ownership of the marker once it is awarded and reserves the right to remove it if the property is altered in a way that "diminishes its architectural integrity." Markers remain with a property even if it is sold or transferred.

Once the agreement is signed, HAF's Director of Preservation Services hand paints the marker in one or more colors according to the building's style or era. The colors are provincial green, terra cotta, bronze, federal blue, verdigris, aubergine, Chesapeake gray, and ochre. A building that represents two architectural styles or eras receives a two-colored marker, and all markers receive two coats of paint.

Provincial Green markers are rare. They appear on 17th Century Vernacular buildings, which date from 1681–1708. These buildings,

Historic Annapolis Foundation historic building marker. Illustration by the author.

such as the Sands House at 130 Prince George Street, are modest, and have gambrel roofs, small windows, and later additions.

Close to the Sands House, Middleton Tavern at 2 Market Space has a Terra Cotta marker. Terra Cotta markers exist on 18th Century Vernacular and Georgian style buildings. Large, evenly spaced doors and windows, dentil moldings, and symmetry define these styles.

Annapolis has a remarkably high concentration of Georgian buildings, especially ones of national importance. These buildings, including the James Brice, and Hammond-Harwood Houses, have solid Bronze markers, unlike the others, which are made of sand-cast aluminum.

Across from Middleton Tavern, Griffin's Restaurant at 22 Market Space also has a marker. Its color is Federal Blue since Griffin's reflects the Annapolis Federal Style of architecture. This style is simpler than high-style Federal architecture, which evolved from the work of English architect Robert Adam.

Federal Blue markers are similar in color to those painted Verdigris. The word "verdigris" has several meanings. *Webster's* defines it as a "greenish-blue

From left to right: Mrs. Howard (Ruth) Keith, then-president of Historic Annapolis, Inc.; Mrs. Spiro T. (Elinor) Agnew, wife of Maryland's governor at the time; Mrs. Joseph W. (Mary) Alton, wife of Anne Arundel County's County Executive at the time; and Mrs. Roger W. (Ellen) Moyer, wife of then-mayor of Annapolis Roger "Pip" Moyer, pose after Mrs. Keith presented historic building markers to the group for placement on buildings. The markers are for the State House, the John Shaw House, shown in the background at 21 State Circle, and the small Greek Revival building (now the Franklin Law Office) to its left. May 4, 1967. Courtesy of The Capital. Photograph by Lee Troutner.

poisonous compound prepared by treating copper with acetic acid, used as a medicine pigment, and dye." The word also refers to "a greenish-blue coating that forms like rust on brass, bronze, or copper."[1]

Appropriately, Verdigris markers are greenish-blue and appear on Greek Revival buildings. Built between 1820–60, they resemble austere, ancient Greek architecture. Square transom lights, large square windows, and "temple-like door surrounds" are all indicators of this style. The James Andrews House, at 16 Maryland Avenue, is an excellent example of a Greek Revival building.

So is 184 Duke of Gloucester Street. Its marker, which includes the phrase "c. 1860–70," presents an opportunity for a vocabulary lesson. The lowercase letter "c." is the abbreviation for circa, a Latin word used to indicate an approximate date or figure. What is most unique about this building's marker is that it contains two colors: verdigris and aubergine.

Aubergine, or purple, markers appear on buildings erected between 1869–1901. They reflect one or more Victorian or "Romantic" architectural styles. 184 Duke of Gloucester Street represents the Gothic Revival Style. Other Victorian styles include French Second Empire, Queen Anne, and Romanesque.

Brackets, bay windows, elaborate brickwork towers, and verandas all define Victorian Architecture. These features appear on many Victorian buildings in Annapolis such as the Banneker-Douglass Museum at 84 Franklin Street. Formerly Mount Moriah AME (African Methodist Episcopal) Church, this building also represents the Gothic Revival Style.

Near the museum, many buildings on Market and Conduit Streets have Chesapeake Gray markers. Buildings with these markers represent 19th- or 20th-century Annapolis Vernacular architecture and were built between 1837–1921. Annapolis Vernacular houses do one or more of the following: They reflect local culture and building materials; their designs use simplified classical, Federal, and Italianate motifs; and, they are sometimes row or paired houses. Row houses called "Rainbow Row" (c. 1850s) on Conduit Street are good examples of this style.

151 Prince George Street has a distinct Chesapeake Gray marker. Most of the marker is gray, except for its Liberty Tree, which is painted a brilliant gold. The home's owners probably painted the tree, since HAF has no record of doing so.

Several blocks up Prince George Street, towards the actual Liberty Tree's former location, is an example of the eighth and final marker color. An Ochre marker appears on 240 Prince George Street. This house was built between 1903–13, and reflects two of many 20th-century distinctive architectural styles: American Foursquare and Colonial Revival. Others include Tudor Revival, the Craftsman Style, and Beaux Arts, which raises a good question.

Beaux Arts buildings are present throughout the Naval Academy's grounds. However, not one has a historic building marker issued by HAF. Why is this the case? Because the Academy is not part of the city's Historic District and, therefore, its buildings are ineligible to receive them.[2]

Fireplace Mantel Preserves Century-old Letters

The home at 203 Duke of Gloucester Street has a historic building marker. This vignette describes how two letters were preserved there for a century, and what they reveal about Annapolis when they were written.

Sallie Wells did something peculiar with her mail in the early 1900s: after reading it, she put some of the letters atop her dining room mantel. Unfortunately, two of them slipped through a crack behind it, well beyond her reach, in about 1905.

George Brown rediscovered the letters in 2002, while renovating his new (and Sallie's former) residence.

Sallie lived with her husband, John B. Wells, at what the letters call "203 Gloucester Street." John was born in 1846 to a prominent Annapolis family. His father, George Wells, Jr., was an esteemed business, civic, and political leader. He served as President of Farmers National Bank, President of the Maryland Senate, and helped to found the Methodist Episcopal Church in the city.

John's older brother George was equally successful. Born in 1843, he studied medicine at the College of Physicians and Surgeons in New York. He graduated from there in 1867, spent a year in France, and then returned to Annapolis to become a physician. In addition to practicing medicine, George was a political leader; he served as a city alderman, a Maryland State Senator and Delegate, and Clerk of the Court for Anne Arundel County.

John was also politically active. He was sheriff of Anne Arundel County, a magistrate under Governor Austin Crothers' administration, and City Treasurer. Upon his death the *Evening Capital* described him as "a remarkable man in many respects . . . a farmer for many years . . . [and] a man of determined will and strong convictions, just and upright in his dealing toward all."[1]

John married twenty-four-year-old Sallie Elizabeth Beach in 1879. The couple had five children, including Beatrice, Frances, John, Jr., Katherine, and Anne, who died in 1905. The letters Sallie received at about that time are amusing; they're also informative and offer insight into life in early 20th-century Annapolis.

Nellie Latimer wrote the first letter to Sallie on February 28, 1904. Nellie lived in South River, Maryland, and her words reveal that some well-to-do local women—including Sallie—relied on domestic help. As she wrote in ornate script,

My dear Sallie,
    I have tried to secure a servant for you, but must give up in despair.
    I was [thinking] of two in town who formerly lived in the Randall's,

the other at John Collinson's Boarding House. I just heard of one going to town shortly [but] find that she has a place engaged. I [do] hope . . . you have been fortunate enough to secure a good woman . . .

Nellie's letter also reveals that winter of 1904 was harsh. She wrote that, "N and I have had invitations . . . The one invitation was for N and myself . . . [It] will be March 2nd. Everyone will attend, but I do not think I would under existing circumstances. Are we not having disagreeable weather? There is quite a lot of sickness in the neighborhood and Dr. C is kept in the wing . . . I wanted to send this note by mail . . . but from present prospects of weather am going to send it—"

Newspaper reports confirm Nellie's comments about the weather. In late February, the *Evening Capital* published these "Snapshots": "More snow," "Sleet comes next," and "The burning question is how many pairs of over shoes have you worn out this winter?"

The weather probably contributed to the "sickness" that kept "Dr. C" busy in Nellie's "neighborhood." "Dr. C" was surely Dr. John Collinson. Born in 1849, he graduated from the University of Maryland Medical School at age twenty. He married Mary E. Brewer in 1880, and the couple had five children, including one who died at birth. They lived in South River, and an 1896–97 directory lists him as a "Physician" there.[2]

Finally, Nellie's letter reveals that locals weren't above a little gossip now

and then. She wrote that, "I hope Louise is all right again . . . She resembled the little fat woman. I could not help but laugh at her . . . With lots of love, your sincere friend, Nellie B. Latimer."

Sallie's niece, Nell, wrote the second letter that Mr. Brown discovered in 2002. Dated April 22, 1905, it began,

"Dear Aunt Sallie, How are you all now? I wish E and I could drop in on you for a little while this Easter but she has no holiday. . . ."

Mr. Brown found Nell's letter in its original envelope. And, although it lists no return address, it suggests that Nell lived in Washington, D.C. The words "Woodward and Lothrop, Washington" appear in black ink on the front of the

203 Duke of Gloucester Street. Courtesy of George T. Brown. Photograph by David Hartcorn, 2005.

Mr. Brown discovered Sallie's letters (as well as a watch, hatpins, and thimbles) behind this walnut mantel, shown above in its original setting, the parlor. Mr. Brown moved it there in 2002, from the dining room, which is shown in the following figure. Courtesy of George T. Brown. Photograph by David Hartcorn, 2005.

The dining room in which the mantel was located in 2002. Mr. Brown made the room's current mantel shown above. Courtesy of George T. Brown. Photograph by David Hartcorn, 2005.

envelope. This department store had recently opened at 1025 F Street in Washington. A postmark also indicates that the letter left Washington on April 21 at 3 P.M., and arrived at Annapolis at 6 P.M. the same day.

Although Nell probably lived in Washington, her words offer information about Annapolis and its residents in 1905. For instance, she wrote this account of John Yellott: "I saw by the paper that John Yellott was to preach at St. Anne's a week or two ago. Did any of you hear him? I used to know him as a boy in St. John's, and it seems funny to think of him as a minister. I don't remember if the girls knew him them or not. . . ."[3]

Nell's letter also suggests that she came from an affluent family. Like Sallie, she also had servants. She noted that, "I am going to have a woman in the house to help me do a little sewing . . . Well, I guess I must hurry now to lunch. Our cook, you know, is still in the hospital, so the girls and Mrs. F. have everything to do. It goes right hard with them for they are not used to much work."

In addition to having domestic help, Nell's family owned a considerable amount of land. As she boasted, "Did you hear of our good fortune? Two more lots have been sold for $900 in all. Isn't that fine? We have now just one small one left. They certainly have been taken up very quickly. . . ."

Finally, Nell's letter suggests what local women wore in 1905. She wrote that, "E and I are sending a little package by express. We will send it this afternoon so you ought to get it tomorrow, Saturday. If the waist and gloves do not fit they can be exchanged but I hope they are all right . . . If you would rather have another kind of waist, Aunt Sallie, don't mind saying so because one got this with the understanding that it could be exchanged for any other kind." She then closed by stating, "With lots of love to you all from us both, Nell."

Shortly after *The Capital* published my column about Sallie's letters, I received a special letter. It was from Mary Lee Thorsby of San Antonio, Texas, whose second cousin, Mary Katherine Kaiser (maiden name Collinson), had sent her a copy of it. Mrs. Kaiser had received the column from her aunt who lived in Southern Anne Arundel County.

Mrs. Thorsby wrote to inform me that Dr. John Collinson was her grandfather, and that Eleanor (Nellie) Latimer was her great-aunt. Nellie's sister, Mary Brewer, was Dr. Collinson's wife. Mrs. Thorsby also contacted Mr. Brown. She visited him at his home in 2003, and, during their meeting, he offered her the letters. She accepted them with much appreciation.

Preserving the Memory of British Convicts

While Sallie traveled all the way from Texas to learn more about her heritage, Philip Sellars made a much longer trip. In 2004, he came to Annapolis from London for two reasons: to learn about the staggering number of British convicts who were shipped there in the 18th century and to create a radio program to preserve their memory. This is his story.

Were your ancestors convicts? If so, you might have been able to help Philip Sellars, an executive producer with the BBC (British Broadcasting Corporation). Mr. Sellars came to Annapolis from London in June 2004 to make a program for the BBC radio series "Document."

This award-winning investigative history series follows a historical document through time to trace its impact on events. In this case, the document was the Transportation Act of 1718. Passed by the British government, the Act radically increased the number of British convicts that were transported between 1718 and 1776 to America, where they were sold as slaves. They remained in slavery for seven or fourteen years, depending on the severity of their crime.

Many lived in Maryland, including Annapolis, which is what brought Mr. Sellars and his team to town. They came to learn what happened to the convicts after they crossed the Atlantic. And to do so, they made several plans for their stay—plans that could have involved you if your relative was among the transported.

Prior to coming, Mr. Sellars said, "Crucially, we'd love to find someone who claims to have been descended from a convict who arrived in this way." Interviewing such a person could answer questions including: What was a convict's life like in America? How did it differ, if at all, from that of indentured laborers who were here? Did the convicts re-offend? And, what did locals think of them; did they view them as cheap labor (the convicts cost less than indentured servants and African slaves) or a "menacing reminder of the old country?"

The team also planned to visit sites where the convicts might have lived in Annapolis, London Town, Baltimore, and Washington, D.C. There, they would search for "documents, portraits, or the like that might help illustrate this little known area of our common heritage," Mr. Sellars said. Finally, the team planned to interview local historians to give context to their discoveries and to help explain the issue to British audiences. Their interviews would appear in the program that summer.

The program would address a crucial topic in British history, as the Transportation Act's impact was enormous and sobering. About 50,000 British convicts were transported to America between 1718 and 1776—including nearly 35,000 from England and Wales, 16,000 from Ireland, and 800 from Scotland—making them the largest group ever forced to come here, next to African slaves. So popular was the punishment that by 1772, three-fifths of all male convicts in England were being transported, and by 1775, only a tenth of British convicts were being sentenced to prison. More than half of the convicts were in their twenties, and four-fifths were male. While most had committed property offenses, especially grand larceny, others were guilty of petty theft, stealing sheep, or were vagabonds.

Transportation was also used to punish children convicted of lesser capital offenses, in order to save their lives. However, transportation didn't always "save lives." Many died during their voyage, due to illness or overexertion. Mr. Sellars

Some of the British convicts who were transported to America served their sentences south of Annapolis, at London Town. The William Brown House at London Town, above, was built between 1758 and 1764. It overlooks the South River and is one of two buildings that survive from colonial London Town. Illustration by the author.

hoped the program would raise awareness about transportation, and dispel one of the greatest myths surrounding it: that convicts were only sent to Australia.

"The transportation of thousands of British citizens to America—against their will—is a lost piece of history for many people in Britain. Mention transporting convicts and they readily think of Australia, not the Chesapeake," he said. "In this program we're hoping to find descendants of these convicts to prove that no matter humble your origins, you can still make good in America."

The Capital announced Mr. Sellars's plan to come to Annapolis one week before his arrival. It asked anyone who was descended from a transported convict to contact him or the newspaper. The response was overwhelming. Over a dozen people

ANNAPOLIS.

On Monday laſt, the Ship *Greyhound*, Capt. *Gracie*, arrived in *Potowmack* from *London*, with Convicts.

Cuſtom Houſe, ANNAPOLIS, *Entered ſince* November 13.
Sloop Molly, George Perkins, from Barbadoes ;
Sloop Nancy, Thomas Price, from Virginia ;
Ship Cheſter, John Lorain, from Briſtol ;
Sloop Haerlem, Daniel England, from Coracoa ;
Sloop Hopewell, Sweetman Burn, from Antigua ;
Schooner Sparrow, Samuel Weſt, from Salem ;
Cleared for Departure,
Ship Speedwell, Nicholas Stephenſon, for London ;
Schooner Peggy, William Davis, for Virginia ;
Schooner Wilcox, Joſeph Berry, for Virginia ;
Sloop Induſtry, John Strup, for Liſbon ;
Brigantine

Brigantine Abington, James Mudie, for Virginia ;
Sloop Dolphin, Thomas Currier, for North-Carolina.

The Maryland Gazette *often announced the arrival of convicts to the greater Annapolis area. Consider this advertisement that appeared on December 11, 1751 (p. 2 and 3). Courtesy of the Maryland State Archives* SPECIAL COLLECTIONS *(Maryland State Law Library Collection of the* Maryland Gazette*)* Maryland Gazette, Advertisement for the arrival/sale of convicts, *Dec. 11, 1751 MSA SC 2311-1-4.*

in the Annapolis area came forward with information about their convict ancestors within seven days. Mr. Sellars was "surprised and delighted" by this result.

John Gadd was among the first to answer *The Capital*'s query. However his ancestor, Thomas Gadd, was transported to America in 1661, before the Transportation Act of 1718.

Ella Rowe also responded. Ms. Rowe, corresponding secretary for the Maryland Genealogical Society, contacted WYPR-88.1 FM during a live panel with Mr. Sellars's associate Mike Thomson; Robert Barnes, a Reference Archivist from the Maryland State Archives; and Historic Annapolis Foundation President Dr. Gregory Stiverson.

Ella's ancestor, Jonathan Ady, was exiled, or "transported," to America in 1737, after London's Old Bailey court found him guilty of stealing a linen handkerchief among other items. He served his seven-year term under Thomas Brerewood in Baltimore County, married, had eleven children, and became a farmer, cooper, and landowner near today's Monkton, Maryland.

Carol Carman's ancestor, Thomas Flory, also settled in Maryland. Ms. Carman, an active member and past president of the Anne Arundel Genealogical Society, contacted WYPR-88.1 FM and *The Capital*. She began researching her family's history in 1989. She soon discovered two distant cousins, who informed her of their mutual convict ancestor.

Thomas was supposed to come to America in 1719 as an indentured servant. Instead, the eighteen-year-old Brit was convicted of stealing a silk handkerchief valued at 2 shillings and was exiled as a convict. He arrived in Annapolis in 1721 aboard the ship *Gilbert,* served his time, and ended up as a landowner, husband, father of eight—and Carol's fifth great-grandfather on her father's side. He lived in Virginia and Anne Arundel County before establishing himself near Fort Frederick in Washington County.

Many of the transported convicts, including Thomas and Jonathan, did modestly well after serving their sentences. Others returned to crime, such as Jeremiah Swift, who was tried, convicted, and hanged for murdering his master's children. And a few, like Charles Peale, became famous. He was transported to Annapolis in the 1730s, after being convicted of stealing money from the London post office where he was employed. After serving his sentence, he became a schoolmaster and landowner, married, had many children including the renowned artist Charles Wilson Peale, and died with a sizeable personal estate.

"He did well for a convict," Mr. Barnes said. "All of this points out that you're never through. We're learning that more and more of them [the convicts] paid their debts to society and then became established citizens."[1]

Charles Peale's name appears in Peter Wilson Coldham's book *The Complete Book of Emigrants in Bondage 1614-1775,* which lists many of those sent here under the Transportation Act. Another famous—or rather, infamous— name appears in another of Coldham's books. According to *Bonded Passengers to American, Volume 2,* Richard Nixon of St. Mary Whitechapel was transported in 1736 to Maryland for an ironic crime: "breaking and entering."[2]

Mr. Sellars's program, "Land of the Unfree," aired on September 6, 2004, on BBC Radio 4. It was a sensation. He and Mr. Thomson attributed much of its success to their Annapolis visit. As Mr. Sellars said, "Mike and I are very grateful to the archivists, historians, and readers of *The Capital* for their assistance . . . It was a real pleasure to see what an important part of life personal history is in this part of the world—as a history programme maker it was a treat to rummage around in a state so steeped in its own past."[3]

Annapolis in December 1904

In 2004, Mayor Ellen O. Moyer commissioned Ginger Doyel to create the city of Annapolis's annual holiday open house invitation. Using watercolor and pencil, the artist drew this image for the front of the card. It depicts Annapolis in December 1904, and features these and other scenes reported by the *Evening Capital* that month:

Skating on the Spa: The boys and girls were skating on Spa creek today. The creek is frozen from shore to shore and the ice is of several inches in thickness . . .

Down at the market house greens are displayed in lavish profusion. Trees of all sizes and many kinds are to be seen and holly and mistletoe in wreaths and crowns are on many stalls. The presence of the snow on the ground seems to stimulate the sale of Christmas greens . . .

In spite of the bad weather which turned . . . the city streets into a loblolly of slush and mud, the town was alive with shoppers today . . . Country teams were seen in great numbers loaded with their freight of Christmas green and happy, though ardor dampened farmers' families . . .

Dozens of boats rode anchor in the Annapolis harbor all day yesterday. Few left the safe anchorage today to proceed on their cruise as the weather was threatening . . . Covered with snow and ice the tied up oyster boats can be seen on all sides. It has been absolutely impossible for them to get out on the tonging grounds . . .

Festooned in a garland of snow, sparkling in the bright lights of a pleasant night and muffled beneath the soft carpet of the hurrying flakes, Annapolis presented a bewildering sight of beauty Saturday night . . . Every tree and shrub, fence and building, telephone and telegraph wire carried its burden of snow, that glistened and gleamed, glared and sparkled . . .

Sleigh riding a dog: A little girl on West Street has attracted considerable attention during the recent snow storms by riding her pet dog up

Annapolis in December 1904. Illustration by the author.

and down the street on her sled. The little dog sits upright and seems to enjoy the sport. The animal holds on as his mistress rides him over the gutters and rough places . . .

The artist chose these scenes for a reason: they are relative to current events and issues in Annapolis. For instance, the boat club, oyster shed, and Fish Market on the waterfront are meant to remind people that the Chesapeake Bay was (and still is) crucial to the city's character and livelihood. The horses and wagons are meant to convey that the city's streets weren't designed for cars. And, that Spa Creek was frozen (as it often was in the early 20th century) suggests that the local climate has changed.

Articles about the illustration appeared in both *The Capital* and *Baltimore Sun* newspapers in December 2004. The artist is currently creating a second edition of the card. It features a similar panorama of the U.S. Naval Academy in 1905 and will be available in December 2005.

Appendix 1. Market Space Deed

On July 28, 1784, eight men granted the city of Annapolis 1.43 acres (approximately today's Market Space) through this deed:

"This Indenture made this Twenty Eighth Day of July in the year of our Lord one thousand seven Hundred and Eighty four Between Nicholas Carroll Jacob Hurst Charles Wallace, Joseph Williams Thomas Harwood John Davidson James Mackubin and James Williams of the City of Annapolis Gentlemen of the one part and the Mayor Recorder Aldermen and Common Council of the City of Annapolis of the other part Witnesseth that the said Nicholas Carroll, . . . for and in Consideration of the Sum of five Shillings sterling to them in hand paid by the said Mayor Recorder Aldermen and Common Council of the City of Annapolis the Receipt wherof is hereby Acknowledged have granted bargained sold aliened enfeoffed released and confirmed by those Presents and said Nicholas Carroll . . . do grant bargain Sell alien enfeoff release and confirm unto the said Mayor Recorder Aldermen and Common Council of the City of Annapolis and their Successors for ever all that portion or parcel of Ground lying and being in the City of Annapolis at the head of the Dock Beginning at a Post Standing at the North East Corner of Mr. James Williams's House and running South forty Degrees West three Hundred and Ninety two feet & a half foot till it intersects the line of Church Street on the South West Side of the Dock, thence with said Street South Seventy four and a quarter Degrees East two hundred and Nineteen feet to a post Thence with a straight line to the beginning and all the Rights Title Interest use property Claim and Demand as well in Law as in Equity of them the said Nicholas Carroll . . . of in and to the said Portion or Parcel of Ground or any part thereof To have and to hold the said Right Title Interest [sic] use property together with all the Claims and Demands as well as in Law as in Equity of them the said Nicholas Carroll . . . of in and to the said portion or parcel of Land or any part thereof unto the said Mayor Recorder . . . provided always and these presence are upon the express Conditions that the said Mayor Recorder Aldermen and Common Council of the said City of Annapolis or their Successors erect or cause to be erected on the said Ground hereby granted to them a good Substantial Brick Stone or framed Market House well fitted with all Accomodations necessary for the Reception and Sale of Provisions of Sixty feet in Length and forty feet in width the said Building to be erected on the Westernmost part of the aforesaid portion or parcel of Ground hereby granted near to the line of Church Street the front of Sixty feet in length to stand in a Line parallel to the line of the large Brick Building facing the Dock now Occupied by Messrs Charles Wallace Joseph Williams Thomas Harwood and John Davidson leaving the Distance of Eighty feet between the Line of the said Building and the aforesaid Line which space of Eighty feet in width to be Continued along the said Lines from the south west to North East the whole extent of the portion or parcel of Ground hereby Granted to be established and used as a publick Street the Westermost end of the aforesaid Building to be erected for a Market House in depth forty feet to be opposed to Church Street that portion of Ground lying between the aforesaid Building and the Water Eighty feet in Width to be Continued from the South West to the North East in a Direction parrallel with said Building the whole Extent of the portion or parcel of Ground hereby granted and be established and used as a publick Street all the Remainder of the said portion of parcel of ground hereby granted excepting a space of Eighty foot in width fronting to the House now occupied by Mr. Gilbert Middleton and connecting the two Streets herein above mentioned to be reserved for the purpose of making further Additions if necessary to the Building to be Erected in Manner above described for the purposes herein before mentioned the aforesaid Building to be erected within the Space of three Years from the Date of these Presents otherwise this Indenture to be void and of no Effect . . ."[1]

Appendix 2. *"Resolution Regarding City Market," Passed by the Annapolis City Council on August 12, 1968*

"Whereas the Municipal Corporation is the owner of property located at Market Space within the City of Annapolis, and heretofore the Mayor and Aldermen have leased space within and about the building upon said premises for use as a public market place;

And whereas, the building upon said premises has deteriorated and depreciated, and is now in a state of disrepair;

And whereas, The Mayor and Aldermen have determined that it is no longer necessary to maintain public premises for a city market place, and that the objects and purposes for which the said premises were originally intended are no longer being served;

And whereas, the Mayor and Aldermen have determined that it would be in the public interest to demolish the building upon the said premises to enhance the appearance of this area and to provide for a free flow of vehicular traffic, and to provide additional parking facilities and open space, and to relieve congestion in the area,

Now therefore, be it resolved this 12 day of August, 1968, by the mayor and aldermen of the City of Annapolis that the building known as the City Market shall be demolished and removed; and the City Attorney is hereby directed to notify all tenants of the said market place that their tenancy of said premises shall terminate effective December 31, 1968, and they shall vacate on or before that date; and the City Engineer is hereby directed to thereafter cause the building to be demolished and removed, and to present to the Mayor and Aldermen, as soon as practicable hereafter, a plan for redevelopment of the said area to relieve the existing congestion therein, to provide for a free flow of traffic in the area, with adequate open space to enhance the beauty and attractiveness of the City."[1]

Notes

F. Marion Lazenby and the Annapolis Dairy Products Company

1. Kendall Banning, *Annapolis Today*, 255.
2. Richard Lazenby, personal interviews: 1 December 2002, 8 April 2003, and 25 October 2003.

Peggy Kimbo Remembers Growing up in a Segregated, Urban Annapolis

1. Peggy Kimbo, personal interviews: 25 September 2003 and 27 September 2003.

Orlando Ridout IV Recalls His Family's Woodlyn Farm Dairy

1. Orlando Ridout IV, personal interview: 12 November 2003.

J. Wilson Macey and The Annapolis Banking and Trust Company

1. *General Assembly January 6–April 4, 1904 Session Laws*, reproduced in William Hand Browne, Edward C. Papenfuse, et al., eds., *Archives of Maryland*, 215+volumes, (Baltimore and Annapolis, Md., 1883–) 209:3881 (hereinafter cited as *Archives of Maryland*). This series is ongoing and available online at http://archivesofmaryland.net where volumes, collectively or individually, can be searched electronically. The new act was called "An Act to repeal and re-enact with amendments Sections 1, 3, and 4 of Chapter 157 of the Acts of the General Assembly of Maryland passed at the January Session, 1900 entitled 'An Act to Incorporate the Annapolis Banking and Trust Company.'"
2. J. Wilson Macey, personal interview: 14 November 2003.

Charles and Edward Weiss: Immigrants, Brothers, and Businessmen

1. Albert E. Walker, ed., *The Evening Capital Historical and Industrial Edition: Portraying the Glorious Past and Future Possibilities of Annapolis, Maryland*, 37 (hereinafter referred to as Walker, *Historical*).
2. Ibid., 36.

The Troublesome Kate Kealy

1. *Evening Capital* (Annapolis, Md.), 18 September 1903 (hereinafter referred to as *Evening*).
2. Ibid., 14 September 1903.

3. Ibid., 18 September 1903.
4. Ibid., 7 October 1903.
5. Ibid., 25 August 1903.
6. Ibid., 14 September 1903.
7. Ibid., 18 September 1903.
8. Ibid., 4 October 1903.
9. Ibid., 7 October 1903.
10. Ibid., 12 October 1903.
11. Ibid., 13 October 1903.
12. Ibid., 30 October 1903.
13. Ibid., 18 November 1903.
14. Ibid., 16 November 1903.

Pearl Gray's Runaway Wedding

1. David Holly, *Steamboat on the Chesapeake*, 98–99.
2. *Baltimore Sun* (Baltimore, Md.), 13 August 1903.
3. Ibid.

Winston Churchill—the American

1. Naval cadet record for Winston Churchill, 1.
2. Winston Churchill, *Army and Navy Register* 13 (1892): 513–14.
3. Winston Churchill, personal notebook. The Papers of Winston Churchill. ML16, Series 3, Box 5. Rauner Special Collections Library,
   Dartmouth College, Hanover, N.H.
4. Charles C. Burlingham, Letters of 6 October 1903 and 28 October 1903
   to unidentified newspaper. The letters are part of a collection of materials
   sent by John H. Dryfout of the Saint-Gauden's National Historic Site to
   Midshipman 3/C Brian T. Smith on 21 March 1988 (hereinafter referred
   to as Dryfout, materials). The package is located in Alumni jacket # 2147.
   U.S. Naval Academy Special Collections & Archives, Nimitz Library,
   Annapolis, Md. (hereinafter referred to as Nimitz).
5. Photocopy of unidentified biographical entry for Winston Churchill. Handwritten citation on the copy reads "DAB suppl.4." Dryfout, materials. Nimitz.
6. Ibid.
7. *The National Cyclopedia of American Biography, Vol. 10*, 178–79.
8. Photocopy of unidentified chronology for Winston Churchill. Dryfout,
   materials. Nimitz.
9. Winston Churchill, *Richard Carvel*, vii–viii.
10. Capt. John P. W. Vest, USN (Ret.), "Ripples from a Novel," *Shipmate* 45,
    no. 7(1982): 31–32.
11. *Evening*, 3 January 1902.
12. Capt. John P. W. Vest, USN (Ret.), "Ripples from a Novel," *Shipmate* 45,
    no. 7(1982): 31–32.

13. Winston Churchill. Letter of 20 June 1899 to Winston Churchill. Photocopy of original letter formerly located at Rauner Special Collections Library, Dartmouth College, Hanover, N.H. Alumni jacket #2147. Nimitz.

Robert Campbell Recalls Prohibition and Politics in Annapolis

1. Robert Campbell, personal interviews: 12 March 2004 and 24 September 2004.

Henry Campbell, the Old Fish Market, and How "Old Bay" Came to Town

1. Robert Campbell, personal interviews: 12 March 2004 and 24 September 2004.
2. McCormick & Co. Inc. "Old Bay: Traditionally Old Bay, An Historical Tale to Tell."
3. Walker, *Historical*, 24.

William Henry Hebron, the "Jewish" Fish Merchant

1. *Johnson's Directory of Annapolis, Maryland for 1896–97*, 29 (hereinafter referred to as *Johnson's*).
2. *Gould & Halleron Annapolis City Directory, 1910*, 3, 53, and 132 (hereinafter referred to as *Gould*).

Edward and Ella Burtis: Market Master, Market Mistress

1. Robert Harry McIntire, *Annapolis Maryland Families, Vol. I*, 105 (hereinafter referred to as McIntire, *Families*); *Evening*, 22 August 1924.
2. *The Code of the City of Annapolis by the Counselor*, 68 (hereinafter referred to as *The Code*).
3. Ibid., 89, 91–92.
4. Ibid., 82–93.
5. Clarence Marbury White, Sr. and Evangeline Kaiser White, *The Years Between: A Chronicle of Annapolis, Maryland, 1800–1900 and Memoirs of Clarence Marbury White, Sr. and Evangeline Kaiser White*, 32–34.
6. Don Riley, "I Remember . . . Sights and Smells of Old Annapolis Market," 2.
7. Hildegarde Hawthorne, *Rambles in Old College Towns*. In Mame and Marion Warren's *Maryland Time Exposures 1840–1940*, 187–88.
8. *Polk's City Directory for Annapolis, Maryland 1924*, 27 (hereinafter referred to as *Polk's 1924*).
9. *Evening*, 22 August 1924.
10. Ibid., 26 August 1924.
11. Ibid., 21 July 1931.
12. Annapolis Mayor and Aldermen (Proceedings) 1931–1935. MSA M49-24, 190. MdHR 19,996-3.
13. Ibid., 231.

14. Ibid., Annapolis Mayor and Aldermen (Proceedings) 1935–1941. MSA M49-25, 21–22. MdHR 19,996-4.
15. Ibid., and *Evening,* 15 October 1935.
16. *Evening,* 10 December 1935.
17. Ibid., and Annapolis Mayor and Aldermen (Proceedings) 1935–1941. MSA M49-25, 31–32. MdHR 19,996-4. The petition did not convince Aldermen Jackson and Spriggs. Both still held that she was "incompetent," and voted against her.
18. *Evening,* 20 July 1937.
19. William J. McWilliams, *Charter and Code of the City of Annapolis, Revised and Annotated,* 182–89 (hereinafter referred to as McWilliams, *Charter*).
20. *Evening,* 14 July 1939.
21. Ibid.

Lou Hyatt, "the King of Shoeboxes"

1. The Hyatt's store was where Mangia Italian Grill & Sports Cafe is today.
2. Louis Hyatt, personal interview: 21 September 2004.

James Strange Spoils Halloween for Local Youths

1. *Evening,* 31 October 1916.
2. Ibid.
3. Ibid., 31 October 1917.
4. Ibid., 1 November 1917.
5. Ibid., 29 October 1918.
6. Ibid.
7. Ibid.
8. Ibid.
9. Ibid., 17 October, 1918.
10. Ibid., 1 November 1918.
11. Ibid.

Peter and Helen Palaigos Recall Pete's Place

1. Kimberly Williams, "163 Main Street, Inventory No. AA-561," Section 8, 1 (hereinafter referred to as Williams, "163"). Her source is Prov. Court Liber BT 4, Folio 393, December 5, 1761.
2. Ibid. Her source is Will Liber 34, Folio 8, recorded June 7, 1766.
3. Ibid. Her source is McIntire, *Families, Vol I,* 209.
4. Ibid. Her source is Liber NH, Folio 597.
5. Shirley Baltz, *Quays of the City,* 44 (hereinafter referred to as Baltz, *Quays*).
6. Ibid. Her source is Diary of Samuel Vaughn. Manuscript Division, Library of Congress.
7. Williams, "163," Section 8, 4.
8. Ibid. Her source is Liber WNN, Folio 148.

9. Peter and Helen Palaigos, personal interviews: 8 December 2003 and 22 April 2004.

Francis R. Geraci, Jr., and the City's Former "Tonsorial Saloons"

1. Francis R. Geraci, Jr., "Descendants of Francesco Geraci." Genealogical report. Courtesy of Francis R. Geraci, Jr., Annapolis, Md., n. date, 2. Will dated 15 November 1905.
2. Ibid.
3. *Evening*, 18 March 1920.
4. Francis R. Geraci, Jr., personal interview: 13 November 2003.

Carolyn Martin's Sandwiches

1. Joseph and Jo Ann Martin, personal interviews: 24 September 2004 and 30 September 2004.

Dr. Faye Allen Reflects on Practicing Medicine and Marrying Dr. Aris T. Allen

1. Jude Thomas May, *Achieving the American Dream: The Life of the Honorable Aris T. Allen, M.D.*, 178–79.
2. Dr. Faye Allen, personal interview: 4 May 2004.

Harry Klasmeier Recalls a "Quiet and Reserved" Annapolis

1. Harry Klasmeier, personal interview: 30 July 2003.

Market House on the Move (1698–1775)

1. Anthony Lindauer, personal interview: 20 October 2003.
2. *Proceedings and Acts of the General Assembly, October 1678–November 1683*, *Archives of Maryland*, 7:612.
3. Anthony Lindauer, *From Paths to Plats: The Development of Annapolis, 1651–1718*, 10 (hereinafter referred to as Lindauer, *From Paths to Plats*).
4. *Proceedings and Acts of the General Assembly, 1693–1697*, *Archives of Maryland*, 19:119 and 227.
5. Lindauer, *From Paths to Plats*, 18.
6. *Proceedings and Acts of the General Assembly, March 1697/8–July 1699*, *Archives of Maryland*, 22:114.
7. Ebenezer Cook, *Sot-weed Factor, or A Voyage to Maryland*, a satyr.
8. David Ridgely, *Annals of Annapolis*, 121–22 (hereinafter referred to as Ridgely, *Annals*).
9. Ibid., 122.
10. Anne Yentsch, *A Chesapeake Family and Their Slaves: A study in historical archaeology*, 245 (hereinafter referred to as Yentsch, *A Chesapeake Family*).
11. Dr. Morris L. Radoff, *Buildings of the State of Maryland at Annapolis*, 57 (hereinafter referred to as Radoff, *Buildings*). His source is Stoddert's Report, f. 3, Ms. Land Office.

12. Radoff, *Buildings,* 57–58.
13. Yentsch, *A Chesapeake Family,* 245.
14. *Proceedings and Acts of the General Assembly, March 1697/8–July 1699, Archives of Maryland,* 22:111.
15. Ibid., 503–04, 292, and 341.
16. Elihu S. Riley, *The Ancient City,* 90 (hereinafter referred to as Riley, *City*).
17. Sir William Blackstone, *Commentaries on the Laws of England (Bk. 3, Ch. 4).*
18. *Proceedings and Acts of the General Assembly, March 26, 1707–November 4, 1710, Archives of Maryland,* 27:358.
19. Riley, *City,* 130.
20. *Proceedings and Acts of the General Assembly, July 7, 1740–June 4, 1744, Archives of Maryland,* 42: 623.
21. Ibid.
22. Ibid.
23. Yentsch, *A Chesapeake Family,* 247.
24. *Proceedings and Acts of the General Assembly, October 10, 1727–August 8,1729, Archives of Maryland,* 36:282–83. The act was called "An Act to appropriate Part of the Land laid out in the City of Annapolis for the building a Custom-House on, to and for the building a Market-house."
25. Ibid.
26. Ibid.
27. Yentsch, *A Chesapeake Family,* 242.
28. Ibid.
29. *Maryland Gazette,* 20 October 1730. Photostat in *The Maryland Gazette December 10, 1778–November 29, 1734.* Maryland State Archives, Annapolis, Md. MSA SC 2626.
30. *Proceedings and Acts of the General Assembly, May 10, 1748–December 14, 1751, Archives of Maryland,* 46:626.
31. Radoff, *Buildings,* 59. The city paid J. Thompson to remove the old market house in 1755. See Baltz, *Quays,* 52.
32. Radoff, *Buildings,* 60, and *Maryland Historical Magazine* 14 (1919): 265.
33. Jane W. McWilliams, *Evening Capital* (Annapolis, Md.), "From the pages of the Maryland Gazette," 9 February 1970.
34. *Maryland Gazette,* 7 February 1754.
35. Ibid., 7 September 1775.
36. Radoff, *Buildings,* 60.
37. Yentsch, *A Chesapeake Family,* 264.
38. *Journal and Correspondence of the Maryland Council of Safety, July 7, 1776–December 31, 1776, Archives of Maryland,* 12:89.

Eight Generous Gentlemen

1. Radoff, *Buildings,* 60–62. Also see Baltz, *Quays,* 55.

2. Mark B. Letzer and Jean B. Russo, eds., *The Diary of William Faris: The Daily Life of an Annapolis Silversmith*, 132 (hereinafter referred to as Letzer and Russo, *Diary*).

3. *Maryland Gazette*, 16 October 1794.

4. Letzer and Russo, *Diary*, 154.

5. Mayor's Court Land Records, MSA M41-1, 428-30. MdHR 7833-3.

6. Letzer and Russo, *Diary*, 427.

7. *Maryland Gazette*, 16 February 1786.

8. Sara Jane Rose, "Facts Pertaining to the Annapolis Market House" (hereinafter referred to as Rose, *Facts*). Her source is Corporation Accounts for the City of Annapolis (1785–1903, folio 6).

9. Rose, *Facts*. Her source is Annapolis By-Laws and Ordinances, Box 1, 1779–1819, 5157A.

10. Letzer and Russo, *Diary*, 130.

11. Ibid.

12. Ibid.

13. Baltz, *Quays*, 55. Her source is Annapolis Records 12: folio 111, 3 February 1787.

14. Letzer and Russo, *Diary*, 304.

15. Ibid., 401

16. Ibid.

17. Ibid., 404. *The Diary* also notes that in 1798 Wells, "owned a one-story frame dwelling, with a brick smoke house and frame slaughter house."

18. Rose, *Facts*. Her source is Corporation Accounts, City of Annapolis, James Brice Treasurer 1784–1802, and A List of Stalls for the Year 1810, Annapolis Records, 9470, Licenses for Auctioneers, Market Stalls & Dogs 1810–1811, 14.

19. Norman Risjord, *Builders of Annapolis*, 37.

20. Letzer and Russo, *Diary*, 189.

21. Ibid., 140.

22. Ibid., 217.

23. Annapolis Mayor, Aldermen, and Councilmen (Proceedings) pp. 141–198 in Annapolis Records 6, 195–96, 1811–1819, MSA M47-15, MdHR 5102-3.

24. The Market Master couldn't charge more than 6¼ cents per hundred weight at the weigh-house, "and if less than one hundred weight, 6¼ cents for each draft weighted in the large scales . . . paid to the Treasurer." He also had to weigh items as needed during non-market hours, but could keep the profits incurred during these times. See *By-Laws of the Corporation of the City of Annapolis, Revised* (hereinafter referred to as *By-Laws, Revised*).

25. Rose, *Facts*. Her source is Annapolis Records #17, p. 57–58.

26. By 1897, the word "minor" had replaced the word "slave"; anyone found guilty of this offense paid no less than $2, but no more than $5 per offense.
27. Rose, *Facts*. Her source is Annapolis Records #17, p. 337.
28. Of this fine, half went to the informer and the other half went to the corporation.
29. *By-Laws, Revised,* 11–16.
30. Radoff, *Buildings*, 62.
31. Annapolis Mayor and Aldermen (Proceedings) 1862–63, MSA M49-8, Box 24, Folder 8, MdHR 5158-25.
32. James Wood Burch, "Report to Historic Annapolis on the Market House Study," 3.

Save the Library!

1. Barrett McKown, *The Annapolis and Anne Arundel County Public Library: A History*, 10 (hereinafter referred to as McKown, *Library*).
2. *Evening*, 23 February 1920.
3. McKown, *Library*, 11.
4. *Evening*, 7 January 1936.
5. *Evening Sun* (Baltimore, Md.), 10 May 1943.
6. Ibid., 10 August 1943.
7. *Baltimore News American*, 28 September 1947.
8. McKown, *Library*, 21.
9. *Baltimore News American*, 28 September 1947.
10. Ibid.
11. Ibid.
12. *Evening Sun*, 2 May 1949.
13. *Evening*, 29 December 1961.

Save the Post Office!

1. *Evening*, 1 November 1900.
2. Ibid., 29 November 1901.
3. This list includes eight of the fifteen reasons that their letter featured.
4. *Evening,* 29 November 1901.
5. Ibid., 2 January 1902.

Gil Crandall Recalls the Opening of the "New" Severn River Drawbridge

1. *Evening*, 14 October 1921.
2. *The National Cyclopedia of American Biography, Vol. D,* 298. Also, see *The National Cyclopedia of American Biography, Vol. 31* (New York: James T. White & Co., 1944) 6–7.
3. Henry B. Wilson. Letter of 1 October 1921 to Albert T. Ritchie. U.S. Naval Academy Records of the Superintendent. General

Correspondence/Support Facilities. Series: Civil Facilities & Relations. Box 1, Folder 1 "Bridges/Severn River."

4. Henry B. Wilson. Letter of 23 November 1921 to John Mackall. U.S. Naval Academy Records of the Superintendent. General Correspondence/Support Facilities. Series: Civil Facilities & Relations. Box 1, Folder 1 "Bridges/Severn River." Nimitz.

5. *Evening*, 29 April 1922.

6. Ibid., 5–15 June 1924, and *The Washington Post*, 15 June 1924.

7. Gilbert Crandall, personal interviews: 5 January 2004 and 4 April 2004.

8. Heather M. Iarusso, " 'Bridge-ing the generation gap," *The Capital*, 1 April 1994.

Oscar and Jean Grimes Lament the Loss of Local Farmland

1. Oscar and Jean Grimes, personal interview: 26 September 2004.

Annapolis High School Becomes Maryland Hall for the Creative Arts

1. Ellen Moyer, personal interview: 28 August 2003.

2. *Evening*, 6 November 1972.

3. *Evening*, 13 and 14 November 1972.

4. Laura Brown. Letter of 15 September 1976 to Alvin Jones. Maryland Hall for the Creative Arts history file. Maryland Hall for the Creative Arts, Annapolis, Md.

5. Melissa Moss, telephone interview: 28 August 2003.

6. *The Capital*, 10 and 28 March 1977.

7. Ibid., 28 December 1978.

8. Ibid.

9. Joel McCord. "Art lovers try to raise the curtain on a new era." *The Sunday Sun*, 4 February 1979, Arundel Living, 1.

10. Ibid.

The Carroll Family—Buried Beneath a Shopping Center?

1. Robert L. Worden, *St. Mary's Church in Annapolis, Maryland: A Sesquicentennial History, 1853–2003*, 68.

2. Ibid.

3. Ibid., 69 and 199. Deed of Richard and Rebecca C. Turner of Washington, D.C., to Samuel J. and Sylvia B. Katcef, dated June 8, 1961, Book 1481, page 523, Anne Arundel County Land Records. The "grave yard lot" was surveyed by J. R. McCrone, Jr., Inc., Registered Land Surveyors, June 1, 1961, Job 5619, Book 1481, page 526, Anne Arundel County Land Records. The cemetery location is based on an analysis of the 1870 deed (Welch to Redemptorists, S.H. 4, folio 355), 1961 McCrone survey; April 11, 1970 topographic map, House Number and Tax Map #51, Planning and Zoning Commission, Anne Arundel County, Sheets T24

and T25; April 1986 Revised Site Plan, Annapolis Harbour Center; July 1, 1988 (rev.), Map 51, Maryland Department of Assessments and Taxation, Property Map Division; and June 1998, Map 51, Maryland Office of Planning, Property Mapping Section.

4. Ibid., 68–69.

5. Ibid., 68.

6. Ibid., 68–69.

7. Robert and Norma Worden, personal interview: 11 December 2003.

The J. F. Johnson Lumber Company Leaves Town

1. Harold E. Slanker, Jr. "The J. F. Johnson Lumber Company: A Composite History." *Anne Arundel County History Notes* 24, no. 4 (1993): 1–2 (hereinafter referred to as Slanker, "Composite History").

2. Ibid.

3. Ibid.

4. The J. F. Johnson Lumber Company, "The J. F. Johnson Lumber Company—75 years," 4.

5. Slanker, "Composite History," 2.

6. Mame Warren, *Then Again . . . Annapolis, 1900–1965,* xxii (hereinafter referred to as Warren, *Then Again*).

7. Harold E. Slanker, Jr. "The J. F. Johnson Lumber Company: A Composite History—Conclusion." Anne Arundel County History Notes 25, no. 1(1993): 1–2.

8. Harold E. Slanker, Jr., personal interview: 4 August 2004.

Admiral Dewey Lays the Chapel Cornerstone

1. Jack Sweetman, *The U.S. Naval Academy: An Illustrated History*, 2d ed., 141 (hereinafter referred to as Sweetman, *History*); James Cheevers, "United States Naval Academy Part III, A Golden Age," 36.

2. Navy Office of Information, Biographies Branch, "Admiral of the Navy George Dewey United States Navy, Deceased." 17 May 1963. Special Collections vertical file for George Dewey. Nimitz.

3. Sweetman, *History,* 51. George Dewey, *Autobiography of George Dewey with an introduction and notes by Eric McAllister Smith* (Annapolis, Md.: Naval Institute Press, 1987), 23. For specific offenses, see Cadet Record for George Dewey, Record Group 405, Cadet Records for Cadets 1853–1882. Nimitz.

4. *Evening,* 2 June 1904.

5. Ibid., 4 June 1904.

6. Ibid., 3 June 1904.

7. Ibid.

8. Alfred Keys Schanze, selected letters from 1904–08 (hereinafter referred to as Schanze, letters). Record Group Alumni/Memorabilia, Personal Papers, Alfred K. Schanze, Class of 1908. Nimitz.

9. *Evening*, 4 June 1904.

Alfred Schanze Records His Naval Academy Adventures

1. Schanze, letters.
2. *Annual Register of the United States Naval Academy, Annapolis, Maryland, 1903–04*, 113–19.
3. Walker, *Historical*, 11.
4. William Oliver Stevens, *Annapolis: Anne Arundel's Town*, 251–52.
5. *Maryland Republican* (Annapolis, Md.), 1901.
6. The USS *Terror*, a monitor, was decommissioned after the Spanish-American War. She was recommissioned in 1901 as a training vessel at the U.S. Naval Academy before being decommissioned a final time on May 8, 1906.
7. *Evening*, 26 August 1904.
8. 1905 *Lucky Bag*, 162–64.
9. *Evening*, 30 January 1905.
10. Sweetman, *History*, 102.

Why Midshipmen Toss Their Hats at Graduation

1. James Cheevers, telephone interview and email correspondences: 25 May 2004 and 26 May 2004.
2. Sweetman, *History*, 149.
3. Schanze, letters.
4. Ibid.

French Soldiers—Buried at St. John's?

1. *Evening*, 17 April 1911.
2. http://www.sjca.edu
3. *Evening*, 18 April 1911.

Annapolis's Other Military School

1. Hanson's *Laws of Maryland*, 1763–1784. *Archives of Maryland*. 203:395.
2. Tench F. Tilghman, *The Early History of St. John's College in Annapolis*, 52 (hereinafter referred to as Tilghman, *College*).
3. Ibid.
4. Ibid., 59–61.
5. Ibid., 92.
6. Ibid., 118.
7. Ibid., 125.
8. *Catalogue of St. John's College, Annapolis, Maryland, for the Academic Year 1884–1885* (Baltimore, Md.: Steam Press of James Young, 1885), 21.
9. Ibid., 18–21.
10. Tilghman, *College*, 167.

11. *Catalogue of St. John's Catalogue, Annapolis, Maryland, for the Academic Year 1886–1887* (Annapolis, Md.: Daily and Weekly Republican Steam Press, 1887), 39–41.
12. *Catalogue of St. John's College, Annapolis, Maryland, for the Academic Year 1907–1908* (Annapolis, Maryland Republican Print, 1908), 55.
13. Tilghman, *College*, 152.
14. *Catalogue of St. John's College, Annapolis, Maryland, for the Academic Year 1907–1908* (Annapolis, Maryland Republican Print, 1908), 56.
15. Ibid., 54–55.
16. Ibid., 56–57.
17. Tilghman, *College*, 163.
18. Ibid., 168.
19. Ibid., 171–72.
20. Ibid., 172.
21. *Catalogue of St. John's College, Annapolis, Maryland, for the Academic Year 1923–1924* (Annapolis, Md.: Capital Gazette Press, 1924), 12, 46–47.
22. *Catalogue of St. John's College, Annapolis, Maryland, for the Academic Year 1924–1925* (Annapolis, Md.: Capital Gazette Press, 1925), 23–25.
23. Tilghman, *College*, 172.
24. Emily A. Murphy, *A Complete and Generous Education: 300 Years of Liberal Arts, St. John's College, Annapolis,* 71 (hereinafter referred to as Murphy, *Complete*).

How Spanish Influenza Attacked St. John's and the Academy

1. Jane W. McWilliams, telephone interview: 19 October 2004.
2. Anne Marie Drew, ed., *Letters from Annapolis: Midshipmen Write Home, 1848–1969*, 123 (hereinafter referred to as Drew, *Letters*).
3. Ibid., 123–24.
4. Ibid., 124.
5. *Evening*, 2 November 1918
6. Jane W. McWilliams, telephone interview: 19 October 2004.
7. Janice Hayes-Williams, telephone interview: 21 October 2004.
8. Warren, *Then Again*, 38.
9. Drew, *Letters*, 124–25.

"A Pretty Piece of Land": How ROTC Saved St. John's from the Academy

1. *Evening*, 17 August 1945.
2. Ibid., 23 June 1945.
3. Murphy, *Complete*, 122.
4. St. John's College *1945–46 Yearbook*, 31.
5. *Evening*, 20 June 1945.
6. Ibid. 23 June 1945.
7. St. John's College *1945–46 Yearbook*, 33.

8. Murphy, *Complete,* 127.

9. Sweetman, *History,* 203.

10. *Evening,* 22 May 1946.

11. Ibid., 12 June 1946.

St. John's Artist Designs a Special Stamp

1. Al Luckenbach, *Providence 1649: The History and Archaeology of Anne Arundel County Maryland's First European Settlement,* 1.

2. *Evening,* 9 February 1949.

3. 1948–49 St. John's College Yearbook, 16. Art was "exclusively an extra-curricular activity."

4. *Evening,* 13 April 1949.

5. Ibid., 24 May 1949.

6. Sarah Corbin Robert, "Report of the 300th Anniversary Celebration of Annapolis, Maryland," 147–53 and 158–61.

Ogle Hall's Many Owners

1. Henrietta Ogle. Letter of 5 February 1776 to her mother-in-law, Mrs. Samuel Ogle. Typescript of the photostat, which was presented to the U.S. Naval Academy Alumni Association by Rear Admiral Frederick Gore Richards and Mrs. Richards, the great-great-great-great granddaughter of Mrs. Samuel Ogle. The typescript appears as an index in Jean Lee Eareckson's report, "Ogle Hall-Alumni House, 1739 to 1982."

2. Ibid.

3. Ibid.

4. Facts from this chapter found in Jean Lee Eareckson, "Ogle Hall-Alumni House, 1739 to 1982."

How Maryland Considered Taxing Bachelors to Fund Education

1. *Proceedings and Acts of the General Assembly, February 22, 1755–October 9, 1756, Archives of Maryland,* 52: 650–56.

2. Ibid., preface 72.

3. Ibid., 504.

4. Ibid., 503.

5. Ibid., 504.

6. Ibid.

7. *Proceedings and Acts of the General Assembly, April 8, 1757–May 13, 1758, Archives of Maryland,* 55: 537.

8. *Proceedings and Acts of the General Assembly, October 23, 1758–May 6, 1761, Archives of Maryland,* 56: 488.

9. Ibid., 488–89.

10. Ibid., 489.

11. *Proceedings and Acts of the General Assembly, March 17, 1762–November 26, 1763, Archives of Maryland,* 58: 310.

12. *Journal of the House of Delegates, 1806, Archives of Maryland,* 554: 40.

13. *Journal of the House of Delegates, 1808, Archives of Maryland,* 556: 65. The entire bill was eventually defeated.

14. *Proceedings of the House [of Delegates] 1841, Archives of Maryland,* 689: 284–85.

Bygone Naval Academy Dating Traditions

1. Banning, *Annapolis Today,* 342.

2. Ibid., 191–92.

3. Ibid., 179–99.

4. Ibid., 196–97.

5. Walter and Mignon Gerich, personal interviews: 25 November 2002 and 8 August 2003.

6. *Fifty Years After: The Class of Nineteen Forty-Five, United States Naval Academy,* 113.

The Naval Academy's Other Golf Course

1. *Evening,* 22 June 1916.

2. WorldGolf.com. "The History of the American PGA." http://www.worldgolf.com/wglibrary/history/ampgahis.html 2 September 2003.

3. *Army and Navy Journal* 51, no. 14 (1913): 430.

4. *Army and Navy Journal* 53, no. 6 (1915): 297.

5. Ibid.

6. Cary Meredith, telephone interview: 29 April 2003.

7. Richard Lazenby, personal interview: 8 April 2003.

8. Daniel Hunt, telephone interview: 9 April 2003.

9. Walker, *Historical,* 20.

10. *Evening,* 20 January 1928.

11. Fred Rhodes, *U.S. Naval Academy Golf Course: a Bit of History,* 5.

12. Ibid., 6–7.

13. Ibid., 9.

14. Ibid., 12.

15. Ibid., 13.

16. Ibid., 14.

17. *Evening,* 19 January 1928.

18. Ibid.

Halligan Hall: Home to Marines and Midshipmen

1. 1921 *Lucky Bag,* 267.

2. *Report of the Secretary of the Navy for the Year 1895,* 65.

3. *Annual Reports of the Navy Department for the Year 1898*, 820.

4. *Annual Reports of the Navy Department for the Year 1899*, 908.

5. *Annual Reports of the Navy Department for the Year 1900*, 1091.

6. Florence M Kelleher. "Henry Ives Cobb, 1859–1931." Yerkes Observatory Virtual Museum. 12 September 2003 http://astro.uchicago.edu/yerkes/ virtualmuseum/Cobb.html; and University of Chicago Magazine Online 12 September 2003 http://magazine.uchicago.edu/9910/html/cobb3.htm.

7. *Annual Reports of the Navy Department for the Year 1902*, 956.

8. Ibid.

9. *Evening*, 29 September 1903.

10. Sweetman, *History*, 167–69.

11. *Evening*, 15 June 1917.

12. Ibid., 9 June 1917.

13. Ibid., 12 June 1917.

14. *Army and Navy Journal* 55, no. 5 (1917): 170.

15. "Life at the Barracks." *The Log* 6, no. 3 (1917): 3 and 15.

16. 1921 *Lucky Bag*, 267.

17. Sweetman, *History*, 167.

Henry Sturdy's Colonial Guide Service

1. Matthew Palus, interviews with Orlando Ridout IV: 13 December 2002 and 18 December 2002.

2. Henry Francis Sturdy and Arthur Trader, *Seeing Annapolis and the Naval Academy*, Tercentenary Revised Edition, inside front cover.

3. Robert Reynolds and Edwin Weber, telephone interviews: 2 September 2004, 4 September 2004, and 5 September 2004; Gilbert Crandall, personal interviews: 10 July 2004 and 28 August 2004.

Rats: Unlikely Preservationists

1. Heather Foster, personal interview: 18 May 2004; Lisa Mason-Chaney, personal interview: 29 March 2005.

Woodworkers Help to Preserve Local History

1. Carter Lively, personal interview: 24 May 2004.

2. Michael Arndt, personal interview: 24 May 2004 and telephone interview: 23 March 2005.

Anne St. Clair Wright: Annapolis's "First Lady of Preservation"

1. "A Tribute to Anne St. Clair Wright." *Historic Annapolis Foundation Journal* 5, no. 1(2002): 4 (hereinafter referred to as "Tribute").

2. Ibid.

3. Dr. Mark Leone, personal interview: 14 April 2004.

4. "Tribute," 4.

5. Nancy Avallone, telephone interview: 12 April 2004.

6. Transcript of interview with Anne St. Clair Wright. 6 August 1981. Unidentified interviewer. Photocopy at Historic Annapolis Foundation, Annapolis, Md.

7. "Daughter of Navy Paints Relief Murals," *Washington Herald*, 29 November 1936.

8. Ronnie Carr, telephone interview: 12 April 2004.

9. "Tribute," 4.

10. Ann Fligsten, telephone interview: 12 April 2004.

11. Linnell Bowen, telephone interview: 13 April 2004.

Saving the Historic Market House

1. Albert J. Goodman. Letter of 21 October 1941 to Robert Campbell.

2. The market-area center would be for white servicemen; the city was also planning to create a USO center for African-American servicemen on Northwest Street.

3. Annapolis Mayor and Aldermen (Proceedings) 1941–1947, MSA M49-26, 1, MdHR 19,996-5.

4. Ibid.

5. Ibid., 22.

6. Ibid., 30.

7. *Evening,* 21 October 1941.

8. Annapolis Mayor and Aldermen (Proceedings) 1941–1947, MSA M49-26, 30, MdHR 19,996-5.

9. Ibid., 31.

10. *Evening,* 7 November 1941

11. Annapolis Mayor and Aldermen (Proceedings) 1941–1947, MSA M49-26, 33, MdHR 19,996-5.

12. Ibid., 34.

13. Ibid., 40.

14. Ibid., 39.

15. Roland A. Brown et al. vs. Mayor, Counselor and Aldermen of the City of Annapolis. Mr. Childs presented three exhibits with the bill: (1) a copy of the Charter of Annapolis; (2) a certificate of Katherine Linthicum, City Clerk, taken from the Journal of Proceedings of the Mayor, Counselor and Aldermen of the city of Annapolis of October 20, 1941; and (3) an original notice that Albert J. Goodman, the city's Special Attorney, had addressed to Robert H. Campbell on 21 October 1941.

16. Ibid.

17. *Evening,* 8 December 1941.

18. Ibid.

19. Ibid.

20. Annapolis Mayor and Aldermen (Proceedings) 1941–1947, MSA M49-26, 50, MdHR 19,996-5.

Saving the Historic Market House—Again

1. The Planning Council of the Greater Baltimore Committee, Inc. *Comprehensive Master Plan Annapolis, Maryland, 1962,* 74.
2. Ibid., 83.
3. Ibid., 79.
4. Ibid., 74.
5. The committee consisted of F. Marion Lazenby (chair), George Nichols, Willis Armbruster, Leonard Berman, Robert Eggleston, Sam Snyder, and William Myers.
6. *Evening,* 29 July 1959.
7. Ibid., 12 August 1959.
8. Ibid., 25 August 1959.

Saving the Market—One More Time

1. *Evening,* 21 December 1968.
2. Ibid., 13 August 1968.
3. See Appendix 2 for the Resolution.
4. "Heir of Original Market Site Owner Enters Annapolis Dispute," *Washington Post.* 19 December 1968 (hereinafter referred to as "Heir").
5. *Evening,* 24 December 1968.
6. Ibid., and Ernest Allen Connally. Letter of 1 August 1968 to Mrs. Howard (Ruth) Keith. Vertical file. Historic Annapolis Foundation, Annapolis, Md.
7. Ibid.
8. The Hilton is the Annapolis Marriott Waterfront Hotel today.
9. *Evening,* 24 July 1968.
10. Ernest Allen Connally. Letter of 1 August 1968 to Mrs. Howard (Ruth) Keith. Vertical file. Historic Annapolis Foundation, Annapolis, Md.
11. *Evening,* 13 August 1968.
12. Ibid.
13. "Heir."
14. Roger "Pip" Moyer, telephone interview: 3 March 2004.
15. *Evening,* 16 September 1968.
16. Ibid., 12 September 1968.
17. Roger "Pip" Moyer, telephone interview: 3 March 2004.
18. Pringle Symonds, telephone interview: 8 March 2004.
19. Ibid.
20. Stephen Carr. Letter to the editor of the *Evening Capital* (Annapolis, Md.). Author's note: I have a print of the letter from microfilm at Nimitz Library, Annapolis, Md. However, I did not record the date of the letter.

21. *Evening*, 14 August 1968.
22. Ibid.
23. Ibid.
24. Douglas Gordon Carroll, et al. vs. the Mayor and Aldermen of the City of Annapolis. No. 19173. Circuit Court for Anne Arundel County. Filed 17 December 1968.
25. L. Harvey Poe, Jr., personal interview: 6 March 2004.
26. *Evening*, 3 January 1969.
27. James Biddle. Letter of 25 July 1968 to Mrs. Howard (Ruth) Keith. Vertical file. Historic Annapolis Foundation, Annapolis, Md.
28. *Evening*, 17 July 1969.

"Hysteric, Historic Annapolis"

1. Dr. Gregory Stiverson and Donna Hole, personal and telephone interviews, and email correspondences: 10–20 August 2004.

Making Sense of Annapolis's Historic Building Markers

1. Joseph H. Friend and David B. Guralnik, eds., *Webster's New World Dictionary of the American Language*, 1618.
2. "Three Centuries of Annapolis Architecture." Educational pamphlet. Annapolis, Md.: Historic Annapolis Foundation, 2001. Patricia Blick and Jennifer Orrigo, personal interviews and email correspondences: 2003 and 2005.

Fireplace Mantel Preserves Century-old Letters

1. *Evening*, 6 May 1919.
2. *Johnson's*, 90.
3. John Yellot graduated from St. John's College in 1892.

Preserving the Memory of British Convicts

1. Robert Barnes, personal interview: 29 June 2004.
2. Peter Wilson Coldham, *Bonded Passengers to America, Vo. 2, Middlesex, 1617–1775*, 197.
3. Philip Sellars, personal interview and email correspondences: June–September 2004.

Appendix 1

1. Mayor's Court Land Records, MSA M41-1, 428–30. MdHR 7833-3.

Appendix 2

1. Mayor and Aldermen (Resolutions) 1959–1970, MSA M96-1.

Bibliography

Annapolis Banking and Trust Company Individual Ledger No. 1, 1905. Annapolis Banking and Trust Company Archives, Annapolis, Md.

"Annapolis Stamp Issued." *Southern Maryland Times.* 2 May 1949.

Annual Register of the United States Naval Academy, Annapolis, Maryland. Washington, D.C.: Government Printing Office, 1903–04, 1910–11, and 1911–12.

Annual Reports of the Navy Department for the Years 1898, 1899, and 1902. Washington, D.C.: Government Printing Office, 1898, 1899, and 1902.

Avery, Catherine H., and Jane W. McWilliams. *A Century of Caring: A History of Anne Arundel Medical Center 1902–2002.* Annapolis, Md.: Anne Arundel Medical Center, 2002.

Baltz, Shirley V. *Quays of the City.* Annapolis, Md.: The Liberty Tree, Ltd., 1975.

Banning, Kendall. *Annapolis Today, Revised Ed.* New York: Funk & Wagnalls Company, 1942.

Blackstone, Sir William. *Commentaries on the Laws of England (Bk. 3, Ch. 4).* Oxford: Clarendon Press, 1765. 10 March 2005, http://www.longang. com.

Brown, Philip L. *The Other Annapolis, 1900–1950.* Annapolis, Md.: Philip L. Brown, 1994.

Brown, Roland A. et al. vs. Mayor, Counselor and Aldermen of the city of Annapolis, a municipal corporation. No. 8289. Circuit Court for Anne Arundel County. 31 December 1941.

Browne, William Hand, Edward C. Papenfuse, et al., eds., *Archives of Maryland,* 215+ volumes, (Baltimore and Annapolis, Md., 1883–). This series is ongoing and available on line at http://archivesofmaryland.net where volumes, collectively or individually, can be searched electronically.

Burch, James Wood. "Report to Historic Annapolis on the Market House Study." 3 January 1969. Vertical file. Historic Annapolis Foundation, Annapolis, Md.

Burlingham, Charles C. Letters of 6 October 1903 and 28 October 1903 to unidentified newspaper (presumably in Cornish, New Hampshire). Alumni jacket #2147. U.S. Naval Academy Special Collections & Archives. Nimitz Library, Annapolis, Md.

By-Laws of the Corporation of the City of Annapolis, Revised. Annapolis, Md.: J. Green, 1839.

Cheevers, James. "United States Naval Academy Part III, A Golden Age." Shipmate 58, no. 6 (1995): 35–40.

Churchill, Winston. "A Plea for the Revival of Boating Interests at the Naval Academy." Letter. *Army and Navy Register* 13 (1892): 513–14.

Churchill, Winston. Letter to unidentified newspaper (presumably in Cornish, New Hampshire). 17 October 1903. Alumni jacket #2147. U.S. Naval Academy Special Collections & Archives. Nimitz Library, Annapolis, Md.

Churchill, Winston. Personal notebook. The Papers of Winston Churchill. ML16, Series 3, Box 5. Rauner Special Collections Library, Dartmouth College, Hanover, N.H.

Churchill, Winston. *Richard Carvel.* New York: The Macmillan Company, 1899.

The Code of the City of Annapolis, by the Counselor. Annapolis, Md.: Evening Capital Print, 1897.

Coldham, Peter Wilson. *Bonded Passengers to America, Vol. 2, Middlesex, 1617–1775.* Baltimore, Md.: Genealogical Publishing Co., Inc., 1983.

Cook, Ebenezer. *Sot-weed Factor, or A Voyage to Maryland, a satyr.* London: 1708. Poets' Corner, Poets' Corner Editorial Staff, 2003, 9 March 2005, http://www.theotherpages.org/poems/cook02.html.

Drew, Anne Marie. *Letters From Annapolis.* Annapolis, Md.: Naval Institute Press, 1998.

Dryfhout, John. Collection of materials sent on 21 March 1988 to Midshipman 3/C Brian T. Smith. Alumni jacket #2147. U.S. Naval Academy Special Collections & Archives. Nimitz Library, Annapolis, Md.

Eareckson, Jean Lee. "Ogle Hall-Alumni House: A History, 1739–1982." Annapolis, Md.: Historic Annapolis, Inc., 1982. Vertical file. Historic Annapolis Foundation, Annapolis, Md.

Evening Capital (Annapolis, Md.). Nimitz Library, Annapolis, Md.

Everstine, Carl. *The General Assembly of Maryland, 1776–1850.* Charlottesville, Va.: The Michie Company, 1982.

Everstine, Carl. *The General Assembly of Maryland, 1850–1920.* Charlottesville, Va.: The Michie Company, 1982.

Fifty Years After: The Class of Nineteen Forty-Five, United States Naval Academy. The Association of the Class of 1945, U.S.N.A.: 1994.

Friend, Joseph H., and David B. Guralnik, eds. *Webster's New World Dictionary of the American Language.* New York: The World Publishing Company, 1968.

Goodman, Albert J. Letter of 21 October 1941 to Robert H. Campbell. Courtesy of Robert H. Campbell, Annapolis, Md.

Gould & Halleron Annapolis City Directory, 1910. Annapolis, Md.: Gould & Halleron, 1910.

Hawthorne, Hildegarde. *Rambles in Old College Towns.* New York: Dodd, Mead & Co., 1917. In Mame and Marion Warren's *Maryland Time Exposures 1840–1940.* Baltimore, Md.: The Johns Hopkins University Press, 1984.

Hokuf, Esther P. Letter of 4 August 2003 to Ginger Doyel.

Holly, David C. *Steamboat on the Chesapeake, Emma Giles and the Tolchester Line.* Centreville, Md.: Tidewater Publishers, 1987.

Iarusso, Heather M. " 'Bridge'-ing the generation gap." *The Capital* (Annapolis, Md.). 1 April 1994.

The J. F. Johnson Lumber Company. "The J. F. Johnson Lumber Company—75 years." 1996. 9 March 2005, http://www.johnsonlumberco.com.

Johnson's Directory of Annapolis, Maryland for 1896–97. Annapolis, Md.: Republican Steam Press, 1896.

Key, Rebecca. "A Notice of Some of the First Buildings with Notes of Some of the Early Residents." *Maryland Historical Magazine* 14 (1919): 256–57.

Kinnaman, John Allen. *The Internal Revenues of Colonial Maryland.* Diss. Indiana University, 1954.

Letzer, Mark B., and Jean B. Russo, eds. *The Diary of William Faris: The Daily Life of an Annapolis Silversmith.* Baltimore, Md.: The Press at the Maryland Historical Society, 2003.

Lichtenstein, Abba G. & Associates. "The Severn River Bridge at Annapolis, Maryland: Report on Historical and Technological Significance. Prepared for the Citizens For a Scenic Severn River Bridge." 1991? Courtesy of Gilbert Crandall, Annapolis, Md.

Lindauer, Anthony. *From Paths to Plats: The Development of Annapolis, 1651–1718.* Crownsville, Md.: Maryland State Archives and Maryland Historical Trust, 1997.

Luckenbach, Al. *Providence 1649: The History and Archaeology of Anne Arundel County Maryland's First European Settlement.* Crownsville, Md.: Maryland State Archives and Maryland Historical Trust, 1995.

Maryland Gazette (Annapolis, Md.). Maryland State Archives, Annapolis, Md.

Maryland Historical Society. *Filming Maryland.* Baltimore, Md.: Maryland Historical Society, 2000.

Maryland Republican (Annapolis, Md.), 1901.

Maryland State Archives, Annapolis, Md. Citations to specific archival materials are found in endnotes throughout the book. These records were researched by the author or obtained upon request from the archives.

May, Jude Thomas. *Achieving the American Dream: The Life of the Honorable Aris T. Allen, M.D.* Baltimore, Md.: Gateway Press, 1990.

McCormick & Co. Inc. "Old Bay: Traditionally Old Bay, An Historical Tale to Tell." Millersville, Md.: McCormick & Co. Inc., n. d.

McIntire, Robert Harry. *Annapolis Maryland Families, Vol. I.* Baltimore, Md.: Gateway Press, Inc., 1980.

McKown, Barrett, ed. *The Annapolis and Anne Arundel County Public Library: A History.* Annapolis, Md.: The Public Library Association of Annapolis and Anne Arundel County, Inc., 1987.

McWilliams, Jane W. "From the pages of the Maryland Gazette." *Evening Capital* (Annapolis, Md.), 9 February 1970.

McWilliams, William J. *Charter and Code of the City of Annapolis, Revised and Annotated.* Annapolis, Md.: Capital-Gazette Press, Inc., 1935.

Miller, Marcia M., and Orlando Ridout V, eds. *Architecture in Annapolis: A Field Guide.* Crownsville, Md.: Maryland Historical Trust Press, 1998.

Murphy, Emily A. *A Complete and Generous Education: 300 Years of Liberal Arts; St. John's College, Annapolis.* Annapolis, Md.: St. John's College Press, 1996.

The National Cyclopedia of American Biography, Vol. 10. New York: James T. White & Company, 1900.

The National Cyclopedia of American Biography. Vol. D. New York: James T. White & Co., 1934. Naval cadet record for Winston Churchill. Alumni jacket #2147. U.S. Naval Academy Special Collections & Archives. Nimitz Library, Annapolis, Md.

Palus, Matthew. Interviews with Orlando Ridout IV: 13 December 2002 and 18 December 2002. Manuscript and sound recording at Historic Annapolis Foundation, Annapolis, Md.

The Planning Commission of the Greater Baltimore Committee, Inc. "Comprehensive Master Plan, Annapolis, Maryland, 1962: A Report to the City of Annapolis Planning and Zoning Commission." Baltimore, Md.: The Greater Baltimore Committee, Inc., 1962.

Polk's City Directory for Annapolis, Maryland 1924. Richmond, Va.: R. L. Polk & Co., Inc., Publishers, 1924.

Polk's City Directory for Annapolis, Maryland 1939. New York: R. L. Polk & Co. Inc., Publishers, 1939.

Polk's City Directory for Annapolis, Maryland 1954. Boston, Mass.: R. L. Polk & Co., Inc., Publishers, 1954.

Radoff, Dr. Morris L. *Buildings of the State of Maryland at Annapolis.* Annapolis, Md.: The Hall of Records Commission, 1954.

Report of the Secretary of the Navy for the Year 1895. Washington, D.C.: Government Printing Office, 1895.

Rhodes, Fred. *U.S. Naval Academy Golf Course: a Bit of History.* n. p., n. d. Copies available at the U.S. Naval Academy Golf Course, Annapolis, Md., and Nimitz Library, Annapolis, Md.

Ridgely, David. *Annals of Annapolis.* Baltimore, Md.: Cushing and Brother, 1841.

Riley, Don. "I Remember . . . Sights and Smells of Old Annapolis Market." *Sunday Sun Magazine* (Baltimore, Md.), 20 September 1959, 2.

Riley, Elihu S. *The Ancient City: a History of Annapolis, in Maryland, 1649–1887.* Annapolis, Md.: Record Printing Office, 1887.

Riley, Elihu S. A *History of Anne Arundel County in Annapolis, Maryland.* Annapolis, Md.: Charles G. Feldmeyer, 1905.

Risjord, Norman K. *Builders of Annapolis: Enterprise and Politics in a Colonial Capital.* Baltimore, Md.: Maryland Historical Society, 1997.

Robert, Sarah Corbin. "Report of the 300th Anniversary Celebration of Annapolis, Maryland." Annapolis, Md.: The Annapolis Tercentenary Commission, 1949. Anne Arundel County Public Library Annapolis Area Library, Annapolis, Md.

Rose, Sara Jane. "Facts Pertaining to the Annapolis Market House." 1976. Handwritten and typed reports. Vertical file. Historic Annapolis Foundation, Annapolis, Md.

Schanze, Alfred Keys. Selected letters from 1904–08. Record Group Alumni/ Memorabilia, Personal Papers, Alfred K. Schanze, Class of 1908. U.S. Naval Academy Special Collections & Archives. Nimitz Library, Annapolis, Md.

Slanker, Harold E., Jr. "The J. F. Johnson Lumber Company: A Composite History." *Anne Arundel County History Notes* 24, no. 4 (1993): 1–2.

Slanker, Harold E. Jr. "The J. F. Johnson Lumber Company: A Composite History—Conclusion." *Anne Arundel County History Notes* 25, no. 1 (1993): 1–2.

Smith, Adam C. "The case of the lost art." *St. Petersburg Times* (St. Petersburg, Fl.), 12 June 2001.

St. John's College. "A Brief History of St. John's." 2003. 9 March 2005, http://www.sjca.edu.

St. John's College yearbooks from the late 19th and mid-20th centuries. See endnotes for specific citations. Greenfield Library, Annapolis, Md.

Stegman, Carolyn B. *Women of Achievement in Maryland History.* University Park, Md.: Women of Achievement, 2002.

Stevens, William Oliver. *Annapolis: Anne Arundel's Town.* New York: Dodd, Mead & Company, 1937.

Stewart, Charles W. *John Paul Jones: Commemoration at Annapolis, April 24, 1906.* Washington, D.C.: Government Printing Office, 1907.

Sturdy, Henry Francis and Arthur Trader. *Seeing Annapolis and the Naval Academy, Tercentenary Revised Ed.* Baltimore, Md.: Pridemark Press, 1949.

The Sun (Baltimore, Md.). 11 August 1898 and 12 August 1903.

Sweetman, Jack. *The U.S. Naval Academy: An Illustrated History.* 2d ed. revised by Thomas J. Cutler. Annapolis, Md.: Naval Institute Press, 1995.

"Three Centuries of Annapolis Architecture." Educational pamphlet. Annapolis, Md.: Historic Annapolis Foundation, 2001.

Tilghman, Tench Francis. *The Early History of St. John's College in Annapolis.* Annapolis, Md.: St. John's College Press, 1984.

"A Tribute to Anne St. Clair Wright." *Historic Annapolis Foundation Journal* 5, no. 1 (2002): 4.

Trieschmann, Laura and Kimberly Williams. "The J. F. Johnson Lumber Company, 1901 West Street, Annapolis, Inventory No. AA-2212." Annapolis Intensive Survey, The Maryland Historical Trust, Maryland Inventory of

Historic Properties. Crownsville, Md.: Maryland Historical Trust, 1993–2002.

Trieschmann, Laura and Kimberly Williams. "The United States Post Office, 1 Church Circle, Annapolis, Inventory No. AA-400." Annapolis Intensive Survey, The Maryland Historical Trust, Maryland Inventory of Historic Properties. Crownsville, Md.: Maryland Historical Trust, 1993–2002.

United States Naval Academy *Lucky Bags* from 1894–1946. U.S. Naval Academy Special Collections & Archives. Nimitz Library, Annapolis, Md.

The United States Naval Academy Alumni Association, Inc. *Register of Alumni, Graduates, and former Naval Cadets and Midshipmen, 1845–1980*. Annapolis, Md.: The United States Naval Academy Alumni Association, Inc., 1980.

United States Statutes at Large. 81st Congress, 1st Session 1949, Vol. 63, Part 1. Washington, D.C.: United States Government Printing Office, 1950.

Vest, John P. "Ripples of a Novel, Richard Carvel of Carvel Hall." *Shipmate* 45, no. 7 (1982): 31–32.

Walker, Albert E. ed. *The Evening Capital Historical and Industrial Edition: Portraying the Glorious Past and Future Possibilities of Annapolis, Maryland*. Annapolis, Md.: The Evening Capital Publishing Company, 1908.

Warren, Mame. *Then Again . . . Annapolis, 1900–1965*. Annapolis, Md.: Time Exposures Ltd., 1990.

White, Clarence Marbury, Sr. and Evangeline Kaiser White. *The Years Between: A Chronicle of Annapolis, Maryland, 1800–1900 and Memoirs of Clarence Marbury White, Sr. and Evangeline Kaiser White*. New York: Exposition Press, 1957.

Williams, Kimberly. "163 Main Street, Inventory No. AA-561." Annapolis Intensive Survey, The Maryland Historical Trust, Maryland Inventory of Historic Properties. Crownsville, Md.: Maryland Historical Trust, 1994.

Worden, Robert L. *Saint Mary's Church in Annapolis, Maryland A Sesquicentennial History, 1853–2003*. Annapolis, Md.: St. Mary's Parish, 2003.

Yentsch, Anne. *A Chesapeake Family and Their Slaves: A study in historical archaeology*. New York: Cambridge University Press, 1994.

About the Author

Ginger Doyel is a fourth generation Annapolitan. She received a B.A. in Leadership Studies from the University of Richmond in 2001, graduating first in her class from the university's Jepson School of Leadership Studies. Upon graduating, Ginger served as a Research Fellow with the Pew Partnership for Civic Change in Charlottesville, Virginia. While in Charlottesville, she also founded the business Art Fore Golfers, which produced original golf art for clients along the East Coast.

In 2002, Ginger returned to Annapolis, where she is an author and artist. She contributes regularly to *The Capital* newspaper and several magazines, has written *Gone to Market: The Annapolis Market House, 1698–2005* (published by the city of Annapolis in 2005), and is currently writing a history of the Annapolitan Club. She has also illustrated multiple books, including *Gertrude the Albino Frog and Her Friend Rupert the Turtle,* and has created artwork for Historic Annapolis Foundation among other organizations. She enjoys golfing, running, and spending time with her family—especially her younger sister and best friend, Cathleen.

More books on the Chesapeake Region from Tidewater Publishers

Annapolis
Elizabeth B. Anderson
ISBN 10: 0-87033-546-4.   ISBN 13: 978-0-87033-546-4.

Bodine's Chesapeake Bay Country
A. Aubrey Bodine
Edited by Jennifer B. Bodine
ISBN 10: 0-87033-562-6.   ISBN 13: 978-0-87033-562-4.

Chesapeake Bay in the Civil War
Eric Mills
ISBN 10: 0-87033-479-4.   ISBN 13: 978-0-87033-479-5.

The Chesapeake Collection: A Treasury of Recipes and Memorabilia from Maryland's Eastern Shore
Woman's Club of Denton, Inc.
ISBN 10: 0-87033-431-X.   ISBN 13: 978-0-87033-431-3.

Chesapeake Rumrunners of the Roaring Twenties
Eric Mills
ISBN 10: 0-87033-518-9.   ISBN 13: 978-0-87033-518-1

A Cook's Tour of the Eastern Shore
Easton, Maryland, Memorial Hospital Junior Auxiliary
ISBN 10: 0-87033-001-2.   ISBN 13: 978-0-87033-001-8

Down on the Shore: The Family and Place that Forged a Poet's Voice
Adele V. Holden
ISBN 10: 0-87033-547-2.   ISBN 13: 978-0-87033-547-1.

Exploring the Chesapeake in Small Boats
John Page Williams, Jr.
ISBN 10: 0-87033-429-8.   ISBN 13: 978-0-87033-429-0.

Ghost Fleet of Mallows Bay: And Other Tales of the Lost Chesapeake
Donald G. Shomette
ISBN 10: 0-87033-480-8.   ISBN 13: 978-0-87033-480-1.

Ghosts & Haunted Houses of Maryland
    Trish Gallagher
    Illustrated by Howard Burns
    ISBN 10: 0-87033-382-8.   ISBN 13: 978-0-87033-382-8.

Lighting the Bay: Tales of Chesapeake Lighthouses
    Pat Vojtech
    ISBN 10: 0-87033-466-2.   ISBN 978-0-87033-466-5

Lost Towns of Tidewater Maryland
    Donald G. Shomette
    ISBN 10: 0-87033-527-8.   ISBN 13: 978-0-87033-527-3.

Maryland Folklore
    George G. Carey
    ISBN 10: 0-87033-396-8.   ISBN 13: 978-0-87033-396-5.

Maryland Lost and Found . . . Again
    Eugene L. Meyer
    ISBN 10: 0-87033-548-0.   ISBN 13: 978-0-87033-548-8.

My Favorite Maryland Recipes
    Helen Avalynne Tawes
    ISBN 10: 0-87033-500-6.   ISBN 13: 978-0-87033-500-6

The Mystery of Mary Surratt: The Plot to Kill President Lincoln
    Rebecca C. Jones
    ISBN 10: 0-87033-560-X.   ISBN 13: 978-0-87033-560-0.

Rivers of the Eastern Shore: Seventeen Maryland Rivers
    Hulbert Footner
    Illustrated by Aaron Sopher
    ISBN 10: 0-87033-092-6.   ISBN 13: 978-0-87033-092-6.

Rudow's Guide to Fishing the Chesapeake
    Lenny Rudow
    ISBN 10: 0-87033-568-5.   ISBN 13: 978-0-87033-568-6.

Shipwrecks on the Chesapeake: Maritime Disasters on Chesapeake Bay and Its Tributaries, 1608–1978
    Donald G. Shomette
    ISBN 10: 0-87033-283-X.   ISBN 13: 978-0-87033-283-8.

Tidewater Time Capsule: History Beneath the Patuxent
    Donald G. Shomette
    ISBN 10: 0-87033-463-8.   ISBN 13: 978-0-87033-463-4.

The Watermen of the Chesapeake Bay
    John Hurt Whitehead III
    ISBN 10: 0-87033-374-7.   ISBN 13: 978-0-87033-374-3.